Instant
VBScript

Alex Homer
Darren Gill

Wrox Press Ltd.®

Instant VBScript

Published by Wrox Press Ltd. 30 Lincoln Road, Olton, Birmingham, B27 6PA.
Printed in Canada
Library of Congress Catalog no. 96-61411

ISBN 1-861000-44-8

Trademark Acknowledgements

Credits

Authors
Alex Homer
Darren Gill

Contributing Author
Steve Jakab

Additional Material
Douglas Shand

Editor
Chris Ullman

Development Editors
Graham McLaughlin
David Maclean

Technical Reviewers
Robert Barker
John Bohrman
Jon Bonnell
Mike Burgess
Andrew Grubbs

Technical Reviewers
Mark Harrison
Oyvind Johannessen
Juan T Llibre
Tony McClay "TheBigMan"
Shawn Murphy
Adwait Ullal

Production Manager
Gina Mance

Design/Layout
Neil Gallagher
Andrew Guillaume

Proof Reader
Pam Brand

Index
Simon Gilks

Cover Design
Third Wave

For more information on Third Wave, contact Ross Alderson on 44-121 236 6616
Cover image by David Maclean

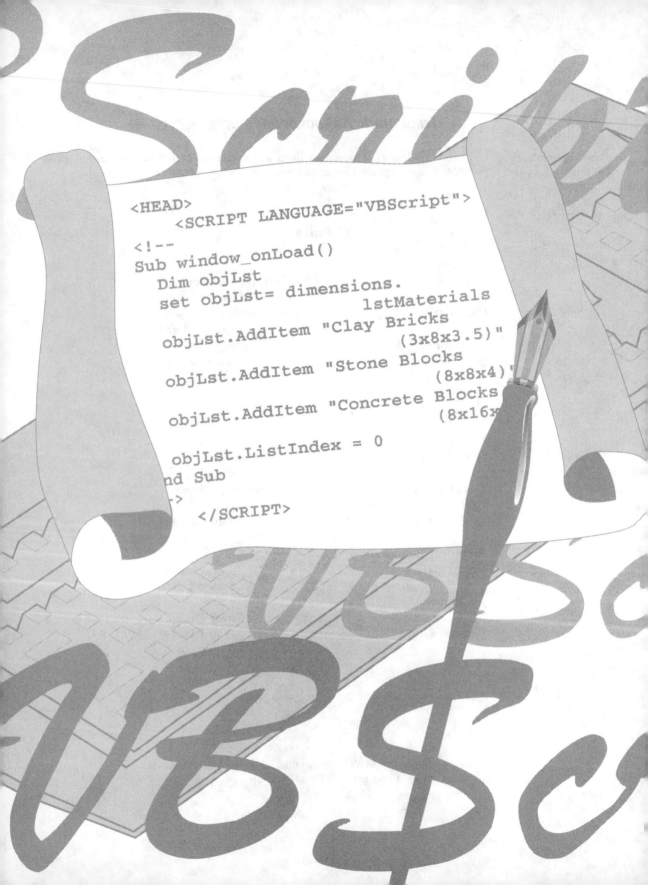

```
<HEAD>
    <SCRIPT LANGUAGE="VBScript">
<!--
Sub window_onLoad()
  Dim objLst
  set objLst= dimensions.
                              lstMaterials

  objLst.AddItem "Clay Bricks
                              (3x8x3.5)"

  objLst.AddItem "Stone Blocks
                              (8x8x4)"

  objLst.AddItem "Concrete Blocks
                              (8x16x

  objLst.ListIndex = 0
nd Sub
-->
    </SCRIPT>
```

VBScript

Table of Contents

```
<HEAD>
    <SCRIPT LANGUAGE="VBScript">

<!--
Sub window_onLoad()
  Dim objLst
  set objLst= dimensions.
                         1stMaterials
  objLst.AddItem "Clay Bricks
                         (3x8x3.5)"
  objLst.AddItem "Stone Blocks
                         (8x8x4)"
  objLst.AddItem "Concrete Blocks
                         (8x16x
  objLst.ListIndex = 0
nd Sub
-->
      </SCRIPT>
```

VBScript

Introduction

Who's this Book For?

This isn't a book for people who are new to programming, but it is for those who are completely new to VBScript. The aim is to show the programmer the vast potential of VBScript, and to get them up to speed without wasting time on relearning simple concepts such as 'what's a variable?' or 'what is the web?'. So to enable us to keep a fast pace throughout this book, we're going to assume two things:

 That you have a working knowledge of either **Visual Basic**, **VBA** (Visual Basic for Applications), or a similar type of language. This doesn't mean that you need to be an 'expert', but that you are comfortable with the common syntax and functionality. We won't be trying to teach you how to multiply variables together, or how a **For...Next** loop works, for example.

 That you can create normal HTML pages, and understand the basics of the language up to the HTML 2 standard. We won't be covering the basic structure and tags. However, there are several elements which have been introduced, since HTML 2, that you're likely to use regularly with VBScript. We'll be looking at these in some detail throughout the book, as they are required.

What's Covered in this Book?

This book begins with a very brief outline of VBScript's position in the Internet world, before diving headlong into VBScript. After going through a few basic examples, we provide a quick overview of HTML tables and frames, and how they can be exploited to extra effect by VBScript within your pages. We introduce functions, and show how to carry out simple calculations within your pages. We then look at how you can get information back from simple HTML controls.

We also introduce the ActiveX Control Pad, a very useful utility that no VBScript programmer should be without, and take a look at how it makes life so much easier. We look at the different properties, events, and methods of the ActiveX Controls, and how these differ from HTML controls. This information will allow you to enhance the functionality and ease of use of your applications.

Gradually, we put together several small programs which form the basis of a large sample application. This utilizes the more interesting and complex controls. Our application illustrates how the different concepts learned earlier can be combined to create a professional looking page, that can handle user interactions with the same efficiency of any stand-alone application.

The later chapters cover a diverse set of topics, from the browser object hierarchy, to component download and database access. These encourage the programmer to explore the lesser known aspects of VBScript. We develop a debugging window to help with testing, and a web page analysis tool to aid maintenance. We end the book by tackling the difficult subject of sending data to your server—and getting an intelligible response back! Finally, there are plenty of useful appendices which allow you to reference various properties, methods, and events at a glance.

What You Need to Use this Book

Apart from a bit of time, and a willingness to learn, you'll need access to a PC running Windows 95/NT, a copy of Internet Explorer version 3.0 or later, and (ideally) a connection to the Internet so that you can run the examples from our web site. It's important to execute the samples from the web site, or type the code as you go along, since the examples form a fundamental part of the learning process.

We also recommend that you download a copy of the ActiveX Control Pad from the Microsoft home site, as it will save you much time and effort in later chapters. It can be found at:

```
http://microsoft.com/ie/download
```

The latest version of Internet Explorer (3.0, as of writing) can be downloaded from:

```
http://microsoft.com/workshop/author/cpad
```

Although this book assumes that you are using Internet Explorer, it is also possible to use the later versions of Netscape Navigator, provided that you install the VBScript add-in. However, we do *not* recommend that you use the add-in with this book, since it does not (at the time of writing) fully implement all aspects of VBScript. Indeed, not all of the examples in the book will work with Netscape, since they are intended to utilize specific features of Internet Explorer. For more information about the add-in, check out Netscape's home site at:

```
http://home.netscape.com/comprod/products/navigator/version_2.0/plugins/
business_and_utilities.html
```

Where You'll Find Our Sample Pages

All the samples you'll see in this book are available from our World Wide Web site at:

```
http://www.wrox.com
```

We haven't included a disk with this book for several reasons. Apart from keeping the price of the book to a minimum, this system actually benefits you in that it's easy to select those samples that are of interest—rather than indiscriminately filling up your hard disk with stuff you'll never look at. More importantly still, the samples that you do choose from our site are always the most up-to-date. You'll also find a selection of other tools and files that you'll find useful when you start building your own interactive Web pages.

The samples which are directly applicable to each chapter are held together in a single directory; the location in which you'll find all these files is:

```
http://www.wrox.com/books/0448/code/
```

You can view these files directly in your browser, and see the source code by selecting Source from your browser's View menu. This opens the raw code into NotePad (or your default text editor), where you can then save it on to your own system if you wish to experiment with it.

Conventions

Finally, we've used a number of different font and layout styles to indicate different types of information in the book. Here are some examples of them, and an explanation of what they mean:

> Comments in boxes like these are bits of interesting information that you should take a look at.

Whereas this style indicates a comment that, while interesting, is more of an aside. It's a bit of friendly chit-chat.

```
In our code examples, this code style shows new and important, pertinent code,
that can be run on Iexplorer;
```

```
while this shows code that's less important in the present context, or code that
has been seen before.
```

When we're talking about **bits of code** in the main text, then they'll be in a **chunky font** as well.

Text that appears on your screen—on a menu or dialog box, for example, also has its own font.

Tell Us What You Think

We've worked hard on this book to make it useful. We've tried to understand what you're willing to exchange your hard earned money for, and we've tried to make the book live up to your expectations.

Please let us know what you think about this book. Tell us what we did wrong, and what we did right. This isn't just marketing flannel: we really do huddle around the e-mail to find out what you think. If you don't believe it, then send us a note. We'll answer, and we'll take whatever you say on board for future editions. The easiest way is to use e-mail:

feedback@wrox.com
Compuserve 100063,2152

You can also find more details about Wrox Press on our web site. There, you'll find the code from our latest books, sneak previews of forthcoming titles, and information about the authors and editors. You can order Wrox titles directly from the site, or find out where your nearest local bookstore with Wrox titles is located. The address of our site is:

```
http://www.wrox.com
```

Errata & Support

We all make mistakes - we try to make as few as possible within this book. That said, there will be an error here and there or maybe a point that is simply not making itself clear. Errata to our text & code is posted on our web site (`www.wrox.com`) and is updated when necessary. If you have further need of assistance please drop a mail to : `support@wrox.com` and we will get right back with an answer.

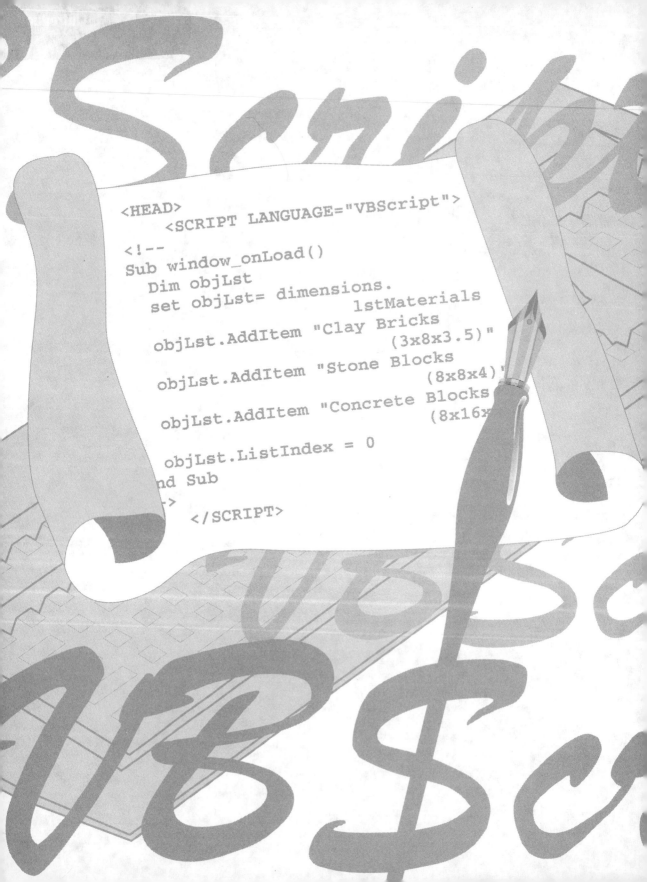

```
<HEAD>
    <SCRIPT LANGUAGE="VBScript">

<!--
Sub window_onLoad()
  Dim objLst
  set objLst= dimensions.
                         lstMaterials

  objLst.AddItem "Clay Bricks
                         (3x8x3.5)"

  objLst.AddItem "Stone Blocks
                         (8x8x4)"

  objLst.AddItem "Concrete Blocks
                         (8x16x

  objLst.ListIndex = 0
nd Sub
->
    </SCRIPT>
```

What Is VBScript?

The **World Wide Web**, or Web for short, has evolved from a group of Internet technologies as a means to publish information that can be viewed by others in remote locations. While these locations may be separated by a few hundred miles, or even an ocean or two, they could just as easily be as close as the next room. For example, the **Intranet**, where you access the information stored on your own network, is a fast growing use of the technology. The client machine uses a **browser** application to display the pages and, as these browsers are available for the majority of computer systems, the data can be used in an environment of genuine machine independence.

Traditionally, Internet pages have been static in nature, consisting mainly of text and simple images and, in recent times, realistic video and sound clips. However, despite the apparent simplicity of such pages, all the work of creating and maintaining the pages must still be done at the server end, and even the smallest amount of interactivity with the viewer requires continual administrative effort if the information is to be kept up to date and interesting. Without such effort the information and content will soon become stagnant, and people may eventually stop visiting your site.

In its most basic form, VBScript is just a way of making your Web pages 'reactive'—enabling them to interact with the user so that they are *more* than just static text and graphics. It's also very easy to use. If you can create normal HTML pages (and we're going to assume that you can) then adding functionality with VBScript is very simple.

But VBScript is more than just that. It also allows you to insert other objects into your pages. These can be taken from any of the hundreds that are already available, or even ones that you create yourself. (The whole future of computing is based around objects, and we'll talk more about what an object actually is later on.) VBScript is also the foundation for the 'coming together' of many of the latest developments in document handling and information storage. In new versions of Windows™, we're already seeing a blurring of the boundaries between local and network-based information, with the desktop itself becoming a browser window.

In this chapter, we'll be looking at:

- The background to VBScript, and other ways of making your Web pages react with the user and 'come alive'.

- The basic structure of an HTML page containing VBScript code.

- How we connect our VBScript code with events which occur in the browser, and how we can implement more complicated techniques such as variables and functions.

- How the features of newer browsers, such as tables and frames, can be especially useful with VBScript.

Making Web Pages Come Alive

There are an increasing number of ways to make your site more interesting so that (hopefully) people will keep coming back. The traditional method is to use HTML forms and server side programs accessed through the **CGI** (Common Gateway Interface). The viewer supplies information by filling in text boxes, making selections in lists, and selecting option or check boxes. They then submit the information by clicking a button, and this will tell your server program to build a new 'virtual' web page on the fly. The page is specially tailored to their wishes, but is virtual in that it doesn't actually exist as a stored page on the server. This way your information is always up-to-date and interesting. The main drawback is the time delay inherent when the client and server machine are communicating across the vast expanses of the Internet. You can build the most dynamic web page in the world, but network traffic and slow servers may significantly reduce the **usability** of your site.

Current Web Technologies

To address this problem of server dependence, several different technologies are appearing which make Web pages themselves more reactive. Not only can they replace the majority of CGI server requirements, but they also allow you to add extra functionality to your pages. One of the first was Java® from Sun Microsystems. Java is a language based loosely on C++, and it allows you to create small applications—called **applets**—which can be placed in a Web page and downloaded to the browser. The applets will then run on the client browser, so eliminating much of the wait for a server response. These applets can mostly achieve the same things as a stand-alone application. For example, moving images or controls that react when you use them. In fact, you can even use Java to create whole stand-alone applications.

Along with Java itself, an HTML scripting language was developed that complemented these applets. It uses special text commands embedded within the actual document, and these can interact with the viewer and manipulate Java applets. This language was licensed by Netscape Communications Corp. and released as part of the Netscape Navigator 2.0 Web browser as JavaScript. Like Java, JavaScript is syntactically similar to C++, but is also much simplified.

VBScript is a Microsoft product, introduced initially into that company's **Internet Explorer 3.0** Web browser, although it's also available to other manufacturers if they want to include it in their products. As well as using it to manipulate your pages directly, you can—as with JavaScript—manipulate other objects (generally **ActiveX**™ controls) within a Web page. You can even create various objects and controls yourself, making use of such development languages as C++, Delphi, and Visual Basic. However, unlike Java applets, which are specially written for use in Web pages, ActiveX objects are usually just ordinary Windows OLE objects: for example, text boxes, labels and buttons. In fact ActiveX is really the new specification for Microsoft's OLE (Object Linking and Embedding) technology, so there's already an established pool of objects that you can employ when building your pages.

JavaScript and VBScript are basically similar technologies, but with a few subtle differences. The main one is the syntax itself—JavaScript has its roots in C++, whereas VBScript's origins are closer to Visual Basic. As long as your browser offers the relevant support then you can use either—or even both together in the same page. However, you've bought this book to learn about VBScript, so from here on in that's where we'll be concentrating. Of course, there are other ways of making Web pages 'come alive'. You can display video clips, play sounds, and use scrolling text and other page items, but none of these are 'reactive' in the true sense of the word—they don't interact with the user in the way that, for example, a Java or ActiveX page does. You'll be seeing this in our first example.

An Example Application

Here's an example of what you can achieve with VBScript and ActiveX objects. It's a page from the fictitious site of Bob's Building Supplies, and it helps a prospective customer calculate how much a project is going to cost.

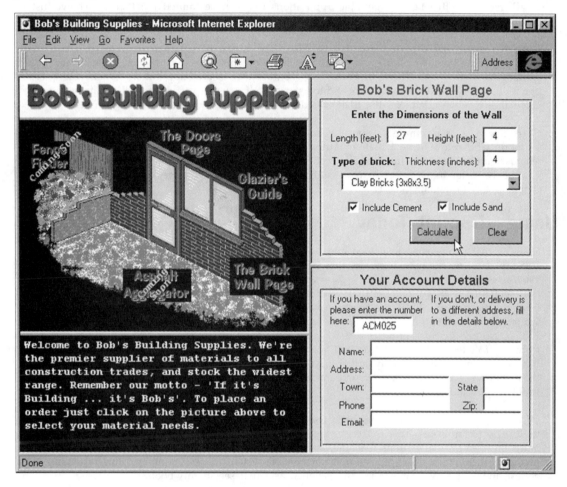

By entering details of a wall they want to build, the page shows what materials they'll need, and adds up the total cost. They can then simply click a button to place their order.

OK, so it's a simple example, but just consider how this could give your company an advantage in its market. It tells the customer exactly what they need to buy, and placing the order is so easy that they're unlikely to go elsewhere! If the future of commerce is Internet-based (like we keep hearing it will be), then you need to know how to build pages like this for your site. We'll be showing you how this page works in the next few chapters, but first we need to consider how VBScript fits into the overall scheme of things. This involves considering exactly what an object is.

About 'Objects'

The term **object** has been floating around in the computing world for many years. In essence, the grand plan is that all computer programs will consist of objects, rather than the monolithic blocks of executable code that we see in evidence today. The promise of object technology is to give us small, reusable, efficient, and portable applications that can be knitted together to achieve just the result that we need.

ActiveX controls are a perfect example of this. They consist of separate programs which contain their own data, and which will carry out functions on this data directly. For instance, the Equation Editor that comes with Microsoft Word is a separate OLE server application. When you insert an equation into a Word document, the Editor starts itself up and carries out all of the necessary calculations. When complete, the final equation is embedded into your Word document.

Of course, you aren't limited to putting an equation into a Word document. Any application that supports OLE can activate Equation Editor, and can display the results in its own documents. Microsoft's Web browser, Internet Explorer, can use OLE Servers in exactly the same way. Ultimately, as far as OLE (or ActiveX) is concerned, your HTML page is just another document that happens to contain objects.

Using VBScript Today

So, now that you're keen to get on and learn about VBScript, we come across the first problem. VBScript only works with browsers that support it. Remember that many people are using non Windows-based systems, or older browsers. All they may see of your beautifully crafted pages are odd scraps of text and static graphics—or even worse, the actual script that is supposed to be bringing the page to life! Until more browsers include full support for the new technology, your work will be wasted on all but a small section of the Web-surfing community. For instance, version 3 of Netscape's popular browser doesn't come with built-in support for VBScript. Just take comfort from the fact that it's every bit as bad with Java and all of the other new standards. If the viewer is using a Unix-based text-only browser, you have little chance of producing an interactive page for them! However, as you work through the book, we'll show you how to overcome some of these problems.

Of course, if you can control which browsers your viewers use then you're free to exploit all of these new technologies. This is true in the case of the company **Intranet**, as you can install the latest browser on every user's machine, and so can practice and master VBScript and ActiveX methods. If you're building an internal information system in *your* company, this represents the easiest and best way to maximize the benefits, as you'll see in this book.

The Future of Web Technologies

Whenever technology moves as quickly as the Internet and the World Wide Web, it's always impossible to be sure where exactly it'll go. However, the latest technologies coming from the major players are all heading in roughly the same direction.

In particular, Microsoft is closing the gap between the Internet and the computer on your own desk. In the current version of Internet Explorer, you can view the contents of your local and network drives, and can display all types of document—besides HTML pages. In future releases, you can expect the word Internet to be dropped from the name altogether. The browser will become just Explorer (sound familiar?), and will seamlessly link information on your own system or network with any of the millions of others that make up the Internet as a whole. In this environment, VBScript can be thought of as the 'glue' that holds it all together.

The Structure of VBScript in HTML Pages

VBScript is inserted into an HTML page using the special **<SCRIPT>** and **</SCRIPT>** tag pair. All of the latest browsers, such as Netscape 3 and Internet Explorer 3, recognize this tag, and react according to the type of script they find there. To identify the type of script, we use a **LANGUAGE** attribute. In our case, the **LANGUAGE** is '**VBScript**', and we've placed it all in the **BODY** section of the page.

```
<HTML>
   <HEAD>
      <TITLE> My First Page </TITLE>
   </HEAD>
   <BODY>
      <SCRIPT LANGUAGE="VBScript">
         . . .
         'some VBScript here
         . . .
      </SCRIPT>
   </BODY>
</HTML>
```

Hiding Code from Older Browsers

However, not all browsers recognize the new **<SCRIPT>** tag pair. One that doesn't will display everything between the tags as simple text, just as it appears in the HTML code—and believe us, this isn't a pretty sight! We therefore have to find a way to hide it from older browsers. The easiest way is to use the **<!--** *comment* **>** tag, like this:

```
<HTML>
   <HEAD>
      <TITLE> My First Page </TITLE>
   </HEAD>
   <BODY>
      <SCRIPT LANGUAGE="VBScript">
         <!-- hide from older browsers
         . . .
         'some VBScript here
         . . .
         -->
      </SCRIPT>
   </BODY>
</HTML>
```

Once it has processed the **<SCRIPT>** tag, the browser ignores any other HTML tags up to the closing **</SCRIPT>** tag, so the comment tag makes no difference to it. However, a browser that doesn't recognize the **<SCRIPT>** tag will just ignore it, and instead process the comment tag—thereby skipping the whole of the VBScript code.

11

> The current release of Internet Explorer is very choosy about the exact syntax and placing of the actual parts of the comment tag. The previous example shows one form it will accept, using two hyphens—one immediately after the exclamation mark, and the other before the closing tag marker. Placing other text on the same lines, or before or after the comment tag, often causes an error when the page is loaded into the browser.

What's Actually 'In' VBScript?

So now that we can see where the script goes, what does it actually look like? Well, if you've used Visual Basic or VBA (Visual Basic for Applications) then you'll feel right at home. In effect, VBScript is a cut-down version of Visual Basic. Although it includes most of the statements and functions that are concerned with mathematics (string, date, and number manipulation), and the common control structures are all there, not much else is...

There's no file manipulation, no graphics, no printing functionality and, rather surprisingly, there are none of the 'real' financial functions either. These could have been useful if you intended to create a Web site concerned with, say, an insurance company.

So you are limited in the tasks that you can achieve, and the reason for such a paucity of features is that security would otherwise be a considerable problem. Bear in mind that simply opening the HTML page in your browser loads the code into memory, ready to run as soon as you click a button or type in some text. Many of the omitted functions and statements could have easily been used by a malicious page creator to damage the data on your system. With VBScript (and JavaScript) the designers have decided that including all of the other functionality is just too much of a risk to the Internet community as a whole.

Neither is there a rich list of variable types. In VBScript, everything is a **Variant**, and this can store any type of value. You can use the normal VB **VarType** function to find out what kind of variable is stored, and can change it using a range of conversion functions such as **CLng** and **CDbl**—just as you can in VB. VBScript also supports arrays.

Other than that, it's so easy that you might as well be using Visual Basic. So let's get on with our first script.

Our First Script: 'Hello Web World'

For our first example, we'll use VBScript in its most simple form. And of course, by tradition we'll do a 'Hello World' program. In fact, you'll soon see how easy it is to create far more than that.

Like Visual Basic, you have to 'connect' your code (in this case, VBScript) to some **event** that occurs in the browser. The most obvious starting point is to use a push button to run the code, and that's what we'll do in the first example. Here's the complete HTML document (**HelloWorld.htm**), and the result is displayed in Internet Explorer—showing what happens when you click the button.

```
<HTML>
  <HEAD>
    <TITLE>Hello Web World</TITLE>
  </HEAD>
  <BODY>
    <H3>The traditional first example</H3>
    <SCRIPT LANGUAGE="VBScript" FOR="MyButton" EVENT="OnClick">
```

```
     <!-- hide from older browsers
        MsgBox ("Hello Web World !")
     -->
     </SCRIPT>
     <INPUT NAME="MyButton" TYPE="Button" VALUE="Click Me" >
   </BODY>
 </HTML>
```

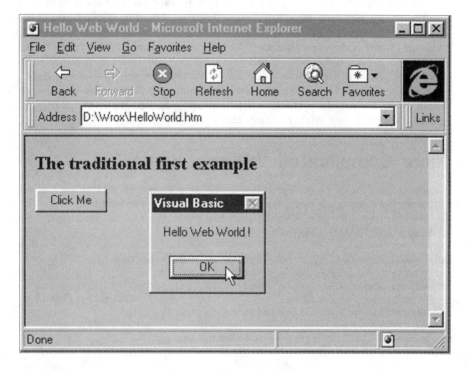

Here we're particularly interested in the section that contains the script itself, and the statement that produces the button. The script is contained between the **<SCRIPT>** and **</SCRIPT>** tags, and you'll see that the opening tag contains several new attributes.

```
<SCRIPT LANGUAGE="VBScript" FOR="MyButton" EVENT="OnClick">
   <!-- hide from older browsers
      MsgBox ("Hello Web World !")
   -->
</SCRIPT>
```

The first argument, as we've seen, simply defines the language of the script. It could be **'JavaScript'** instead, if that was the language that we were using. The other two form the connection between the script and the control on the page which calls it. The **FOR** attribute contains the name of the control, and the **EVENT** attribute defines which event of that control it'll react to.

We've linked the script to a button named **MyButton** and, because buttons (like most other controls) have several events associated with them, we've defined the **OnClick** event as the one we want to react to, so our code will run when the user clicks the button. All we have to do now is to create the button on the page:

```
<INPUT NAME="MyButton" TYPE="Button" VALUE="Click Me" >
```

This uses the standard HTML **<INPUT>** tag to create a push button, giving it the name **MyButton**, and the caption **Click Me**. Clicking it runs the VBScript code which simply makes use of a normal VB message box to display the text. We told you it was easy!

> The samples which are directly applicable to each chapter are together in a directory on our Web site. You'll find this next example, **HelloWorld.htm**, at:
>
> **http://www.wrox.com/books/0448/code/chapter01/HelloWorld.htm**
>
> You can view it directly in your browser, and can see the source code by selecting **Source** from your browser's **View** menu. This opens the raw code into **NotePad** (or your default text editor) and you can then save it onto your own system if you wish to experiment with it.

Using More Complicated VBScript Code

We can make our page more useful by adding more code to the **<SCRIPT>** section. Here's an example using an **If..Then..Else** construct. Again, it's very similar to the code that you would use if you were writing directly in Visual Basic. The complete page is called **Opinion.htm**, and we've just included the code section here:

```
<SCRIPT LANGUAGE="VBScript" FOR="MyButton" EVENT="OnClick">
    <!-- hide from older browsers
    If MsgBox ("Don't you think VBScript is really COOL ?",36,"Opinion
                                                    Poll") = 6 Then

        Msgbox "So do I...",,"My Opinion"
    Else
        Msgbox "Well I do...",,"My Opinion"
    End If
    -->
</SCRIPT>
```

The result is a different type of message box, which contains a question mark icon and both Yes and No buttons. We're using the function form of **MsgBox**, and the second argument (36) defines the various attributes of a message box in the same way as in Visual Basic. The third argument is just the message box title.

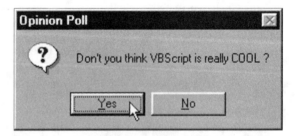

The VBScript **MsgBox()** function only returns a value of **6** if the Yes button is clicked, so we can then take a decision about which message to display. Again, this is pretty basic stuff, but it shows how, with just a little code, you can add instant functionality to your pages. We've used message boxes on purpose, because they represent a quick and easy way to react with the viewer of your page. Similarly, we can use the **InputBox()** function to get values from them, and this leads us on to using **variables** in a page.

As we mentioned in the introduction to the book, we're assuming that you're familiar with Visual Basic or VBA (Visual Basic for Applications). You can get information on the VB language, and help on its syntax, from the Help files that are included with most Microsoft Office applications. There are also Help pages available from Microsoft's Web site, and if you've installed the ActiveX Control Pad then you'll find a language reference topic in its Help menu.

Variables and Calculations in VBScript

Here's the code for an example (**Variables.htm**) which uses variables. We declare three variables within our script, using the **Dim** keyword. Then we use an input box to obtain the values for the number of hours and the hourly rate. Finally, we can calculate the result and display it in a message box.

```
<SCRIPT LANGUAGE="VBScript" FOR="MyButton" EVENT="OnClick">
   <!-- hide from older browsers
      Dim NumHours, HourlyRate, TotalDue
      NumHours = InputBox("How many hours?")
      HourlyRate = InputBox("How much per hour?")
      TotalDue = NumHours * HourlyRate
      MsgBox "You owe me $" & TotalDue
   -->
</SCRIPT>
```

Here's the result, and you'll notice that the input box looks distinctly 'out-of-place' in Windows 95. Later versions of Internet Explorer will probably sort this out!

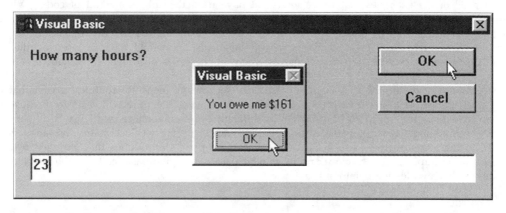

You don't actually have to declare a variable before you use it. VBScript will accept the **implicit declaration** of variables—where you use one that doesn't exist already by placing it in the left-hand side of an assignment statement, like this:

```
NewVariable = 365
```

The only catch here is that, if you misspell a variable name in your code, VBScript will assumes that it's a new variable, and will create one for you, assigning an empty string (or zero value) to it. The likely result is that your code won't work.

To prevent this happening, you can insert an **Option Explicit** statement directly after the **<SCRIPT>** tag and opening comments. Then you *do* have to declare all your variables 'up front', but at least if you misspell the name of one in your code, the browser will present you with a helpful error message.

15

```
<SCRIPT LANGUAGE="VBScript" FOR="MyButton" EVENT="OnClick">
<!-- hide from older browsers
    Option Explicit    'force declaration of all variables
    Dim NumHours, HourlyRate, TotalDue
```

All this will be pretty familiar stuff if you've used VB or VBA before, and we don't intend to spend a lot of time covering basic methods like this. However, notice the effect of making the variables a type **Variant**. When you use VB or VBA, you should be selecting your variable types to achieve maximum efficiency in your code, rather than taking the easy option of just using the **Variant** type.

In VBScript, you don't have a choice—they're all variants. But it does mean that you don't have to worry about type mismatch errors in most cases. In our example code, we've collected the values as strings, multiplied them together like numbers, and have then displayed the result as text again, and we've done all this without having to even consider the variable types.

> Of course, there will be occasions where you need to be more careful about assigning values between variables. You'll see more of this later on, and we'll also discuss the standard naming conventions for variables. Right now, however, we can just take advantage of the freedom that working with Variants gives.

'Inline' Script Code, Subroutines, and Functions

So far, all of the examples that we've looked at have used the 'inline' method of coding VBScript. In other words, there's only one set of statements between the **<SCRIPT>** and **</SCRIPT>** tags which is called for by the specific event defined by the **FOR** and **EVENT** arguments in the opening tag. If we want to create more than one set of statements, we would have to insert another **<SCRIPT>** and **</SCRIPT>** pair of tags elsewhere in the same document to contain it.

Instead, we can divide the code in the **<SCRIPT>** section into separate routines, except that now we can't use the **FOR** and **EVENT** tags to define which event the code will react to, because the various routines may need to be called from different events. Therefore, we'll use a different method of coding the script part. In the opening **<SCRIPT>** tag we just define the language, and then, in the section of the page used for the script, we place the routines that we want to use. Here's an example page (**Subroutine.htm**) which uses the same basic code as the previous example, but divides it up into subroutines:

```
<HTML>
    <HEAD>
        <TITLE>Using VBScript Subroutines</TITLE>
        <SCRIPT LANGUAGE="VBScript">
        <!-- hide from older browsers

            Sub GetOpinion
                If MsgBox ("Don't you think VBScript is really COOL ?",
                                    36,"Opinion Poll") = 6 Then
                    Msgbox "So do I...",,"My Opinion"
                Else
                    Msgbox "Well I do...",,"My Opinion"
                End If
            End Sub
```

```
            Sub MyButton_OnClick
                GetOpinion
            End Sub


        -->
        </SCRIPT>
    </HEAD>
    <BODY>
        <H3>A demonstration of VBScript subroutines</H3>
        <INPUT NAME="MyButton" TYPE="Button" VALUE="Click Me">
    </BODY>
</HTML>
```

This is even more similar to the way Visual Basic works. The button that is created by the **<INPUT>** tag will automatically have an **OnClick** event associated with it. By simply defining a subroutine called **MyButton_OnClick** (**MyButton** is the name of the button control), we form the connection between the subroutine and the button. The **MyButton_OnClick** subroutine will be run when the latter is clicked.

Of course, like VB, we can also create our own user-defined subroutines and functions. In this example, we've taken the code that displays the message boxes, and put it into a separate subroutine called **GetOpinion**. We can call the subroutine from **MyButton_OnClick**. Later on we'll look at how functions can be used.

> One other way of using the **<INPUT>** tag is to specifically define the script for each event that you want the control to react to. For example:
>
> **INPUT NAME="Firstbutton" TYPE="Button" VALUE="Click Me" LANGUAGE = "VBScript" OnClick="MsgBox 'You did it!'">**
>
> And if we have a subroutine called **WhenButtonClicked,** we can insert an **<INPUT>** tag like this:
>
> **INPUT NAME="MyButton" TYPE="Button" VALUE="Click Me" LANGUAGE = "VBScript" OnClick = "WhenButtonClicked">**
>
> This method tends to make your code more difficult to follow, however, and isn't generally recommended.

One other point to notice is that the **<SCRIPT>** section is now within the **<HEAD>** of the page, rather than in the **<BODY>** section as we saw before. Where you place the code depends on when you want it to be loaded by the browser. It also affects the **context** of any variables or routines you create, as you'll see next.

When is the Script actually Executed?

As your browser loads a page containing a **<SCRIPT>** section, it analyzes and interprets the code contained there. Any code that isn't within a procedure (i.e. a function or subroutine) is executed as soon as that section of the page has loaded. So if you put code in the **<HEAD>** section, it'll be executed after the header has loaded, but before the rest of the page loads. If you put the code in the **<BODY>** section, it'll be executed when the complete page has loaded. Any normal HTML code and text (before the **<SCRIPT>** section in the source document) is displayed first, and then the rest is displayed after the code has loaded and has been stored and analyzed by the browser.

17

However, this is all different with code that *is* in a procedure. The browser stores this in memory and only executes it when a call is made to that procedure. This could be explicitly from a line in your script (for example, `GetOpinion`—as in the previous example), or implicitly if the routine has a name which automatically links it to a control, and that specific event has occurred (such as `MyButton_OnClick`).

The other point to note, which we'll come back to in more detail in later chapters, is that code placed in the `<HEAD>` section will be run before the rest of the page is created, or **rendered**. This is often necessary if you want to change some aspects of the page, which can include using VBScript commands to write text or create HTML tags. Once the complete page has been rendered, some of the VBScript commands will be unavailable.

How the Placing of Code Affects Context

Variables that are defined within a `<SCRIPT>` section, but outside any procedure (subroutine or function), are automatically **global**, and available to any other code in that page. They are also accessible from pages which are displayed in other frames. (The procedures themselves can be executed from pages in other frames.) However, variables that are defined within a procedure are **local** to that procedure, and can't be referenced from outside it. So, if you want some variables to be global, you'll need to define these outside all the other procedures—generally at the start of a `<SCRIPT>` section.

The following code sample shows the rules of context in more detail. You'll see why much of this is so important when we come to look at how frames can be used to display several different pages in your browser simultaneously.

```
<SCRIPT LANGUAGE="VBScript">
   <!-- hide from older browsers

   Dim MyGlobal      'is available to all procedures in the script

   Sub MySubroutine
      Dim MyLocal     'is only available within this procedure
      . . .
   End Sub

   -->
</SCRIPT>
```

Using Functions in VBScript

We've now seen how a simple script is included in an HTML page, and we've used a push button control to start it running. We've also examined how the code can be broken down into separate subroutines, some of which are explicitly named so as to create a connection between the control (in our case, a push button) and the VBScript code.

While these particular 'connecting' routines are always created as a subroutine, you often use a **function** if you're writing some more general user-defined procedures. For example, if you're calculating how many bricks you need to build a wall then you're likely to have a separate procedure that, given the length and height of the wall, calculates the result.

You could declare a global variable called **NumBricks**, and then update it in the procedure before retrieving the value in the calling code, but a neater way of doing this is to create a function which accepts the values for length and height, plus the size of a brick, as arguments (or **parameters**), and then returns the result by assigning it to the function itself. Here's an example of this type of function, taken from our sample page **HowManyBricks**.htm:

```
Function HowManyBricks (BrickHeight, BrickLength, WallHeight,
                                                  WallLength)
    Dim TheResult
    TheResult = Int(WallLength / BrickLength) + 1
    TheResult = TheResult * (Int(WallHeight / BrickHeight) + 1)
    HowManyBricks = TheResult
End Function
```

The main body of the code can call this function and, when it does so, it supplies the values for the four arguments **BrickHeight**, **BrickLength**, **WallHeight** and **WallLength**. The function declares a local variable to hold the result, and then calculates this value from those values in the four arguments. Finally, we return the result by assigning it to the function name.

As in Visual Basic, the built-in **Int()** function returns the integer part of a number, and so by dividing the length by the size of a brick and adding one to the integer result, and then doing the same with the height, we're sure to have enough bricks.

> Unlike most other languages, VBScript code within a subroutine or function *can't* change the values in the arguments that are supplied upon the code being called. Attempting to do so will cause a script error. This is generally a desirable effect anyway, because changing values in this way is an easy method of creating bugs that are almost impossible to locate. If you *do* need to change the value of any argument within a subroutine or function, you can always use the **ByVal** keyword with that argument, although the original value (outside the subroutine or function) will be unchanged.
>
> ```
> Function  MyProc(CannotBeChanged,  ByVal  ChangeWithinOnly)
> ```
>
> Normally, when you call a function, it receives the address in the memory where the values of the arguments are stored. This makes the process quick and efficient because the values themselves don't need to be sent to it. Using **ByVal** means that the function actually receives a copy of the value, instead of its address. Within the function, you can modify the value of the copy, but the original argument will remain unchanged. The same also applies to subroutines which accept arguments, as well as functions, as we've been discussing here.

Using other <INPUT> Controls with VBScript

To complete our first look at VBScript, we'll see how other standard HTML controls can be used in a page. So far, we have used only a push button, so let's add some text boxes. In the next chapter we'll see code that manipulates list boxes, check boxes, option buttons, and other controls.

The most obvious application of simple VBScript is to provide calculation capabilities within a Web page. Previously you would have had to place a **<FORM>** section in the page, containing various controls into which the user could enter values. When they clicked the Submit button, the values would have been sent back to the server from the browser, and a special program there would have carried out the manipulation of the values. It would have then sent a new page back to the browser, and this would contain the result. This is called **Server Side Processing**.

Modern browser technology is moving more and more towards **Client Side Processing**. In this case, the actual browser carries out the manipulation required on the values, and it then displays the result—often in the same page. VBScript is an ideal (and simple) way to accomplish this type of action. Here's how the **HowManyBricks** function we introduced earlier can be used directly in a page:

```
<HTML>
   <HEAD>
      <TITLE>A Simple Calculation</TITLE>
      <SCRIPT LANGUAGE="VBScript">
      <!-- hide from older browsers

      Function HowManyBricks (BrickHeight, BrickLength, WallHeight,
                                                       WallLength)
         Dim TheResult
         TheResult = Int(WallLength / BrickLength) + 1
         TheResult = TheResult * (Int(WallHeight / BrickHeight) + 1)
         HowManyBricks = TheResult
      End Function

      Sub btnCalc_OnClick
         Dim NumBricks, BHigh, BLen
         BHigh = 0.33
         BLen = 0.75
         NumBricks = HowManyBricks(BHigh, BLen, txtWHigh.Value,
                                                txtWLen.Value)
         MsgBox "You'll need " & NumBricks & " bricks."
      End Sub

      -->
      </SCRIPT>
   </HEAD>
   <BODY>
      <H3>How many bricks do you need?</H3>
      Length of wall in feet: <INPUT NAME="txtWLen" TYPE="text" SIZE=5>
      <P>
      Height of wall in feet: <INPUT NAME="txtWHigh" TYPE="text" SIZE=5>
      <P>
      <INPUT NAME="btnCalc" TYPE="Button" VALUE="Calculate">
   </BODY>
</HTML>
```

And here's the result in Internet Explorer. To keep the script simple, we've used a message box for the result, but, as you'll see later, it could just as easily have been another text box on the page:

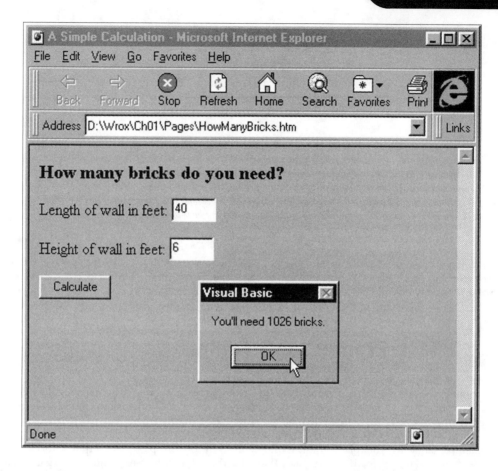

In the **<BODY>** section of the page are two text controls and a button, produced again with normal HTML **<INPUT>** tags. We've named the text boxes **txtWLen** and **txtWHigh**, and have set their display size to **5** characters. The button is named **btnCalc**, and has the caption Calculate.

```
<BODY>
   <H3>How many bricks do you need?</H3>
   Length of wall in feet: <INPUT NAME="txtWLen" TYPE="text" SIZE=5>
   <P>
   Height of wall in feet: <INPUT NAME="txtWHigh" TYPE="text" SIZE=5>
   <P>
   <INPUT NAME="btnCalc" TYPE="Button" VALUE="Calculate">
</BODY>
```

To connect the button with the code, we've written a subroutine called **btnCalc_OnClick**. It sets the size of a brick in **BHigh** and **BLen**, and then calls the **HowManyBricks** function. The result is assigned to the variable **NumBricks**, and this is displayed in a message box.

```
Sub btnCalc_OnClick
   Dim NumBricks, BHigh, BLen
   BHigh = 0.33    'the height of one brick in feet
   BLen = 0.75     'the length of one brick in feet
   NumBricks = HowManyBricks(BHigh, BLen, txtWHigh.Value,
```

```
                                                        txtWLen.Value)
        MsgBox "You'll need " & NumBricks & " bricks."
    End Sub
```

Notice how we refer to the values in the text box controls. Even though they are simple **<INPUT>** tags, the browser actually creates them as **objects**. They have their own **properties** and **methods**, and one of these properties is the **Value**—the text they contain.

> *While we're discussing objects, three words you'll be meeting all the time are **properties**, **methods**, and **events**. A **property** of an object is merely an aspect of it that we can access (and often change) from outside the object, such as the **Value** property used above. A **method** concerns some processing that an object can do internally, often upon its own data. (For example, a method called **Clear** which could delete the data stored in the object.) Finally, an **event**—as you've seen earlier—is some occurrence that the object recognizes, such as a mouse click or key press. Bear in mind that this doesn't have to be something that the viewer does—it could be in response to the browser loading a new page or similar.*

The standard way of referring to an object's properties or methods is with the **period** notation: **objectname.propertyname** or **objectname.methodname**. So, to retrieve the value in the **txtWHigh** and **txtWLen** text boxes, we just use **txtWHigh.Value** and **txtWLen.Value**. In the next couple of chapters, you'll be seeing a lot more about how we refer to and manipulate an object's properties.

Using HTML Frames and Tables

Two of the features that have been introduced in later versions of the HTML language are **tables** and **frames**. These give a huge increase in the freedom of design of Web pages, allowing really complex and artistic results to be produced. However, they also offer some more basic benefits to VBScript programmers and users of other scripting languages.

For example, they let you place controls more precisely on the page, or output information to the user without having to load a new page that fills the whole browser window. In particular, frames make the creation of truly interactive Web pages a reality. You can dynamically update one frame while the user is working within another. You'll see both tables and frames used in many of our sample pages, and you need to be conversant with these to fully appreciate what's going on. In particular, understanding the hierarchy of the browser and the pages being displayed requires a real grasp of the way frames are constructed.

So even though knowledge of tables and frames isn't actually *required*, they are so useful that you can't really afford to ignore them. While your excuse for avoiding them in the past may have been to maintain maximum compatibility with older browsers, remember that VBScript will only work on the more recent browsers, and they will all support tables and frames.

Creating Tables in a Web Page

This isn't designed to be a tutorial on using tables, but more a quick refresher. We'll show you how to structure a table, and some of the extra effects you can apply to it. Although defining a table looks complicated (a jumble of tags which define the appearance), it really is quite easy to do. It uses four basic tags:

 <TABLE>, which defines the whole table.

 <TR>, which defines a complete row.

<TH>, which defines a table heading cell.

 <TD>, which defines the details of an individual cell.

Here's a simple example. We've added the **BORDER=1** argument so that you can see the table borders—by default, they're not visible.

```
<TABLE BORDER=1>
   <TR>
      <TH> Column 1 Heading </TH>
      <TH> Column 2 Heading </TH>
   </TR>
   <TR>
      <TD> Detail for Row 1, Column 1 </TD>
      <TD> Detail for Row 1, Column 2 </TD>
   </TR>
   <TR>
      <TD> Detail for Row 2, Column 1 </TD>
      <TD> Detail for Row 2, Column 2 </TD>
   </TR>
</TABLE>
```

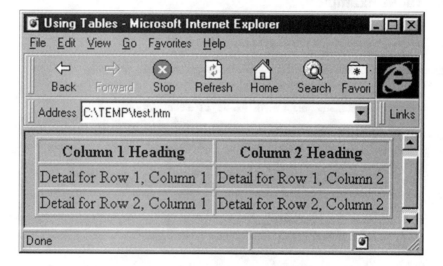

The only difference between the **<TH>** tag and the **<TD>** tag is the way in which the result is formatted. **<TH>** generally makes the text bold, and centers it in the cell. **<TD>** aligns text to the left, unless you add an **ALIGN** argument to change this.

Aligning Text in a Table Cell

In any cell, you can align text **LEFT**, **RIGHT** or **CENTER**. You can also change the vertical alignment of text, which is useful if some cells have text which wraps over several lines. By default, text is aligned centrally in a cell, but you can add the **VALIGN** argument with the values **TOP** or **BOTTOM** to change this—if you don't specify anything, the default is **MIDDLE**.

Changing the Appearance of a Table

Other arguments allow you to change the color of the cell background or the borders, and use a background image in the table. And of course, you can display images in the cells themselves by placing the **<IMG>** tag within the **<TD>** and **</TD>** tags. With only a little extra effort you can create tables which are really striking (or alternatively, unbelievably hideous) in appearance.

Adding Captions to a Table

One other tag that's useful with tables is the **<CAPTION>** tag. With this you can display a text caption above or below a table. The two common arguments are **ALIGN** and **VALIGN**. **ALIGN** controls the horizontal alignment, and can be **LEFT** or **RIGHT**. Otherwise, the default is centered. **VALIGN** can be **TOP** or **BOTTOM**, to place the caption above or below the table. This code places a caption to the left and above a table:

```
<TABLE>
   <CAPTION ALIGN=LEFT VALIGN=TOP> Text of the caption </CAPTION>
   . . . rest of table definition . . .
</TABLE>
```

A Simple Table Example

Here's an example of some of these various table tags used together, and the result is displayed in Internet Explorer. It's called **UseTable.htm**.

```
<TABLE BORDER BORDERCOLORLIGHT=Black BORDERCOLORDARK=White>
   <TR >
      <TH ALIGN=LEFT> <IMG SRC="Wrox.gif"> </TH>
      <TH BGCOLOR=Red> <H2> Wrox Press Limited </H2> </TH>
   </TR>
   <TR>
      <TD ALIGN=RIGHT BGCOLOR=#EED6C6> <STRONG> Where? </STRONG> </TD>
      <TD ALIGN=CENTER>
         <STRONG> Chicago, USA <I> and </I> Birmingham, England </STRONG>
      </TD>
   </TR>
   <TR>
      <TD ALIGN=RIGHT BGCOLOR=#EED6C6> <STRONG> Why? </STRONG> </TD>
      <TD ALIGN=CENTER > Publishing the best computer books around. </TD>
   </TR>
   <TR>
      <TD ALIGN=RIGHT BGCOLOR=#EED6C6> <STRONG> Contact? </STRONG> </TD>
      <TD ALIGN=CENTER>
         <A HREF="http://www.wrox.com"> http://www.wrox.com</A> or e-mail
         to <A HREF="mailto:feedback@wrox.com"> feedback@wrox.com</A>
      </TD>
   </TR>
   <TR>
      <TD ALIGN=RIGHT VALIGN=TOP BGCOLOR=#EED6C6>
         <STRONG> More Info: </STRONG>
      </TD>
      <TD> Wrox are one of the <I> premier </I> publishers . . </TD>
   </TR>
</TABLE>
```

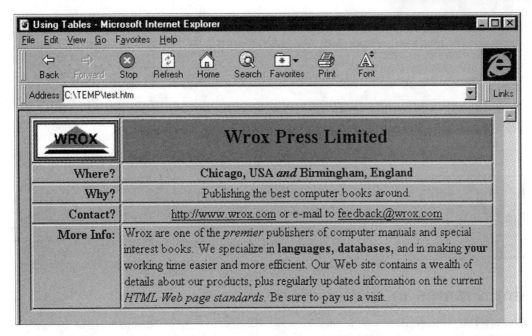

Here we've used several arguments to change the color of the cell background and borders. The
BGCOLOR argument can be set to a color name, such as Black, Red, etc., or to the **RGB triple**—the
values between **0** and **255** for each of the three primary colors Red Green and Blue. It's usual to
specify these in hexadecimal form, preceded by a hash sign. So **#EED6C6** gives a kind of light
pink color. You can also change the color of the table borders using the **BORDERCOLOR** argument,
together with a color name or RGB triple.

In our example, though, we've taken advantage of two other arguments—**BORDERCOLORLIGHT** and
BORDERCOLORDARK. These are the colors of the 3-D effect border lines, and by reversing them
from their normal colors we've got a table that appears to have etched lines between the cells—a
lot nicer.

> You can use the color (and other) arguments in any of the table tags. For
> example, you can set the background color of the table in the opening
> **<TABLE>** tag, and then you can set individual cells to a different color in
> the **<TR>**, **<TH>** or **<TD>** tags. The settings in the **<TH>** and **<TD>** tags override
> those in the **<TR>** tag, which in turn overrides those in the **<TABLE>** tag.

ROWSPAN and COLSPAN Attributes

Another feature of tables that can help to produce a really good presentation style is the ability to
have one cell span multiple rows or columns. This is achieved very simply within the **<TD>** (or
<TH>) tags with the **ROWSPAN** and **COLSPAN** attributes. The following example demonstrates this:

```
<TABLE BORDER=2>
  <TR >
    <TH COLSPAN=3 ALIGN=CENTER> Big Heading</TH>
```

```
   </TR>
   <TR>
      <TD ROWSPAN=2> Side <BR>Head</TD>
      <TD> R1C1</TD>
      <TD> R1C2</TD>
   </TR>
   <TR>
      <TD> R2C1</TD>
      <TD> R2C2</TD>
   </TR>
</TABLE>
```

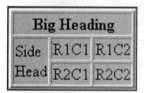

As you can see, the single cell of the first row spans three columns in total, and the first cell of the second row spans two rows. Notice that the third row only has two **<TD>** entries. The first cell has effectively already been declared in the previous **ROWSPAN** entry.

Using Frames in a Web Page

Many HTML writers never use **frames**, basically because they can't be sure that the majority of viewers will be using the latest browser. Viewing a document which contains frames on a normal browser means that you can miss much of the functionality and information in the pages. However, frames are supported in the recent releases of both the Netscape and Microsoft browsers, and many proprietary browsers also contain such support. VBScript is particularly good at manipulating information in a multiframe page.

We'll cover frames in a bit more depth than tables, just to make sure that you really grasp the concepts. Later, when we're knee-deep in VBScript, you'll need this knowledge to fully understand what's going on.

A Hierarchy of Pages

If you've never used frames before, you probably think of the browser window as only holding one page at a time. When you click on a link, or type a new URL into the Address box, the browser closes the current page and opens a new one. You can load another page into a new window instead of the existing one, but then you effectively have two independent copies of the browser running.

When you use frames, you divide the browser window up into rectangular sections (the frames), and then load a different page into each frame. Instead of a single document, you can display several, and they then form a fixed hierarchy. This gives you far more control over the way the information is presented, but it does mean that you have to be able to grasp how the documents are related, and you must be able to navigate through the hierarchy.

Defining the Frames

To create frames, you use two new tags:

 <FRAMESET>, which replaces the **<BODY>** tags and defines how the window is subdivided.

<FRAME>, which defines the document that appears in each frame and how that frame behaves.

Here's a simple example, and the result is shown in Internet Explorer:

```
<HTML>
   <HEAD>
      <TITLE> Frame Test</TITLE>
   </HEAD>
   <FRAMESET COLS="150,*">
      <FRAME SRC="leftpage.htm">
      <FRAME SRC="rightpage.htm">
   </FRAMESET>
</HTML>
```

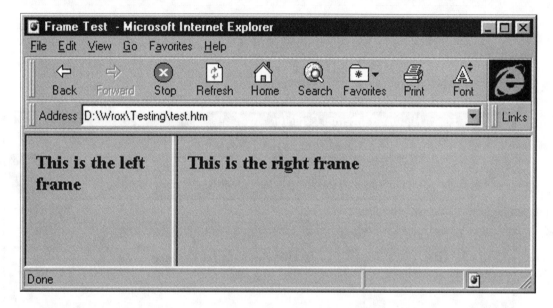

The opening **<FRAMESET>** tag contains the **COLS** argument, and this defines the width of the columns. We've used **COLS="150,*"**, which makes the first (left-hand) column 150 pixels wide, and the asterisk means 'the rest'—so the second column takes up the remainder of the browser window width. If you resize the window, the left column stays at the same width. To define three columns, we could use **COLS="75,*,150"**, for example. Now the left- and right-hand columns are of fixed width, and the central column will take up the remaining space. As well as specifying the size of the frame in pixels, we can use a percentage of the browser window. To make a frame use a quarter of the window width, we would enter **COLS="25%,*"**.

Notice the subtle difference here. Specifying the size in pixels means that the frame will always stay at that size, irrespective of how the browser main window is resized while the page is displayed. However, using the percentage method means that the frames will be resized to match the new window size.

Within the **<FRAMESET>** and **</FRAMESET>** tag pair, we place a **<FRAME>** tag for each frame that we've defined, and use an **SRC** argument with it to identify which document is to be loaded into each frame. In this case, there are two, and they reference simple documents which contain just the text you can see in the screenshot. The documents are called **leftpage.htm** and **rightpage.htm**, and are stored in the same folder as the main document.

> The **SRC** argument behaves just as it does with an **<IMG>** tag. If the documents are not in the same folder then you have to supply the path to them. For example, if they are in a sub-folder called **MyDocs** then you would use **SRC="MyDocs/leftpage.htm"**. Alternatively, you can use the full URL if they are stored elsewhere, for example: **SRC="http://www.wrox.com/ MyDocs/leftpage.htm"**
>
> If the document specified as the **SRC** doesn't exist, you'll generally get an error message when you come to load the page.

If you want to split the browser window horizontally, rather than vertically, you use the **ROWS** attribute in the **<FRAMESET>** tag instead. And to split it both ways you just use both attributes together:

```
<FRAMESET ROWS="100,*" COLS="150,*">
```

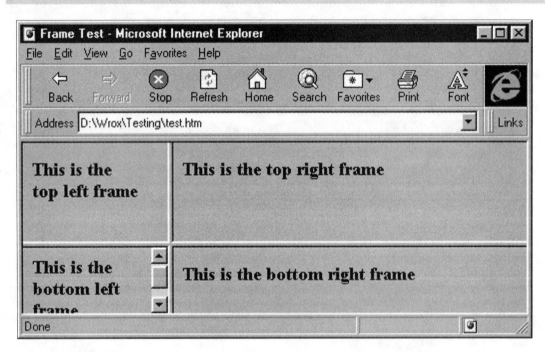

Instead of specifying the frame sizes in pixels, you can define what **proportion** of the available window width they should use. This is similar to using tables. The tag:

```
<FRAMESET ROWS="50%,*" COLS="10%,*">
```

will divide the window into two halves horizontally, and will produce a left column which is one tenth of the widow width.

You'll see from the screenshot that the browser automatically adds scroll bars to a frame where there isn't room to display all of the page. This is just one of the things that you can control by adding extra attributes to the **<FRAME>** tag. Several of the other standard HTML arguments can be used as well, such as:

- 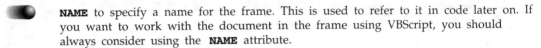 **NAME** to specify a name for the frame. This is used to refer to it in code later on. If you want to work with the document in the frame using VBScript, you should always consider using the **NAME** attribute.

- **SCROLLING** can be set to **YES** or **NO** to make scroll bars always or never available—even if the document won't all fit in the window. If omitted, **AUTO** is assumed, and they are only added if required, as you've seen.

- **NORESIZE** prevents the user from being able to change the size of the frame by dragging the divider bar. If you've specified the size of a frame to suit a particular graphic (in pixels), this can prevent users upsetting the look of your page.

- **FRAMEBORDER** can be set to **YES** or **NO** to control if a border is displayed for the frame. This is useful if you want adjacent frames to appear as though they are a single frame.

- **MARGINHEIGHT** and **MARGINWIDTH** control the size of the vertical and horizontal margin in that frame—in the same way that they can be used in the main **<BODY>** tag of a normal HTML document.

Here are some examples of the various **<FRAME>** tag arguments:

```
<FRAMESET COLS="100,200,*">
   <FRAME SRC="menu.htm" SCROLLING=NO NORESIZE>
   <FRAME SRC="values.htm" NAME="inputpage">
   <FRAME SRC="results.htm" NAME="resultspage" MARGINWIDTH=20>
</FRAMESET>
```

The first and leftmost column is fixed at 100 pixels wide. This allows us to display a narrow graphic as the menu without showing the scroll bars, and it prevents the user from changing the frame width. The second column is named **inputpage**, so that we can retrieve values from controls on it in our code. The third column is again named, and we've defined a 20 pixel wide margin for it.

Nesting <FRAMESET> Tags

The previous examples show a simple hierarchy of pages. The **main** page is the **parent** of the pages that fill each frame. However, we can nest **<FRAMESET>** tags within one another to create more complex frame layouts. For example:

```
<FRAMESET ROWS="50,*,35%" >
   <FRAME SRC="toppage.htm" SCROLLING=NO>
   <FRAMESET COLS="100,*">
      <FRAME SRC="mleftpage.htm">
      <FRAME SRC="mrightpage.htm">
   </FRAMESET>
   <FRAMESET COLS="70%,*">
      <FRAME SRC="bleftpage.htm">
      <FRAME SRC="brightpage.htm">
   </FRAMESET>
</FRAMESET>
```

This splits the window into three rows first, and then the second and third rows are split again with nested **<FRAMESET>** tags. The result is a much more complex layout, and one that you can easily imagine would allow tremendous freedom when designing your pages.

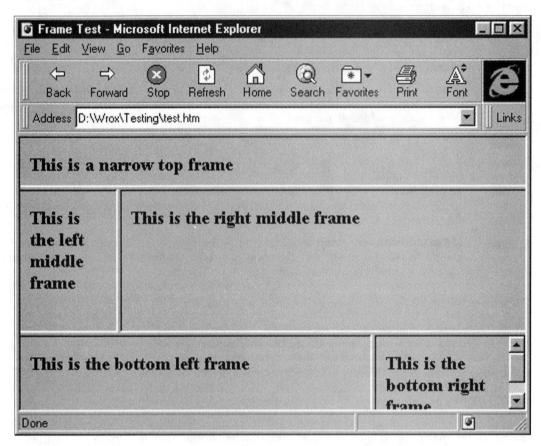

An alternative method of creating this type of complex frame layout is to move the nested **<FRAMESET>** tags down the hierarchy and into the documents that are defined in the **<FRAME>** tags of the main document. In other words, each document has only one **<FRAMESET>**, but the documents that it defines can each have their own **<FRAMESET>** tags. We could achieve the same effect as above by using the following three separate documents. The first is the main document that we're actually loading into the browser:

```
    . . .
    <FRAMESET ROWS="50,*,35%" >
        <FRAME SRC="toppage.htm" SCROLLING=NO>
        <FRAME SRC="middle.htm" >
        <FRAME SRC="bottom.htm" >
    </FRAMESET>
    . . .
```

The document **toppage.htm** is just the text that you see in the screenshot. However, **middle.htm** defines a **<FRAMESET>** which divides its own window (the middle row) into two columns:

30

```
. . .
<FRAMESET COLS="100,*">
   <FRAME SRC="mleftpage.htm">
   <FRAME SRC="mrightpage.htm">
</FRAMESET>
. . .
```

Similarly, the document **bottom.htm** divides up its own row:

```
. . .
<FRAMESET COLS="70%,*">
   <FRAME SRC="bleftpage.htm">
   <FRAME SRC="brightpage.htm">
</FRAMESET>
. . .
```

And, of course, there's no reason why the documents that these pages reference shouldn't contain yet another level of **<FRAMESET>** tags. However, now the parent of these documents is no longer the main document. To refer to it, you have to start looking for the parent of the parent of the current document.

> You'll see more about how pages are related in frames, and how we reference the main and parent windows later. For the time being, it's enough to understand how the hierarchy comes about, and how the methods used to create the frames will affect it.

There are two more things that we need to consider before we leave the subject of frames. Next we'll see how to select which frame the documents are loaded into when the user clicks on a hyperlink, or when our VBScript code comes to display a different page. Finally, we must consider what happens when an older type of browser loads a page which contains frames.

Targeting Documents to Specific Frames

When you click on a hyperlink in a frame to load a new page, it's loaded into the same frame as the hyperlink. This may be the effect that you want, but in some cases you'll want the page to be loaded into a different frame. For example, if you use a small frame to display a menu bar, you'll probably want to display each new page in the larger main frame instead.

To do this, you use the **TARGET** argument in the **<A>** tag that creates the link. You can also specify the default frame for all links using the **<BASE>** tag in the page's **<HEAD>** section.

To set the default for all links to be a frame which is named **resultspage**, we just add the following to the **<HEAD>** section of the page. (Of course, we have to have named the frame using the **NAME** argument in its **<FRAME>** tag.)

```
<BASE TARGET="resultspage">
```

To specify a particular frame in a hyperlink, we add a **TARGET** argument to the **<A>** tag. It overrides the default set in the **<BASE>** tag for this link only:

```
<A HREF="newresult.htm" TARGET="anotherpage"> . . . </A>
```

31

We can also redirect the results of a form submission. When you click Submit in a normal form, where the results are processed by the server, it generally sends back a 'thank you' page to acknowledge receipt. Adding the **TARGET** argument to the **<FORM>** tag means that we can control which frame receives the page:

```
<FORM METHOD="POST" ACTION="/cgi_bin/fmhndl.pl" TARGET="resultspage">
```

There are also four special values that you can use with the **TARGET** argument to control where new pages are loaded:

- **TARGET="_top"** forces the new page to be loaded into the topmost main window in the hierarchy. If you're struggling to get rid of frames once you've 'switched them on', this is the answer. The new document removes existing frames, and will create any new frames that it defines itself.

- **TARGET="_parent"** loads the new page into the immediate parent of the window where the hyperlink resides. This could be the entire main window, but it may not be if you have used nested frame tags.

- **TARGET="_self"** loads the new page into the same window as the one where the hyperlink is situated, ignoring any settings for the **<BASE TARGET=..>** tag.

- **TARGET="_blank"** loads the page into a new window, effectively opening a second instance of the browser. Use this with care, because unless the viewer remembers to keep closing them, they'll end up with several copies open.

Coping with Older Browsers

When a browser that doesn't support frames loads a page with **<FRAMESET>** and **<FRAME>** tags, it simply ignores them. Any pages that they reference won't appear, and as your main document will probably only contain the **<FRAMESET>** definition, they'll get a totally blank screen. This isn't terribly useful. Instead you should make use of the **<NOFRAMES>** tag.

All browsers that recognize the **<FRAMESET>** tag will also recognize the **<NOFRAMES>** and **</NOFRAMES>** tag pair, and so will ignore everything between these opening and closing tags. But of course, older browsers won't recognize **<NOFRAMES>**, so they'll display this. It means that you can design part of a page which you know will only be displayed by browsers that don't have support for frames.

```
<HTML>
<HEAD>
   <TITLE> Frame Test</TITLE>
</HEAD>
<FRAMESET ROWS="50,*,35%" >
   <FRAME SRC="toppage.htm" SCROLLING=NO>
   <FRAME SRC="middle.htm" >
   <FRAME SRC="bottom.htm" >
</FRAMESET>
<NOFRAMES>
   <H3>This page uses frames for full effect. Because your browser
   doesn't support frames, we suggest you use our
   <A HREF="altmenu.htm">alternative menu</A>.</H3>
</NOFRAMES>
</HTML>
```

This is how it would look in an older version of the Netscape navigator:

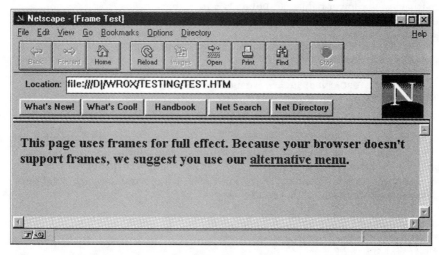

A Simple Tables and Frames Example

Just so that you can see the techniques in use, here's a simple example that uses frames and tables. It's called **WroxVBBooks.htm**, and contains details of four of the books we publish which cover Visual Basic and VBA. It also looks very different from the other sample pages that we've seen in this chapter.

The main HTML page that you load, **WroxVBBooks.htm**, divides the browser window into three **frames**, and names the lower-right one **DetailPage** using:

```
<FRAMESET ROWS="50,*">
   <FRAME SRC="VBBHead.htm" SCROLLING=NO NORESIZE>
   <FRAMESET COLS="140,*">
      <FRAME SRC="VBBMenu.htm" SCROLLING=NO NORESIZE>
      <FRAME SRC="VBB559.htm" NAME="DetailPage" MARGINWIDTH=20>
   </FRAMESET>
</FRAMESET>
```

The top frame contains just the page title, but you can see that it doesn't appear in the normal browser font or color. We've taken advantage of another tag which is slowly becoming standardized across newer browsers. This is the **<STYLE>** tag, and it allows you much more control over the way text is presented on a page. Here's the complete page **VBBHead.htm**, which is loaded into the top frame by the **<FRAME>** tag:

```
<HTML>
   <HEAD>
      <TITLE>Wrox Books</TITLE>
      <STYLE>
        <!--
        H2 { color: white; font-family: courier }
        -->
      </STYLE>
   </HEAD>
   <BODY BGCOLOR="red">
      <CENTER><H2>Visual Basic Books from Wrox Press</H2></CENTER>
   </BODY>
</HTML>
```

The background color of the page is set to red using the **BGCOLOR** attribute of the **<BODY>** tag. Immediately after that is the new **<STYLE>** tag pair. Between the opening and closing tags, we place one or more lines which define a particular style for our text. In this example, we've set the style for Heading 2 **<H2>** text to a white **Courier** font. Notice the unusual syntax of curly brackets, colons and semicolons, and the use of the comment tag to prevent older browsers displaying the contents of the tag.

In the pages that show the details of the books, we've used the style tag in the same way, but this time we have defined the style to apply to all text, by omitting the **H2** part:

```
<STYLE>
  <!--
  { color: black; font-family: arial }
  -->
</STYLE>
```

> There are a whole range of ways in which you can use the **<STYLE>** tag to change the way your pages look. Check out the details by pointing your browser to **http://microsoft.com/workshop/design/des-gen/ss/css-des-f.htm** for more information.

The two lower frames are filled with pages that both include tables. The left-hand frame is a menu, where you can select the book that you want to read about. Here's the HTML code, **VBBMenu.htm**, which creates the page:

```html
<HTML>
    <HEAD>
        <TITLE>VB Books List</TITLE>
        <BASE TARGET="DetailPage">
        <STYLE>
            <!--
            H4 { color: black; font-family: arial }
            -->
        </STYLE>
    </HEAD>
    <BODY BGCOLOR="white" LEFTMARGIN=20>
        <TABLE WIDTH=100><H4>
            <TR>
                <TD><A HREF="http://www.wrox.com" TARGET="_top">
                    <IMG SRC="Wrox.gif" BORDER=0></A></TD>
            </TR>
            <TR><TD><HR></TD></TR>
            <TR>
                <TD><A HREF="VBB559.htm">
                    Beginner's Visual Basic 4.0</A></TD>
            </TR>
            <TR><TD><HR></TD></TR>
            <TR>
                <TD><A HREF="VBB370.htm">
                    Visual Basic 4 Professional</A></TD>
            </TR>
            <TR><TD><HR></TD></TR>
            <TR>
                <TD><A HREF="VBB648.htm">
                    Access VBA Programming</A></TD>
            </TR>
            <TR><TD><HR></TD></TR>
            <TR>
                <TD><A HREF="VBB788.htm">
                Instant Animation With VB</A></TD>
            </TR>
        </TABLE>
    </BODY>
</HTML>
```

It uses a single column table, with each book title contained in a cell. To separate the titles we've placed a horizontal rule **<HR>** between each one, in the alternate rows. Each title is enclosed in an **<A>** tag, and the **HREF** attribute is the name of the page that contains details about that book. Notice that we've set the default **TARGET** for these pages by using the line **<BASE TARGET="DetailPage">** in the **<HEAD>** section of the page. This is to make sure that each detail page is loaded into the other (lower-right) frame, and that it doesn't replace the menu page in the lower-left frame.

However, when the user clicks on the Wrox logo in the top row of the table, we want to load our Wrox home page into the entire browser window, replacing the existing frame structure. So we've added **TARGET="_top"** to this **<A>** tag, which then overrides the default set by the **<BASE>** tag.

Finally, the details about the four books are created with four other pages, and these again use frames. They are the pages **VBB559.htm**, **VBB370.htm**, **VBB648.htm**, and **VBB788.htm**, which you can see referenced in the other **<A>** tags. They only differ in the actual text they contain, and they use a two column by two row table in order to produce the layout that you can see in the screenshot.

```
<TABLE><H4>
   <TR>
      <TD><IMG SRC="370.gif"></TD>
      <TD VALIGN="bottom"> <B>Instant Animation with VB</B></TD>
   </TR>
   <TR>
      <TD VALIGN="TOP">ISBN:<BR>1874416788<P><B>Price: $34.95</B></TD>
      <TD>Professional techniques for using and improving . . .  </TD>
   </TR>
</TABLE>
```

> Like all the examples in this book, you can find this page on our Web site. All the samples which are directly applicable to each chapter are together so that, in the case of this example, **WroxVBBooks.htm**, you'll find it at:
>
> `http://www.wrox.com/books/0448/code/chapter01/WroxVBBooks.htm`
>
> You can view it directly in your browser, and you can even examine the source code. When you're viewing a page containing frames, the browser's **View | Source** menu shows the page that creates the frames (i.e. the 'top' page). To view the other pages that fill each frame, you need to right-click on that page and select **View Source** from the short-cut menu that appears.

Summary

You had a glimpse of one 'real world' application of VBScript in the example page from the fictitious Bob's Building Supplies Web site that we briefly saw at the beginning of the chapter. So far, we've intentionally spent a lot of time on the basics of VBScript so that you're comfortable with how it fits into an HTML page. We've used simple techniques, mainly small routines and message boxes, so that the examples are easy to follow. We've looked at:

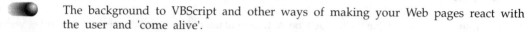

- The background to VBScript and other ways of making your Web pages react with the user and 'come alive'.

- The basic structure of an HTML page containing VBScript code.

- How we connect our VBScript code with an event in the browser, and how to use more complicated techniques such as variables and functions.

- How the new browser support for tables and frames works. Both of these features are especially useful with VBScript.

By now you should be happy with what VBScript is, and you should also have some idea of what it can do. No doubt you're already itching to get on and build your first pages, but before you do, there are some other basic techniques that you'll need to know.

In the next chapter, we need to further explore the relationships between the different items in the hierarchy of the browser: for example, the window itself, the frames it contains, and the documents displayed in each frame. At the same time we'll see how you can output information in ways other than a message box, and so make your pages look more professional. In fact, we'll take all of the things that you've learned about so far and we'll put them together in another small 'real world' application.

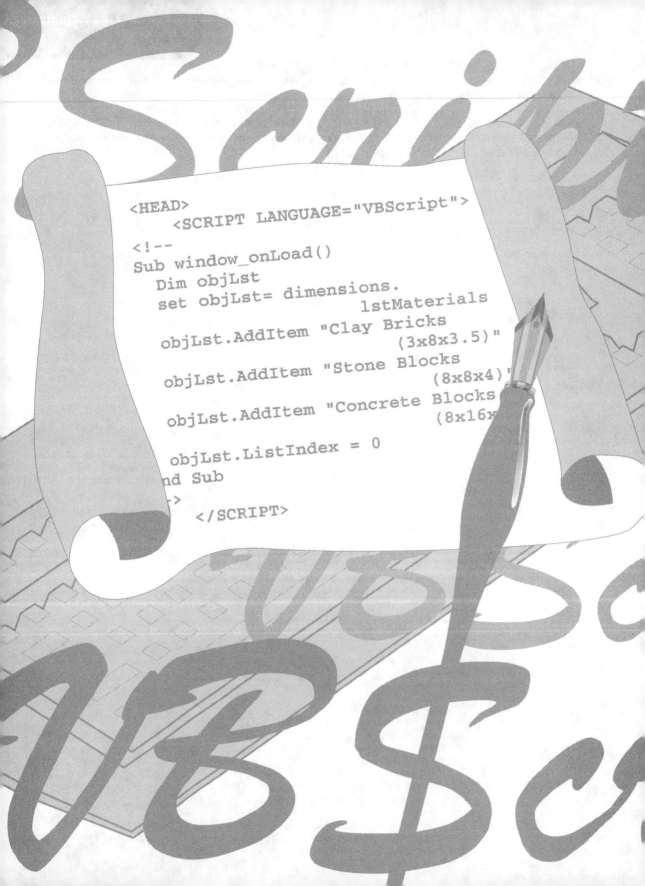

```
<HEAD>
    <SCRIPT LANGUAGE="VBScript">

<!--
Sub window_onLoad()
   Dim objLst
   set objLst= dimensions.
                             lstMaterials
   objLst.AddItem "Clay Bricks
                             (3x8x3.5)"
   objLst.AddItem "Stone Blocks
                             (8x8x4)"
   objLst.AddItem "Concrete Blocks
                             (8x16x
   objLst.ListIndex = 0
nd Sub
-->
    </SCRIPT>
```

Simple VBScript Pages

In Chapter 1, we looked at various basic techniques that you needed to grasp before you could start working with VBScript. These included the background to VBScript and what it can do, the ways in which you can insert VBScript into a Web page, and the behavior patterns of some of the simple controls. We also looked at the way you create tables and frames in your pages, because these are two of the more recent additions to HTML that you'll find very useful when you work with VBScript.

In this chapter, we'll put together all of the things that we've seen so far—such as the background and basic structure of VBScript, how to connect our code with events in the browser, and how tables and frames help to lay out a page. Then we'll go on to discuss some of the other issues that arise when you start to produce VBScript pages that actually do something useful. In particular, we'll be concentrating on different types of controls you can use and, at the end of the chapter, we'll introduce you to some of the simpler ActiveX controls.

So we'll be covering:

- How you create a working VBScript page, using ordinary HTML controls
- Controlling the errors that can arise as your scripts are executed
- Ways of outputting the results and other information to the user
- Using simple ActiveX controls instead of the HTML ones

First, let's see how a page that uses VBScript can perform some 'real-life' applications.

Doing Something Useful with VBScript

You've already had a glimpse of one 'real world' application of VBScript—the example page from Bob's Building Supplies Web site that we saw briefly at the beginning of Chapter 1. Here's a less complex example to help you get to grips with the various methods we introduced in that chapter. Again, it takes the form of a page that Bob could use on his Web site.

The Glass Load Calculator

This example calculates the weight of a load of ordinary window glass (with a small W!), given the total area required. Often customers will be working from the architect's drawings, and so will only know the total area of glass required for their building. Using this page, they can see how many packs of a particular standard stock size of glass they'll have to buy to be able to cut all of the panes that they need.

Of course, you could adapt it to work with any material that comes in stock sizes or standard packs, such as sheets of timber or cans of paint. It could even be changed to tell you how many cases of cola you need to buy to get, say, 17 gallons for your thirsty football team.

You can load this page yourself from our Web site. The address you need is:

> http://www.wrox.com/books/0448/code/chapter02/loadcalc.htm

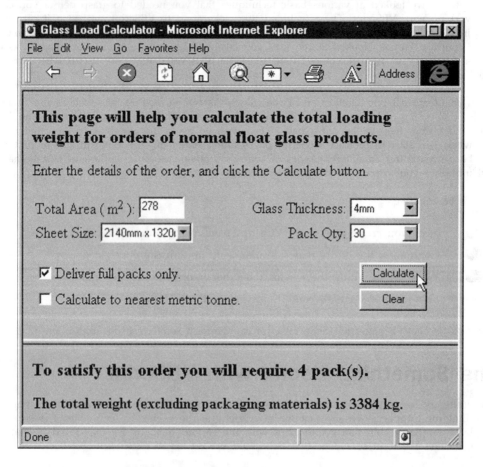

The screenshot shows the result of a calculation. Most of the world's producers specify glass in metric sizes, and so that's the unit of measurement that we've used here. Once again you can easily adapt the code to use other measurement systems. It's quite a simple example, but it demonstrates how the various techniques are used.

Frames within the Glass Load Calculator

The page is made up of two frames. The main page that you load (called `LoadCalc.htm`) contains just this:

```
<HTML>
  <HEAD>  <TITLE>Glass Load Calculator</TITLE>  </HEAD>
  <FRAMESET ROWS="75%,*">
    <FRAME SRC="CalcPage.htm" NAME="calcframe">
    <FRAME SRC="" NAME="resultframe">
  </FRAMESET>
</HTML>
```

> A frame with no source will always attempt to load `Blank.htm` (which is found in the `Windows\System` folder). If it can't be found then an error is generated. If `Blank.htm` is indeed missing then you'll need to create another one along the lines of:
>
> <HTML>
> </HTML>

It divides the browser window into two frames, and loads a different page (`CalcPage.htm`) into the top frame which we've named `calcframe`. The bottom frame is named `resultframe`, and is left empty ready for the results to be displayed.

Tables within the Glass Load Calculator

The HTML code in `CalcPage.htm` creates the header text for the page, and then uses two tables populated with normal `<INPUT>` or `<SELECT>` tags in each cell. These create the controls that you see on the page:

```
<TABLE WIDTH=100%>            <! An extract from CalcPage.htm >
  <TR>
    <TD>
      Total Area M2: <INPUT NAME="txtArea" TYPE="text" SIZE=6>
    </TD>
    <TD ALIGN=RIGHT> Glass Thickness:
      <SELECT NAME="lstThick" SIZE=1 >
        <OPTION> 3mm
        <OPTION SELECTED> 4mm
        <OPTION> 5mm
        <OPTION> 6mm
        <OPTION> 8mm
        <OPTION> 10mm
        <OPTION> 12mm
        <OPTION> 15mm
      </SELECT>
    </TD>
  </TR>
  <TR>
    <TD> Sheet Size:
      <SELECT NAME="lstSize" SIZE=1>
        <OPTION> 2100mm x 920mm <OPTION> 2100mm x 1220mm
```

```
              <OPTION SELECTED> 2140mm x 1320mm
              <OPTION> 2250mm x 1220mm <OPTION> 2500mm x 1605mm
          </SELECT>
      </TD>
      <TD ALIGN=RIGHT> Pack Qty:
          <SELECT NAME="lstPack" SIZE=1>
              <OPTION> 10 <OPTION> 15 <OPTION> 20
              <OPTION SELECTED> 30 <OPTION> 55
          </SELECT>
      </TD>
   </TR>
</TABLE>
<P>
<TABLE WIDTH=100%>
   <TR>
      <TD>
          <INPUT NAME="chkFullPack" TYPE="checkbox" CHECKED=TRUE>
          Deliver full packs only.
      </TD>
      <TD ALIGN=RIGHT>
          <INPUT NAME="btnCalc" TYPE="button" VALUE="Calculate">
      </TD>
   </TR>
   <TR>
      <TD>
          <INPUT NAME="chkTonne" TYPE="checkbox" >
          Calculate to nearest metric tonne.
      </TD>
      <TD ALIGN=RIGHT>
          <INPUT NAME="btnClear" TYPE="button" VALUE="Clear">
      </TD>
   </TR>
</TABLE>
```

As you can see, there's nothing unusual about the way the controls are built into the page. If we were using a normal `<FORM>` section to send information back to the server for processing—and there's no reason why we shouldn't—we would define the controls in the same way.

Event Handling within the Glass Load Calculator

The VBScript section is in the `<HEAD>` of the page, and it contains two subroutines called `btnCalc_OnClick` and `btnClear_OnClick`. These run when the relevant button on the page is clicked. Here's the full code listing from **CalcPage.htm**. Afterwards we'll consider some of the issues it raises, and will examine parts of it in turn.

```
<SCRIPT LANGUAGE="VBScript">         'from CalcPage.htm
<!-- hide from older browsers
Option Explicit        'prevent errors from misspelled variable names

Sub btnCalc_OnClick   'runs when the Calculate button is clicked

    Dim intSheetQty    'the total number of sheets
    Dim sngSheetArea   'the total number of sheets
    Dim intNumPacks    'the total number of packs
    Dim intNumLoose    'the total number of loose sheets
    Dim intPackQty     'the number of sheets in a pack
```

```
      Dim intThickness   'the glass thickness
      Dim sngWeight      'the total weight in kilograms
      Dim strWeight      'the total weight as a string value
      Dim strOutput      'the results output string

      ' check that we have an area entered
      If (Not IsNumeric(txtArea.Value)) Then
         MsgBox "You must enter a total area for the order"
         txtArea.Focus
         Exit Sub
      End If
      If (txtArea.Value = 0) Then
         MsgBox "You must enter a total area for the order"
         txtArea.Focus
         Exit Sub
      End If

      'get the area of each sheet
      Select Case lstSize.SelectedIndex
         Case 0 : sngSheetArea = CSng(1.93)
         Case 1 : sngSheetArea = CSng(2.56)
         Case 2 : sngSheetArea = CSng(2.82)
         Case 3 : sngSheetArea = CSng(2.75)
         Case 4 : sngSheetArea = CSng(4.01)
      End Select

      'calculate the quantity of sheets required
      intSheetQty = Int(txtArea.Value / sngSheetArea) + 1

      'get the quantity in a pack
      Select Case lstPack.SelectedIndex
         Case 0 : intPackQty = 10
         Case 1 : intPackQty = 15
         Case 2 : intPackQty = 20
         Case 3 : intPackQty = 30
         Case 4 : intPackQty = 55
      End Select

      'calculate how many packs this represents
      intNumPacks = Int(intSheetQty / intPackQty)
      If intNumPacks > 0 Then
         intNumLoose = intSheetQty Mod intPackQty
      Else
         intNumLoose = intSheetQty
      End If
      If chkFullPack.Checked And intNumLoose > 0 Then
         intNumPacks = intNumPacks + 1
         intSheetQty = intNumPacks * intPackQty
         intNumLoose = 0
      End If

      'get the glass thickness
      Select Case lstThick.SelectedIndex
         Case 0 : intThickness = 3
         Case 1 : intThickness = 4
         Case 2 : intThickness = 5
         Case 3 : intThickness = 6
         Case 4 : intThickness = 8
```

43

```
        Case 5 : intThickness = 10
        Case 6 : intThickness = 12
        Case 7 : intThickness = 15
    End Select

    'calculate the weight
    sngWeight = CSng(intSheetQty * sngSheetArea * intThickness * 2.5)
    If chkTonne.Checked Then
        strWeight = CStr(Int(sngWeight / 1000) + 1) & " tonnes"
    Else
        strWeight = CStr(Int(sngWeight * 100) / 100) & " kg"
    End If

    'create the results string
    strOutput = "<H3>To satisfy this order you will require "
    strOutput = strOutput & intNumPacks & " pack(s)"
    If chkFullPack.Checked Then
        strOutput = strOutput & "."
    Else
        strOutput = strOutput & " plus " & intNumLoose & " sheets."
    End If
    strOutput = strOutput & "</H3><H4>"
    If chkTonne.Checked Then
        strOutput = strOutput & "You will need to schedule a vehicle"
        strOutput = strOutput & " of " & strWeight & " for this load."
    Else
        strOutput = strOutput & "The total weight (excluding packaging"
        strOutput = strOutput & "materials) is " & strWeight & "."
    End If
    strOutput = strOutput & "</H4>"

    'and print it in the other frame
    top.resultframe.document.Open
    top.resultframe.document.WriteLn strOutput
    top.resultframe.document.Close

End Sub  'btnCalc_OnClick


Sub btnClear_OnClick  'runs when the Clear button is clicked
    top.resultframe.document.Clear
    top.resultframe.document.Close
    txtArea.Value = ""
    txtArea.Focus
End Sub

-->
</SCRIPT>
```

We've laid out the code so that it's easy to read and follow—it won't win any prizes for compactness or efficiency! For example, we've avoided using separate functions and subroutines for the repeated tasks. We'll work through the code examining the different techniques it brings into play.

The first line, **Option Explicit**, helps avoid potential variable problems later on, as we discussed in Chapter 1. Then we define the subroutine **btnCalc_OnClick**, which executes when the user clicks the Calculate button. In this routine, we first define the variables we need, using

44

the standard notation which indicates which type of value they will hold. This is another useful way of preventing errors (for example, forgetting what a variable called `TotalWeight` is supposed to contain—a string or a number) from creeping into your code.

> Remember that all VBScript variables are of the `Variant` type, and so can hold any type of data. Simply adding the type to the name doesn't change this, but it means that you're aware of how you should be storing the data. You'll see more of this later on when we look at variable naming conventions.

Validating the User's Entries

The first step with any script like this is to check that, before the user has clicked the Calculate button, they have entered all of the values we need to complete the calculation. Because we've used drop-down lists for most of the options, we know there will be valid data there as they can only select one of the options lists.

However, the Area text box requires the user to type in a value, so we need to check that this is valid before we go any further. Normally, if they typed something like 'six square metres', or left it blank altogether, we would get an error message later on because the code wouldn't be able to correctly convert the entry into a number. However, in our example, we've added a check which prevents invalid values being entered.

To check if the value is a number, we use the `IsNumeric()` function. And because we don't want to accept zero, we test for this as well. You may have expected to perform this action in one go, using code similar to the following:

```
If (Not IsNumeric(txtArea.Value)) Or (txtArea.Value = 0) Then . . .
```

If you try it, you'll find that entering non-numeric values produces a script error, because the browser tries to evaluate both sides of the **OR** condition—even though the first test fails. To get around this, we test the two conditions separately, only checking for zero if we know it's an actual number. Hence the code to handle these cases is duplicated. All it does is display a message, set the focus back to the Area text box using the **Focus** method of the control, and then exit from the subroutine.

```
'check that we have an area entered
If (Not IsNumeric(txtArea.Value)) Then
   MsgBox "You must enter a total area for the order"
   txtArea.Focus
   Exit Sub
End If
If (txtArea.Value = 0) Then
   MsgBox "You must enter a total area for the order"
   txtArea.Focus
   Exit Sub
End If
```

> Many languages allow short-circuit Boolean evaluation in condition tests like the previous code. This simply means that with conditional expressions containing two tests which are separated by **AND** or **OR**, evaluation stops when enough information is available to decide the outcome. For example, in an

> OR condition, where only one of the tests has to be **True** for the whole condition to be satisfied, it stops if the first test is **True**. Similarly, in an **AND** condition, where *both* of the tests have to be **True** for the whole condition to be satisfied, it stops if the first test is **False**. VBScript *doesn't* support this method of evaluation.

Getting the Values from the Controls

The next step in our example is to collect the values from the other controls. To get the value from the Area text box, we simply check its **Value** property using:

```
If (Not IsNumeric(txtArea.Value)) Then . . .
```

However, this won't work with a list box control. The only property which does reveal the current selection is the **SelectedIndex** property, which returns the index of the first item selected. Our lists are all single selection lists, so we know that the number returned will be the index (starting at **0**) of the item we want. To get the area of the sheet that the user selects, we use this code:

```
'get the area of each sheet
Select Case lstSize.SelectedIndex
    Case 0 : sngSheetArea = CSng(1.93)
    Case 1 : sngSheetArea = CSng(2.56)
    Case 2 : sngSheetArea = CSng(2.82)
    Case 3 : sngSheetArea = CSng(2.75)
    Case 4 : sngSheetArea = CSng(4.01)
End Select
```

It reads the value of the **SelectedIndex** of the **lstSize** control, and then uses it to obtain the sheet area directly from the **Select Case** statement—which contains the actual area of each sheet. To make sure it's stored in the correct format in the variable **sngSheetArea**, we've used the **CSng()** function to convert the result into a **Single** data type (which can hold non-integer values).

We've used the same methods with the other list boxes, although in these cases we've just taken the value that appears in the list and have put it into the **Select Case** statement, for example:

```
'get the quantity in a pack
Select Case lstPack.SelectedIndex
    Case 0 : intPackQty = 10
    Case 1 : intPackQty = 15
    Case 2 : intPackQty = 20
    Case 3 : intPackQty = 30
    Case 4 : intPackQty = 55
End Select
```

There's another way you can do this, however. In VBScript, a list box control has an **Options** property, an array-like data structure (usually called a **collection**) containing the values in the list. To get the actual text of the selected item in our **lstPack** control, we could use:

```
'get the quantity in a pack
intItemIndex = lstPack.SelectedIndex
intPackQty = CInt(lstPack.Options(intItemIndex).Text)
```

This first gets the value of **SelectedIndex** for the control, just as in the previous example. But then it uses this index to access the **Options** collection directly, retrieving the text of the currently selected item and converting it to an integer value.

> Remember that you can define a list box as a multiselect list, instead of a single-select list like ours, by including the **MULTIPLE** argument within the **<SELECT>** tag. In this case, you won't be able to retrieve all of the selected values because **SelectedIndex** only returns the first one.

Calculating the Results

As we go along, we carry out the various steps of the calculation. Once we've got the sheet area, we can calculate the quantity of sheets required by dividing it into the total area required. (For simplicity's sake, we're ignoring the waste element that cutting the sheets into individual panes would cause.) We convert the result to an integer and then add one, because unless the area is an exact multiple of a sheet, the customer will need an extra one for the fractional part of the result. If, by an incredibly slim chance it's an exact multiple, we'll actually end up sending them one extra sheet using this method. To be really accurate, you could check this before adding the extra one:

```
'calculate the quantity of sheets required
intSheetQty = Int(txtArea.Value / sngSheetArea) + 1
```

To work out the number of packs and loose sheets required, we just divide by the pack quantity. The integer result is the number of packs, and we can then use the **Mod** operator to find the number of loose sheets:

```
'calculate how many packs this represents
intNumPacks = Int(intSheetQty / intPackQty)
If intNumPacks > 0 Then
    intNumLoose = intSheetQty Mod intPackQty
Else
    intNumLoose = intSheetQty
End If
```

The **Mod** operator divides one number by another and returns only the remainder, discarding the multiples of the first number. So, for example, **32 Mod 7** gives **4**.

If the user has selected the Deliver Full Packs Only option, and they need loose sheets to make up the required area, we need to round up to the next pack and recalculate the total number of sheets. To get the setting of a check box control, we just have to read its **Checked** property, like this:

```
If chkFullPack.Checked And intNumLoose > 0 Then
    intNumPacks = intNumPacks + 1
    intSheetQty = intNumPacks * intPackQty
    intNumLoose = 0
End If
```

The final task in the calculation of the results is to find the total weight. We already know how many sheets there are, and the area of each sheet. To get the weight, we first obtain the total area (by multiplying the number of sheets by the area of each sheet), and then multiply this by the thickness in millimetres, and the weight per millimetre thickness (2.5 kg per mm thick per square metre). We assign the result to the variable **strWeight**, converting it to a string-type using the **CStr()** function.

```
'calculate the weight
sngWeight = CSng(intSheetQty * sngSheetArea * intThickness * 2.5)
If chkTonne.Checked Then
    strWeight = CStr(Int(sngWeight / 1000) + 1) & " tonnes"
Else
    strWeight = CStr(Int(sngWeight * 100) / 100) & " kg"
End If
```

Notice that we check the setting of the Calculate To Nearest Tonne check box first. If this is set (i.e. **chkTonne.Checked** is **True**), we make the weight up to the next complete tonne. Otherwise, we use the weight in kilograms, truncating it to two decimal places.

> VBScript doesn't support the very useful **Format()** function found in VB and VBA, so you have to format values for output using the **Int()** or **Fix()** functions instead. Here we've truncated the value to two decimal places by multiplying by **100**, taking the integer result, and dividing by **100** again.

Outputting the Information

Now we've got all the results we need, we can output them to the user. This could be done by using other text boxes on the page and setting their **Value** property to the values of the variables, like this:

```
txtTotalPacks.Value = CStr(intNumPacks)
```

However, we've chosen to use a separate frame for the results and to output them just like a new Web page. This is the way that the server would do it if you were returning the values to it for processing in the traditional way. But how do we actually get information into the other page?

Later on, we'll look in more detail at how the structure of the browser allows us to communicate with other pages. For the moment, you just need to know that the other frame can be accessed by referencing the name allocated to it within the **<FRAMESET>** structure (the structure responsible for its creation). In the **LoadCalc.htm** page that created the two frames, we named the lower frame **resultframe**, using the **NAME** argument in the **<FRAME>** tag:

```
<FRAMESET ROWS="75%,*">
    <FRAME SRC="CalcPage.htm" NAME="calcframe">
    <FRAME SRC="" NAME="resultframe">
</FRAMESET>
```

You'll recall how we mentioned in Chapter 1 that the different parts of the browser, and the pages being displayed, form a hierarchy. The main browser window is referred to simply as **top**, and each frame is a **child object** of this window. So we can refer to the **resultframe** frame using the syntax **top.resultframe**. Within this frame is the document we want to write to, and, because it's a child object of the frame, this is referred to with **top.resultframe.document**.

There are many ways in which you can refer to the main browser window and the other frames within it. In Chapters 4 and 5, we'll be looking in detail at how best to refer to the other parts of the hierarchy.

The document object supports **methods**, and among them are ones which can be used to place output into the document. For example, **Write** outputs the text directly to the page, and **WriteLn** does the same but adds a carriage return. **Open** and **Close** set up the document to receive text, and then display it afterwards. First however, we have to create the text string that we want to output.

> Methods are the way in which an object can carry out some action on its own data. Don't worry too much about this for the time being, as you'll be seeing much more about objects and their properties and methods later in this chapter, and throughout the rest of the book.

Building a String

The next section of code builds the result into a single string, **strOutput**, and you'll see that this includes the various HTML tags we want to use within the text—just as we would if we were creating the page in a text editor. When we write the text to the new page, the tags are interpreted by the browser in the same way as when it reads a normal HTML page.

```
'create the results string
strOutput = "<H3>To satisfy this order you will require "
strOutput = strOutput & intNumPacks & " pack(s)"
If chkFullPack.Checked Then
    strOutput = strOutput & "."
Else
    strOutput = strOutput & " plus " & intNumLoose & " sheets."
End If
strOutput = strOutput & "</H3><H4>"
If chkTonne.Checked Then
    strOutput = strOutput & "You will need to schedule a vehicle"
    strOutput = strOutput & " of " & strWeight & " for this load."
Else
    strOutput = strOutput & "The total weight (excluding packaging"
    strOutput = strOutput & "materials) is " & strWeight & "."
End If
strOutput = strOutput & "</H4>"
```

So now we're ready to print it. We **Open** the page in the lower frame, write the output string using **WriteLn**, and **Close** it again. As soon as the document's **Close** method is called, the browser updates the page to show the new text.

```
'and print it in the other frame
top.resultframe.document.Open
top.resultframe.document.WriteLn strOutput
top.resultframe.document.Close
```

Clearing the Results Page

The other subroutine in our script clears the display so that the user can perform a new calculation. Technically it's not required, because changing the value in the Area text box and clicking the Calculate button performs the actions again, and they'll see the new result. When you call the document's **Open** method and write to the document, you automatically clear any existing text in it. However, to be tidy, we've included the Clear button on the page, and when the user clicks it then the following code runs:

```
Sub btnClear_OnClick   'runs when the Clear button is clicked
   top.resultframe.document.Clear
   top.resultframe.document.Close
   txtArea.Value = ""
   txtArea.Focus
End Sub
```

This uses the document's **Clear** method, which removes any existing text and prepares the document to be written to. To leave it empty, we just use the **Close** method immediately afterwards. Finally, we clear the Area text box and place the input focus in it ready for another value to be entered.

Hints for Simple VBScript Pages

The Glass Load Calculator example you've just seen is proof of how easily you can use VBScript to create a useful working page when you have only standard HTML input controls for company. Before we go on to look at ActiveX controls, we should consider some of the other techniques which are important in VBScript code similar to the previous example.

Working with Radio/Option Buttons

One control often used in a standard HTML page is the **Radio** or **Option Button**. We could have used it in our Glass Load Calculator and, in fact, it might have made a neat way of selecting the number of sheets in a pack.

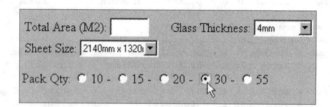

So why didn't we use this method? Well, when you create an option group in a Web page, you give the same name to all of the radio buttons in the same group. This is how the browser knows to switch off the other ones in the same group when you select one.

```
Pack Qty:
<INPUT TYPE=RADIO NAME="optPack">10 -
<INPUT TYPE=RADIO NAME="optPack">15 -
<INPUT TYPE=RADIO NAME="optPack">20 -
<INPUT TYPE=RADIO NAME="optPack" CHECKED=TRUE>30 -
<INPUT TYPE=RADIO NAME="optPack">55
```

The problem now is that you can't refer to the different controls using their name, because they all have the same one. And, the browser doesn't provide an **option group** object containing the value of the one that's selected. Of course, you could give each radio button a different name, but then when you clicked one, the others would remain selected because they wouldn't form a group.

We can get round this using a **global variable** in VBScript. For each button we specify the same subroutine for the code that gets executed when it is clicked, but we send a different value as the parameter. For example, the value of the radio button on the page:

```
Pack Qty:
<INPUT TYPE=RADIO NAME="optPack" OnClick="SetPackQty(10)">10 -
<INPUT TYPE=RADIO NAME="optPack" OnClick="SetPackQty(15)">15 -
<INPUT TYPE=RADIO NAME="optPack" OnClick="SetPackQty(20)">20 -
<INPUT TYPE=RADIO NAME="optPack" CHECKED=TRUE OnClick="SetPackQty(30)">30-
<INPUT TYPE=RADIO NAME="optPack" OnClick="SetPackQty(55)">55
```

The `<SCRIPT>` section of the page does three things. It defines a global variable called `gintPackQuantity` and then sets its initial value to **30**—the same as the value for the radio button that is checked when the page first loads. (Remember that as soon as the page is loaded, any VBScript code that isn't in a subroutine is automatically executed.) It also defines the subroutine `SetPackQty`, which is called each time one of the buttons is clicked. This accepts the value parameter from the option button, and simply assigns it to the global variable.

```
<SCRIPT LANGUAGE="VBScript">
   Dim gintPackQuantity
   gintPackQuantity = 30

   Sub SetPackQty(intPackQtyValue)
      gintPackQuantity = intPackQtyValue
   End Sub
</SCRIPT>
```

Now at all times, the variable `gintPackQuantity` contains the current setting of the option group, and this can be used in the calculation.

Using a <FORM> Section with VBScript

You'll have noticed that we haven't placed our `<INPUT>` tags within the usual `<FORM>` and `</FORM>` tags. These are used to define which area of a page is to act as a form, and the opening `<FORM>` tag defines how, when the user clicks a Submit button, the browser should communicate the form data back to the server.

```
<FORM METHOD=POST ACTION="http://www.myserver.com/cgi-bin/handler.pl">
```

In our application, we don't need a server, except perhaps to supply the page in the first place, and we certainly have no wish to communicate with it while the page is open. This is one of the reasons for using VBScript in a page like our Glass Load Calculator—it does all the work itself and the server has no involvement, so we don't need to use a Submit button or define areas of the page which contain input controls.

However, there are some cases where you might want to do this. We saw how to validate the user's input in a text box before we processed the data in our script. You could just as easily validate it by using VBScript and then sending it all off to the server for 'real' processing—for example, as the criteria for a database search. In this case, you would need to use the `<FORM>` tags to delineate the area of the page that the browser should use when sending the data. We'll look at these techniques in more detail in a later chapter.

Avoiding Errors in Your Scripts

Before we move on from simple uses of VBScript, we should consider one more useful technique. No matter how carefully you validate user's input and code your VBScript routines, there is always the possibility of an error occurring. You can aim to avoid errors in several ways. For example:

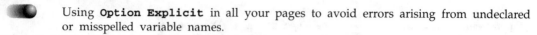 Using **Option Explicit** in all your pages to avoid errors arising from undeclared or misspelled variable names.

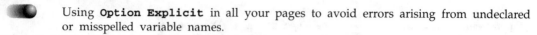 Avoiding the use of global variables where possible, because changing their value within a subroutine can lead to all manner of bugs that will prove very difficult to find.

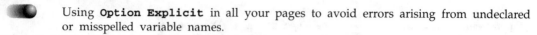 Using a proper naming convention for your variables, and giving subroutines and functions meaningful names. You should also consider commenting your code to help make future maintenance easier.

Microsoft suggest a standard system for naming variables:

Data Type	Prefix	Example
Boolean	bln	blnAccepted
Byte	byt	bytPixelValue
Date or Time	dtm	dtmFirstTime
Double	dbl	dblTotalDistance
Error	err	errOverflow
Integer	int	intCount
Long	lng	lngFreeSpace
Object	obj	objListBox
Single	sng	sngLength
String	str	strAddress

If you declare a script level variable, Microsoft suggest that you precede it with 's', such as **sintMyCurrentValue**. If you're used to VB or VBA, you may prefer to use 'g' (for global) instead. For example, **gintMyCurrentValue**. Either way, it helps to make clear which variables have global (or script-level) scope.

Variants, Conversions, and other Mysteries

You may have noticed in all of the code samples used so far that, when we declare variables using **Dim**, we can't allocate a specific **data type** to them. Unlike its VBA origins, VBScript has only one intrinsic variable type—the **Variant**. As such, whenever we use a variable in a calculation, or as an argument to some object's method, the script engine will do its best to select an appropriate variant subtype.

However, sometimes it can get the wrong idea and we could end up with anything—from a type mismatch error at run time to a well-hidden logical error arising from an incorrect rounding of some value. For example, trying to divide 'Boo' by **15** would obviously not give you a valid result! This error is easy enough to track down, but some are a lot harder. Fortunately, VBScript has numerous variant conversion functions to add to your code arsenal in the war against bugs.

Although all data is of type **Variant**, and so equally useful, some variants are more equally useful than others. This is because each variant has a **SubType**—you have your floating points, strings, and integer values after all! The trick is knowing what data you have and converting it to the type you require. In the Glass Load Calculator example, we've been using the intrinsic VBScript functions **CSng()** and **Int()**. **CSng()** is used to take text which represents a valid number, and to convert it into single precision floating point data. This means that the user can express the required area accurately to as many decimal places as they wish, and this offers a better approximation of how many packs and loose sheets they need. Yet we can still convert it into other types when we use it in our calculations.

The following table summarizes a few of the more useful functions involved in converting variant data:

Function	Use
Asc(), AscB(), AscW()	Takes a character and returns its ASCII numeric value. The '**B**' and '**W**' forms are for byte and word size character sets, respectively.
Chr(), ChrB(), ChrW()	Converts an integer value to the ASCII character equivalent. For example, **Chr(169)** gives the copyright symbol.
CBool()	Converts a numeric expression (or numeric string) to a Boolean result. If the expression is zero, **False** is returned; otherwise, **True** is returned. If an expression can't be interpreted as a numeric value, a run-time error occurs.
CDate()	Converts a valid date expression to a date value. For example, **MsgBox CDate("12 january 1996")** produces a message box containing "01/12/96" or "12/01/96", depending on which side of the Atlantic your computer thinks it's sitting on!
CDbl(), CSng()	These convert an expression to a double or single precision value thereby forcing arithmetic to use floating point calculation.
CInt(), CLng()	These convert expressions to either integers or long integers.
Hex()	Returns a hexadecimal value of any numeric expression.
Int(), Fix()	Removes the fractional part of its argument, rounding down.

As mentioned earlier, there's one obvious omission in VBScript, and that's the **Format()** function. This flexible and widely used function could convert data to almost any textual form. The other omission is a function to convert to currency format, such as VB's **CCur()** function.

There are also a number of functions that can be used to determine just what *kind* of data your variant is holding, or what it can be converted to. We have already seen **IsNumeric()** function in action. Here's a full list of the '**Is-**type' functions:

Function	Return
IsArray()	**True** if the variable being tested is an array.
IsDate()	**True** if the expression being tested can be converted to a date value.
IsEmpty()	**True** if the variable has not been initialized or set equal to **Empty**.
IsNull()	**True** if a **Null** value exists within the expression evaluated.
IsNumeric()	**True** if the expression can be converted to a numeric value.
IsObject()	**True** if the expression represents an object or a reference to an object.

These are primarily useful in preventing errors in the conversion functions. If you suspect you have dubious data in a text box, for example, trap it early and avoid errors from arising later in your code.

Trapping Errors in Your Scripts

Good coding techniques can't always protect you from errors. If you enter **999999** for the Area in our Glass Load Calculator, you'll get an error. It happens when we try to work out the number of packs using the **Mod** operator.

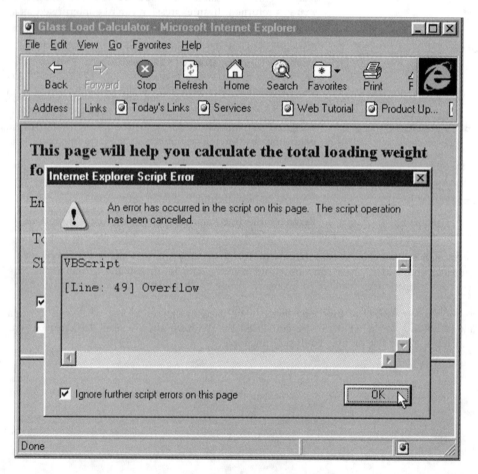

This is rather embarrassing, and it doesn't give a very good impression to our page users. We could get around this error by checking and validating the user's input more thoroughly, but there is one way in which we can prevent the Script Error dialog ever appearing.

Placing the statement **On Error Resume Next** in our code forces the browser to ignore any errors it encounters, and to continue executing the code from the next statement. VBScript also supports the new **Err** object, which we can use to get information about whether an error has occurred, and what type it is. If no error has occurred, **Err.Number** returns zero. Otherwise it returns the number of the error, and we can get the source and description of it using **Err.Source** and **Err.Description**.

Here's how we could have protected our code against this overflow error. First, we place **On Error Resume Next** at the beginning of the **btnCalc_OnClick** subroutine. Then, before the code that actually displays the results, but after all the calculations have been done, we check **Err.Number** to make sure it's still zero. If not then we display a message and exit gracefully from the procedure.

```
If Err.Number <> 0 Then
   strErrMesg = "Sorry this value cannot be calculated. An error of type "
   strErrMesg = strErrMesg & Err.Description & " has occurred while "
   strErrMesg = "processing " & strErrMesg & Err.Source & "."
   MsgBox strErrMesg
   Exit sub
End If
```

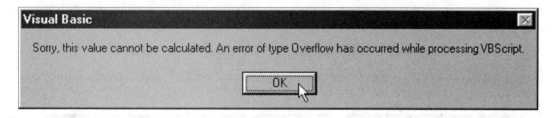

Notice that the **source** of the error is '**VBScript**'. This is where the error occurred. However, if an error occurs inside an ActiveX or other object which is inserted into our page, as you'll see in coming chapters, the name of the object will be the source.

The way that your code behaves when you use **On Error Resume Next** is one subject that we'll be looking at in far more detail in Chapter 6, where you'll see some useful techniques for debugging your code and handling errors properly.

Looking inside VBScript

A particular word crept into the previous section, one that we've tried not to talk about so far. We mentioned the **Err object** and talked about its **properties** and **methods**. If you've been trying to hide from the growing clamor about objects because you think it's more hype than reality, VBScript is a perfect place to start your acclimatization.

Over the next few chapters, you're going to see more and more uses of objects of various kinds. More to the point, you've already been using objects in various ways, but without having to understand too much about them. Even the browser, Internet Explorer, is now an object rather than a normal application, so there's going to be no escape!

Properties, Methods, and Events of the Standard Controls

When you first used controls in your HTML pages, by inserting **\<INPUT\>**, **\<SELECT\>**, and **\<TEXTAREA\>** tags, and before the arrival of VBScript and other scripting languages, you probably never thought of them as objects. They were just 'ordinary' text boxes and buttons that magically did something, thanks to the **METHOD** and **ACTION** arguments in the **\<FORM\>** tag, and the quaintly named programs in the server's **cgi-bin** directory.

In Internet Explorer (and other browsers which support scripting languages), these simple HTML tags do more than just create an ordinary control. They actually encapsulate them in **pseudo objects**—which, as we've already seen, have their own properties, methods and events. To get the setting of a check box, or to place a value in a text box, we can use their properties, like this:

```
intUserChoice = chkDecision.Checked
txtBrowserName.Value = "Internet Explorer"
```

We can also execute the methods of a control. For example to place the input focus on a text box in our Glass Load Calculator example, we used this technique:

```
If (Not IsNumeric(txtArea.Value)) Then
    MsgBox "You must enter a total area for the order"
    txtArea.Focus
    Exit Sub
End If
```

In the same example, we also saw how the events of a control were used. To react to a button being clicked, we wrote a subroutine whose name automatically connected it to the button:

```
Sub btnCalc_OnClick   'runs when the Calculate button is clicked
```

However, there are only a limited set of properties, methods, and events available for the normal HTML controls. Here's the full list:

Element	Properties	Methods	Events
Button, Reset, Submit	form, name, value, enabled	click, focus	onClick, onFocus
Check box	form, name, value, checked, defaultChecked, enabled	click, focus	onClick, onFocus
Radio	form, name, value, checked, enabled	click, focus	onClick, onFocus
Combo	form, name, value, enabled, listCount, list, multiSelect, listIndex	click, focus, removeItem, addItem, clear	onClick, onFocus
Password	form, name, value, defaultValue, enabled	focus, blur, select	onFocus, onBlur
Text, Text Area	form, name, value, defaultValue, enabled	focus, blur, select	onFocus, onBlur, onChange, onSelect

Table continued on next page

Element	Properties	Methods	Events
Select	name, length, options, selectedIndex	focus, blur	onFocus, onBlur, onChange
Hidden	name, value	*<none>*	*<none>*

Property	Description
form	Returns the form object containing the control
name	Sets or returns the name of the control
value	Returns the value of the control
defaultValue	Sets or returns the default value of the control
enabled	Sets or returns whether the control is enabled
checked	Sets or returns the checked state of a check box or radio button
defaultChecked	Sets or returns the default checked property of a check box
listCount	Returns the number of items in the list
list	Returns the list from the control
ListIndex	Sets or returns the list index
selectedIndex	Returns the index of the first option selected in a list
multiSelect	Sets or returns whether the combo is multiselect or not
options	Returns a collection containing the various settings in the **<OPTIONS>** tag for a select element
length	Returns the number of options in a select element

Method	Description
click	Clicks the control
focus	Sets the focus to the control
blur	Removes the focus from the control
select	Selects the contents of the control
removeItem	Removes an item from the control's list
addItem	Adds an item to the control's list
clear	Clears the contents of the control

Event	Description
onClick	Occurs when the control is clicked
onFocus	Occurs when the control gets the focus
onBlur	Occurs when the control loses the focus
onChange	Occurs when the contents of the control change
onSelect	Occurs when the user makes a selection in the control

As you can see, there are several methods, properties, and events associated with each type of control. Many of the properties are similar to those you specify in the HTML tag that creates the control. For example:

```
<INPUT TYPE=TEXT NAME="MyTextBox" VALUE="Hello World!">
```

creates a text box which has a **name** property of **MyTextBox**, and a **value** and **defaultValue** property of **Hello World!** You can retrieve and, in most cases, set a control's properties with VBScript. For example, you can change the **enabled** and **checked** properties of a control like this:

```
MyCheckBox.Checked = -1  'Setting this property to True sets it
MyCheckBox.Enabled = 0   'Setting this property to False disables it
```

We've seen the **Focus** method used on a text box, and likewise you can execute the other methods. To **select** the text in a text box we could use:

```
MyTextBox.Select    'Selects all the text in the text box
```

We've also seen the events used in our Glass Load Calculator example. Any code we place in a subroutine called **btnCalc_OnClick** will be run when that button is clicked. To run code when a text box receives the focus, we would place it in a subroutine called **txtMyTextBox_OnFocus**. Similarly, the code in a subroutine **txtMyTextBox_OnChange** would be run when the contents of the text box changed.

Remember, these are properties, methods, and events for the standard HTML-style controls, such as those you would create by including **<INPUT>**, **<SELECT>** or **<TEXTAREA>** tags directly in the HTML code of the page. Later, we'll be looking at ActiveX controls, which also have a wide range of properties, methods, and events. However, their properties, methods, and events are subtly different from the HTML ones, and generally have different names as well.

Accessing Different Parts of the Browser Window

We've seen how you can write directly to a page in another frame using VBScript. By making use of the way that the different parts of the browser are related (i.e. the hierarchy of objects within it), we can freely access any other part of the browser window. You'll see a lot more of this in Chapter 5, but in the meantime, to write to the lower frame in our Glass Load Calculator we used:

```
top.resultframe.document.Open
top.resultframe.document.WriteLn strOutput
top.resultframe.document.Close
```

where **top** refers to the main browser window, **resultframe** is the name we gave to the lower frame when we created it, and **document** is the page that this frame displays.

It should by now come as no surprise to learn that a document has its own properties and methods, although currently there are no events:

Property	Description
LinkColor	Sets or returns the color of the links in a document while it's being loaded.
ALinkColor	Sets or returns the color of the active links (where the mouse pointer is held down over the link but not released) in a document. Internet Explorer doesn't have this feature, but it's supported for compatibility with other browsers.
VLinkColor	Sets or returns the color of the visited links in a document.
BgColor	Sets or returns the background color of the document.
FgColor	Sets or returns the foreground color of the text.
anchors	Returns a collection containing the anchors in a document.
Links	Returns a collection containing the links in the current document.
Forms	Returns a collection containing the forms in a document.
Location	Returns the location of the document (read only).
LastModified	Returns the last modified date of the document.
Title	Returns the document's title (read only).
Cookie	Sets or returns the cookie for the current document. (We'll be looking at cookies in more depth in later chapters.)
Referrer	Returns the URL of the document which contains the link followed to this document, or NULL if not available.

Method	Description
Write	Writes a string into a document at the current position unless specified to be written elsewhere.
WriteLn	Similar to **write**, but adds a carriage return.
Open	Opens the document for writing.
Close	Updates the screen, displaying all the text written since the last **open**.
Clear	Clears the document and updates the screen.

So we can do a lot more then just write to a document. By using its properties and methods we can tailor it as it's created, and get information about it once it's displayed. For example, we can change the background and foreground colors, using either the **RGB color triple** (by specifying the red, green, and blue values) or one of the predefined standard color names.

```
document.bgColor="#FFFFFF"    'sets the background to white
document.fgColor="green"      'sets the foreground to green
```

59

The way you use the RGB color triple is exactly the same as with normal HTML. The number itself consists of three pairs of hexadecimal digits. The first pair defines the red component, the second pair the green component, and the third pair the blue component. #FFFFFF is white and #000000 is black. An easy way to find the color values is to run Microsoft Paint *and select* Edit Colors *from the* Options *menu, and then to click* Define Custom Colors. *Of course, you'll have to convert the numbers for each component into hexadecimal, but it does help you get an idea of the values you need. There are plenty of shareware 'color picker' programs around as well.*

Some properties of the objects in the browser, such as the **links** and **forms** properties of the **document** object, are **collections**. You access them by specifying an index, which corresponds to their position on the page, or a unique name. So the third link on a page would be `document.links[2]` (remember that all arrays start at zero), or it could be `document.links("MyLink")`.

This fits in with the structure of the browser and its objects, generally referred to as the **object model** or **scripting object model**. We can refer to other elements currently displayed by the browser—even those in another frame—and then work with their properties and methods. If it all seems a little vague at the moment, don't worry. In Chapter 5, we'll look in detail at the object model, and see how all the different elements, including the frame and the document you've already seen, fit together.

Starting to Use Objects

So far in this book, we've only been working with standard VBScript and the HTML-type input controls, such as those you would use in the `<FORM>` section of a normal Web page. If this was all VBScript could do, it certainly wouldn't be the subject of all the attention it's getting at the moment.

As we suggested when we looked at the background to the latest developments in browser technology, the real power is revealed when you start to use objects in your pages. While we described Internet Explorer's implementation of the normal HTML input controls as 'pseudo objects', they are really only a half-way house compared to the functionality available in modern browsers.

The HTML standards laid down by the World Wide Web Consortium (W3C) define different 'levels' of HTML code. Initially, HTML 1 covered the basic tags and how they should be interpreted by browsers. HTML 2 introduced a lot of new tags which made Web pages more attractive, and now there are several releases of HTML 3 which support all of the latest functions—tables, frames, and multimedia. However, the new tag that we're interested in is the `<OBJECT>` tag.

You'll find the W3C object specifications at their Web site:

`http://www.w3.org/pub/WWW/TR/WD-object.html`

This allows you to insert various types of objects into your Web pages. These can be any of the thousands of objects that are now available, and Microsoft is pushing forward in this area by developing their OLE and COM technologies as the new **ActiveX** object standard.

And you aren't be limited to using ActiveX objects in your VBScript pages. It'll be just as easy to use objects created in Java, or other COM-compatible objects. In fact, there will soon be almost no limit to the effects that you can achieve.

60

The HTML <OBJECT> Tag

The **<OBJECT>** tag is a standard way of inserting an object into *any* HTML page, not just those that'll be displayed in Internet Explorer or those that use VBScript. Within the opening and closing tag, normal HTML arguments (or **attributes** as we prefer to call them) are used to set the width, height, and alignment just as you would with an **<IMG>** image tag. However, the **<OBJECT>** tag supports much more than just these. Here's an example:

```
<OBJECT
    ID="MyObject"
    CLASSID="clsid:1A4DA620-6217-11CF-BE62-0080C72EDD2D"
    WIDTH=200
    HEIGHT=200
    ALIGN=CENTER
    BORDER=1
    HSPACE=5>
    <PARAM NAME="ForeColor" VALUE="0">
    <PARAM NAME="FontName" VALUE="Courier New">
    <PARAM NAME="FontSize" VALUE="10">
    <PARAM NAME="Caption" VALUE="Hello World!">
</OBJECT>
```

Notice that this block of text consists of an opening and closing **<OBJECT>** tag, and within the opening tag are the normal HTML-style attributes for **WIDTH**, **HEIGHT**, **ALIGN**, **BORDER**, and **HSPACE**. There are also two extra attributes which only apply to the **<OBJECT>** tag, **ID** and **CLASSID**.

Following the opening tag are a series of **<PARAM>** tags. For each one there is the **NAME** attribute and its **VALUE**. These **<PARAM>** tags define extra values which are proprietary *for that type of object*, rather than for all objects in general.

Finally, after the list of **<PARAM>** tags, there's the closing **</OBJECT>** tag. The bonus with this type of structure is that, like all other tags, a browser that doesn't support objects won't recognize the **<OBJECT>** or **<PARAM>** tags, and so will ignore everything within them, meaning that your pages can still be read by older browsers—of course, this may not be terribly useful if you've taken advantage of objects to perform the main functions of your page!

However, browsers that *do* recognize the **<OBJECT>** tag will ignore any text within the opening and closing **<OBJECT>** tags not enclosed in a **<PARAM>** tag, so you can use this to warn viewers with older browsers that the page contains an object which they won't see:

```
<OBJECT
    ID=MyObject
    CLASSID="clsid:1A4DA620-6217-11CF-BE62-0080C72EDD2D"
    . . etc . .
    HSPACE=5>
    <PARAM NAME="ForeColor" VALUE="0">
    <PARAM NAME="FontName" VALUE="Courier New">
    Sorry, but you need to get a new browser to see this object.
</OBJECT>
```

Object Attributes

As we've seen, the basics of inserting an object are very simple. The hard part is knowing what all the attributes and parameters mean, and what exactly they do. Here's a list of the `<OBJECT>` attributes that Internet Explorer supports, and these will be standard through all of the recently updated browsers:

Argument	Description
`ALIGN=textvalue`	Controls how the object is aligned in the page. **BASELINE**—bottom of object lies on baseline of surrounding text. **CENTER**—object is placed centrally between left and right margins, and following text starts on a new line. **LEFT**—object is placed against the left margin, and following text wraps to the right of it. **MIDDLE**—middle of object lies on the baseline of surrounding text. **RIGHT**—object is placed against the right margin, and following text wraps to the left of it. **TEXTBOTTOM**—bottom of object aligns with the bottom of surrounding text. **TEXTMIDDLE**—middle of object aligns with the midpoint of surrounding text. **TEXTTOP**—top of object aligns with the top of surrounding text.
`BORDER=number`	Width of border displayed when object is defined as a hyperlink using an `<A>` tag.
`CLASSID=UUID`	Defines the object's unique identifier (UUID). ActiveX controls use a UUID of `CLSID:`*class-identifier* which identifies it in the Windows Registry.
`CODEBASE=URL`	Specifies the location and version of the code file for the object.
`DATA=URL`	Data for the object.
`DECLARE`	Declares the object but doesn't instantiate it. Used when cross-referencing or when the object is a parameter in another object.
`HEIGHT=number`	Height for displaying the object in the browser.
`HSPACE=number`	Space in pixels between the object and any text or images to the left or right of it.
`ID=text`	Identifier, or name, used to refer to the control in code.
`ISMAP`	Indicates that mouse clicks on the object should be sent back to the server for processing there.
`NAME=text`	Name to be used for the object when it's submitted on a form.
`SHAPES`	Indicates that the object has a MAP with shaped hyperlinks.
`STANDBY=text`	Text message which is displayed while loading the object.
`TYPE=type`	(Used to be **CODETYPE**) Internet media type for the object, e.g. **TYPE** = `"application/x-oleobject"`

Table continued on next page

Argument	Description
`USEMAP=URL`	Location of the image map which is to be used with the object.
`VSPACE=number`	Space in pixels between the object and any text or images above or below it.
`WIDTH=number`	Width for displaying the object in the browser.

The **CLASSID** attribute is the key to the whole thing. This is a value that is unique for every version of every object, and through it the browser knows which object to load into the page. The Windows Registry uses a similar convention to store details of all the objects installed on your system, so the browser can check to see if the object is already available, and if so then it won't need to download it from the server. If it isn't available on the local machine, the **CODEBASE** argument tells the browser where to download it from.

We'll look at **CLASSID** and **CODEBASE** in more detail later in this chapter, though we won't be spending a lot of time here on the other attributes of the **<OBJECT>** tag. Many will already be familiar, and in coming chapters you'll see more about how they can be used. For the time being, it's enough that you understand the broad outline of the **<OBJECT>** tag and its intrinsic attributes.

Between the opening and closing **<OBJECT>** tags are the **<PARAM>** tags. Each one of these defines a particular attribute of the actual object you are using, and they are broadly equivalent to the object's properties. As all objects have different properties, there's no standard list of **<PARAM>** tags. However, in our previous example for a Label control, we used:

```
<PARAM NAME="ForeColor" VALUE="0">
<PARAM NAME="FontName" VALUE="Courier New">
<PARAM NAME="FontSize" VALUE="10">
<PARAM NAME="Caption" VALUE="Hello World!">
```

The **Label** control isn't a standard HTML type control, but an ActiveX control which is supplied with the full version of Internet Explorer. You can immediately see how ActiveX can extend the functionality of your pages. You have access to a set of intrinsic objects, such as these labels and the equivalents for the other controls you use on forms, plus many other new ones. And the great advantage is that they don't always need to be downloaded before you can use them, because they are likely to be already installed on the user's system.

If you're used to using Visual Basic or VBA, you'll feel right at home with these control objects, as they are very similar to the controls you use when creating an application in VB. Internet Explorer also includes a new object called a **layout control**. This enables you to design a **form** (in the VB sense of the word) onto which you place ActiveX controls. Then you can simply display the completed layout control on your page. We'll be using this and other ActiveX controls throughout the book.

Before we take a look at what you can do with ActiveX controls, we should examine in more detail where all these objects actually come from. It can be disconcerting if, when you come to load an ActiveX-enabled page, you don't understand what's going on behind the scenes, especially if, as has been known to happen, the 'Net is having a little trouble dealing with traffic!

How ActiveX Controls Get into the Browser

The **CLASSID** and **CODEBASE** attributes of the `<OBJECT>` tag are closely related, and between them they control how an object, such as an ActiveX control, is retrieved for display in your pages. If you haven't already got it, or if you only have an older version, the browser will automatically download it from the correct location on the Internet and will then install it. What's more, all of this will happen while the page is loading. With standard controls, generally all you'll see is a brief message in the browser's status bar saying 'Installing Controls', together with a progress bar.

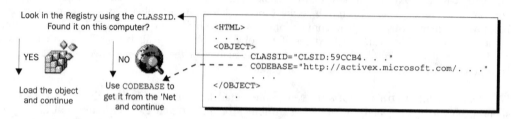

So what can go wrong? Well, what happens if the site defined by **CODEBASE** is busy, or down? Even if it's working, the 'Net may be in one of it's turgid moods. If the user has a 28.8 Kbps dial-up modem and an indifferent Internet service provider, he's likely to hit the Stop button after a couple of minutes wondering why nothing's happening. In all these cases, it's 'no control, no page'. Or at least, not one that's going to look right or work correctly. There's not a lot you can do about any of these problems, but you should at least be aware of how it all works and the potential down sides.

CLASSIDs

When using ActiveX controls, it's imperative that you understand what the **CLASSID** actually is, and where you can find it. In Microsoft-speak, it's a **GUID** (Globally Unique IDentifier) for that particular **PE** (Portable Executable). The PE will normally be an ActiveX control (**.ocx**), but it can also be a dynamic link library (**.dll**) or an OLE server created with, among other tools, Visual Basic.

The GUID is a 'signature' for the control, and the browser uses the Windows Registry to obtain information about the object in question. If you load Registry Editor (**regedit.exe**) and look in HKEY_CLASSES_ROOT, you'll find Forms.Listbox.1. The name Forms.ListBox.1 is a programmer-friendly way of referencing the object which, in this case, is a version 1 control from a group of ActiveX controls called Microsoft Forms 2.0. Within this folder, you'll find a subfolder called CLSID that contains the **CLASSID** that you would need to specify in the `<OBJECT>` tag if you wanted to place an object of this **class** into your web page.

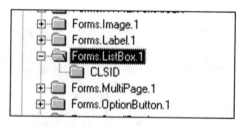

If you now use the CLSID value to search the Registry, you'll find a separate section dedicated to that object which contains a lot more information about it. In our example, you can see that this is in fact a control, because it has a Control folder. Other useful information covers where the code for this control is kept on your system, i.e. the path to the executable file that has the *blueprints* for this control. Take a look at the InprocServer32 folder. In this case, it'll probably be `C:\Windows\System\FM20.dll`—which contains the information for all of the standard Internet Explorer controls.

So, the **CLASSID** attribute gives Internet Explorer the information it needs to interrogate the registry and find out how to actually load the control into your web page. And of course, as a Web developer, you need to know these **CLASSID**s. You could try looking for them in the registry, although this is laborious in the extreme. What you need is some way of doing this simply and intuitively, and in the next chapter, we'll meet a tool that does just that.

We'll finish this chapter with a quick look at what you can do with ActiveX controls. Here's an example which shows you just how bland a normal static page can be when compared to one which takes advantage of VBScript and ActiveX technology.

The Scrolls and Labels Example

While you can achieve a lot using just the normal HTML controls and some VBScript code to tie them together, **objects** provide new opportunities for livening up your pages which simply aren't available using traditional methods. This example, which you can obtain from our Web site under the filename **Label&Scroll.htm**, shows just a few of those possibilities:

> Like all of the examples in this book, you can find this page on our Web site. All the samples which are directly applicable to each chapter are together, so that for this example, **Label&Scroll.htm**, you'll find the relevant files at:
>
> `http://www.wrox.com/books/0448/chapter02/Label&Scroll.htm`
>
> You can view it directly in your browser, and can see the source code by selecting **Source** from your browser's **View** menu. This opens the raw code into **NotePad** (or your default text editor) and you can then save it onto your own system if you wish to experiment with it.

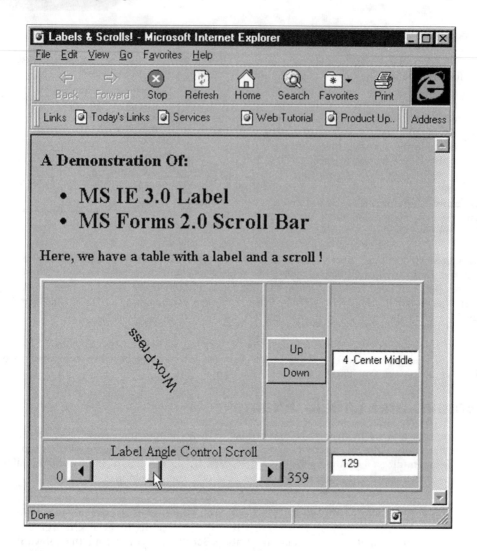

The text, Wrox Press, starts off in a horizontal position, but by using the scroll bar you can rotate it through 360 degrees. The text box next to the scroll bar shows the current angle, although you can't edit this directly. At the top right of the table is another text box containing the current alignment of the text within the label control (which actually fills all of the top left cell of the table). By clicking the Up and Down buttons, you can cycle through the different alignment settings available.

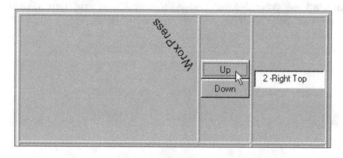

How It Works

The Labels & Scrolls! page uses six ActiveX objects. These consist of: one label, two text boxes, one scroll bar, and two command buttons. The rest of the page is made up of a table and the descriptive text—created in the usual way with HTML code. The ActiveX controls have particular properties that the ordinary HTML controls lack, and of course, there's no HTML equivalent to a label or scroll bar anyway.

The two **command buttons** on the page are similar, differing only in the captions and the actions they carry out. Here's the **<OBJECT>** tag that creates the Up button:

```
<OBJECT
    ID="cmdUp" WIDTH=65 HEIGHT=25
    CLASSID="CLSID:D7053240-CE69-11CD-A777-00DD01143C57">
        <PARAM NAME="Caption" VALUE="Up">
        <PARAM NAME="Size" VALUE="2540;661">
        <PARAM NAME="FontCharSet" VALUE="0">
        <PARAM NAME="FontPitchAndFamily" VALUE="2">
        <PARAM NAME="ParagraphAlign" VALUE="3">
        <PARAM NAME="FontWeight" VALUE="0">
</OBJECT>
```

In the **ID** parameter you can see the 'name' **cmdUp**. This is the name that we've allocated to it so that we can refer to it later. You can also see the **WIDTH** and **HEIGHT** parameters for displaying it on the page. After that, the **CLASSID** defines the exact description and version of the object. This allows the browser to find it on your system, using the Windows Registry. Next come the object-specific parameters, which define the text of the caption itself, and the font used to display it.

The **scroll bar** object is defined in a similar way, but notice here that the object-specific parameters are different. For a scroll bar you'll want to be able to specify the maximum value, the interval for each of its changes, and of course the orientation (horizontal or vertical). We haven't set the **Min** property of the object because the default is zero and we're happy with that value in our page. We only need to include **<PARAM>** tags where we wish to use a value other than the default for that object.

```
<OBJECT
    ID="hsbRotation" WIDTH=240 HEIGHT=23
    CLASSID="CLSID:DFD181E0-5E2F-11CE-A449-00AA004A803D">
        <PARAM NAME="Size" VALUE="3545;580">
        <PARAM NAME="Max" VALUE="359">
        <PARAM NAME="SmallChange" VALUE="5">
        <PARAM NAME="LargeChange" VALUE="15">
        <PARAM NAME="Orientation" VALUE="1">
</OBJECT>
```

If you're used to Visual Basic, you'll recognize these arguments as the normal scroll bar properties. **SmallChange** is the amount by which the value changes when you click on the arrow at either end of the scroll bar, and **LargeChange** is the amount by which the value changes when you click on the gray background area of the scroll bar between the arrows.

The two text boxes on the page are also similar, and are used purely to display the values of the alignment and rotation of the Wrox Press label. To preset their value, we've placed it in the **'Value'** argument of the relevant **<PARAM>** tag.

67

```
<OBJECT
    ID="txtAlignment" WIDTH=96 HEIGHT=24
    CLASSID="CLSID:8BD21D10-EC42-11CE-9E0D-00AA006002F3">
        <PARAM NAME="VariousPropertyBits" VALUE="746604575">
        <PARAM NAME="Size" VALUE="2540;635">
        <PARAM NAME="Value" VALUE="4 - Center Middle">
        <PARAM NAME="FontCharSet" VALUE="0">
        <PARAM NAME="FontPitchAndFamily" VALUE="2">
        <PARAM NAME="FontWeight" VALUE="0">
</OBJECT>
```

The real 'gee-whiz' effect is achieved by using a special label control. This isn't actually the standard Version 2 ActiveX control, which doesn't have an **Angle** property. Instead, we've used the special version which is often referred to in Visual Basic as the 'super-label', and because it's likely that this won't be installed on the user's system, we've included a **CODEBASE** argument in the **<OBJECT>** tag so that, if required, the browser can download it directly from Microsoft.

```
<OBJECT
    ID="lblTheText" WIDTH=240 HEIGHT=163
    CLASSID="CLSID:99B42120-6EC7-11CF-A6C7-00AA00A47DD2"
    CODEBASE = "http://activex.microsoft.com/ . . ."
    TYPE="application/x-oleobject">
        <PARAM NAME="_ExtentX" VALUE="6350">
        <PARAM NAME="_ExtentY" VALUE="4313">
        <PARAM NAME="Caption" VALUE="Wrox Press">
        <PARAM NAME="Angle" VALUE="0">
        <PARAM NAME="Alignment" VALUE="4">
        <PARAM NAME="Mode" VALUE="1">
        <PARAM NAME="FillStyle" VALUE="0">
        <PARAM NAME="FillStyle" VALUE="0">
        <PARAM NAME="ForeColor" VALUE="#000000">
        <PARAM NAME="BackColor" VALUE="#C0C0C0">
        <PARAM NAME="FontName" VALUE="Arial">
        <PARAM NAME="FontSize" VALUE="12">
        <PARAM NAME="FontItalic" VALUE="0">
        <PARAM NAME="FontBold" VALUE="0">
        <PARAM NAME="FontUnderline" VALUE="0">
        <PARAM NAME="FontStrikeout" VALUE="0">
        <PARAM NAME="TopPoints" VALUE="0">
        <PARAM NAME="BotPoints" VALUE="0">
</OBJECT>
```

At the present time, the full **CODEBASE** for the 'super-label' is:

```
'http://activex.microsoft.com/controls/iexplore/ielabel.ocx
#Version=4,70,0,1161'
```

So now that we've defined all of the controls and have laid them out on the page, how does it work? Here's the full code that connects all of the controls together, and you can see that there isn't much needed to achieve the functionality we want:

```
<SCRIPT LANGUAGE="VBScript">
<!--
Option Explicit
```

```
    Dim gintAlign              ' stores the current alignment of the label

    Sub Window_OnLoad()
       gintAlign = 4           ' sets Center Middle alignment on page load
    End Sub

    Sub cmdUp_Click()
       If gintAlign > 0 Then
          gintAlign = gintAlign - 1
          SetAlign               ' set the new alignment
       End If
    End Sub

    Sub cmdDown_Click()
       If gintAlign < 8 Then
          gintAlign = gintAlign + 1
          SetAlign               ' set the new alignment
       End If
    End Sub

    Sub SetAlign()
       lblTheText.Alignment = gintAlign     ' set the label's property
       Select Case (gintAlign)              ' then update the text box
          Case 0:
            txtAlignment.Value = gintAlign & " - Left Top"
          Case 1:
            txtAlignment.Value = gintAlign & " - Center Top"
          Case 2:
            txtAlignment.Value = gintAlign & " - Right Top"
          Case 3:
            txtAlignment.Value = gintAlign & " - Left Middle"
          Case 4:
            txtAlignment.Value = gintAlign & " - Center Middle"
          Case 5:
            txtAlignment.Value = gintAlign & " - Right Middle"
          Case 6:
            txtAlignment.Value = gintAlign & " - Left Bottom"
          Case 7:
            txtAlignment.Value = gintAlign & " - Center Bottom"
          Case 8:
            txtAlignment.Value = gintAlign & " - Right Bottom"
       End Select
    End Sub

    Sub hsbRotation_Change()
       lblTheText.Angle = hsbRotation.Value     ' set the label's property
       txtAngle.Value = hsbRotation.Value       ' and update the text box
    End Sub
    -->
    </SCRIPT>
```

Firstly, we'll define a global variable **gintAlign** to hold the current alignment of the label. The text box on the page already contains 4—Center Middle because we defined its **Value** property using:

```
    <PARAM NAME="Value" VALUE="4 - Center Middle">
```

so we need to set **gintAlign** to this. You can see that we're using one of the browser **window** events here, **Window_OnLoad**, which occurs when the browser loads the page. We'll use it to preset **gintAlign** to **4**. (You'll see more of these events in Chapter 5 when we come to a detailed look at the object hierarchy of the browser.)

Changing the alignment of the text in the **lblTheText** label is done with the two command buttons, **cmdUp** and **cmdDown**. We've defined event procedures for their **Click** events which just change the value of **gintAlign**, and then run the **SetAlign** procedure. This simply changes the **Alignment** property of **lblTheText** and then updates the text box with the new description of the alignment by assigning it to its **Value** property.

> In VBScript routines, when you're using the ActiveX text box controls, as with our example, you can change the text that's displayed in a text box by setting its **Text** property rather than its **Value** property. This makes adapting existing VB code much simpler. For example:
>
> `txtAlignment.Text = gintAlign & " - Left Top"`
>
> has the same effect as:
>
> `txtAlignment.Value = gintAlign & " - Left  Top"`

Handling the rotation of the text in **lblTheText** is just as easy. A **Change** event occurs every time the setting of the scroll bar changes, so we define an event procedure **hsbRotation_OnChange**. In this procedure, we collect the new setting by examining its **Value** property, and assign this to **lblTheText** and its matching text box **txtAngle**.

Changing the **Angle** of the text in the label is all well and good when **Alignment** is **4** (the default we set for when the page was first loaded), and the text in the label control is centrally aligned in both directions. The text is being displayed as close to its anchoring point in the label controls display area as possible, and when you move the scroll bar, it simply rotates about its own midpoint. However, with **Alignment** values other than **4**, the display can be quite interesting. The diagram shows the display text in four positions anchored at the bottom left corner of the label control, when **Alignment** is **6**:

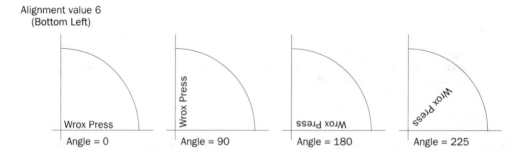

Alignment value 6
(Bottom Left)

Angle = 0   Angle = 90   Angle = 180   Angle = 225

> When using this control, you should always ensure that you make the **Height** and **Width** attributes large enough for your control, whatever angle you intend to use it at. Otherwise, your text will be cropped. Experiment with the sample page a little to understand how the text is displayed for various values of **Alignment** and **Angle**.

That's all there is to it. Using ActiveX controls or other objects, including Java applets, is no more difficult than creating pages in simple VBScript. Once you grasp how the **<OBJECT>** tag works, you can track down which objects you want to use, and, as you're able to find their **CLASSID** values, there's no problem. In fact, in the next chapter, we'll look at an even easier way to build pages like this.

Summary

A lot of this chapter has been about the theory of using VBScript, and the associated techniques which connect your script with the browser itself. You can use just the standard HTML-style **<INPUT>** controls and VBScript to create pages which are interactive. But, as we found in the last section, there's a lot more you can do by taking advantage of the new object-based features of Internet Explorer and other object-enabled browsers.

We've been careful not to go into too much depth in this chapter, so that you wouldn't get bogged down in the gory details of how things work. In the following chapters, however, we'll develop and expand these techniques so that we can produce more powerful and far-reaching methods.

We've looked at:

 How you create a working VBScript page using ordinary HTML controls

 Controlling the errors that can arise as your scripts are executed

 Ways of outputting the results and other information to the user

 Using simple ActiveX controls instead of the HTML ones

The next chapter will introduce you to some of the tools that will make working with objects much easier, and will start to further unravel the ActiveX objects that are part of the browser. So far, we've only been scratching the surface—now it's time to start unleashing the true power of objects.

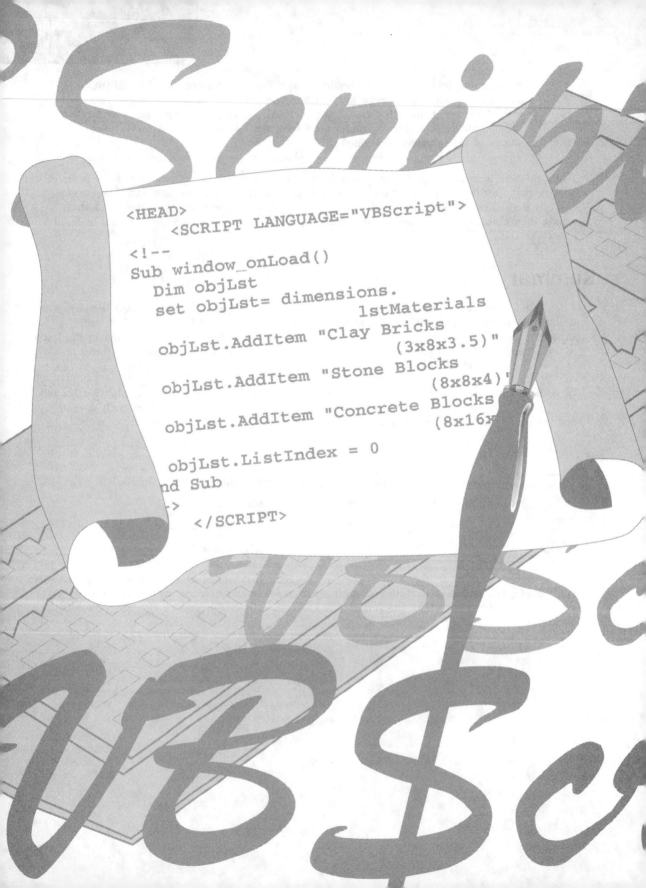

```
<HEAD>
    <SCRIPT LANGUAGE="VBScript">

<!--
Sub window_onLoad()
   Dim objLst
   set objLst= dimensions.
                          lstMaterials
   objLst.AddItem "Clay Bricks
                          (3x8x3.5)"
      objLst.AddItem "Stone Blocks
                          (8x8x4)"
         objLst.AddItem "Concrete Blocks
                          (8x16x
      objLst.ListIndex = 0
nd Sub
-->
      </SCRIPT>
```

Using ActiveX Controls

In the previous chapter, we saw how to improve functionality by using ActiveX controls instead of the more usual HTML **<INPUT>** controls. ActiveX controls (and, in fact, any other objects you insert in your Web pages), will generally provide you with a range of **properties** that you can manipulate, **methods** you can call, and **events** that you can react to. Altogether they provide a much more controllable and customizable environment than the HTML-style controls.

However, we also identified some of the problems they bring to the party. Because they include all this extra functionality, there's a lot more information that you have to provide, and a lot more that you need to know in order to use them. For example, how do you find out what the properties, methods, and events actually *are*? And then, of course, there's the question of the **CLASSID** and **CODEBASE**. Unless you get these right, the page simply won't work. After all, a phrase like **CLSID:8BD21D10-EC42-11CE-9E0D-00AA006002F3** doesn't exactly trip off the tongue!

In this chapter, we'll be looking at:

- Easier ways of inserting **<OBJECT>** tags into your pages
- How we combine traditional HTML **<INPUT>** controls with ActiveX ones
- The standard ActiveX controls that are specifically designed for Web pages
- How we tie together ActiveX controls and the VBScript in the page
- A way of exerting more control over the layout of controls in a page
- Where the **CODEBASE** attribute comes in, and what values to use

First though, we'll examine a better way to insert ActiveX controls and other objects into your HTML pages.

A Better Way to Insert Controls

You could be forgiven for thinking that writing VBScript code was going to be really arduous and time consuming, what with all of the **<OBJECT>** tags that you have to insert, and the various parameters that need to be set for each one. If nothing else, there's plenty of potential for errors caused by typos while entering the HTML code. Fortunately, there's a tool that eliminates a lot of the work of inserting object and parameter tags into the page—the Microsoft ActiveX Control Pad. We'll be using this extensively throughout the rest of the book.

Control Pad is designed to simplify the process of inserting objects into your Web pages, and it'll automatically provide most of the code required to create a working **<OBJECT>** tag in your HTML page. You don't have to go delving into Windows Registry looking for the **CLASSID** of a control, and you certainly don't have to worry about the names and syntax of its properties, methods, and events. What it doesn't help you with is the **CODEBASE** attribute. You may recall that this tells the browser where to get the control from if it isn't found on the user's system. However, later in the chapter, we'll give you some pointers as to where you should look for this information.

Where to Get Control Pad

Fortunately for the world at large, Microsoft have allowed everybody to download this tool free of charge. You can get it directly from the Web at **http://microsoft.com/msdownload**, where you just follow the links from the Internet Technologies section. You can also use FTP to download it from: **ftp.microsoft.com/msdownload/MSDN/CPAD/SETUPPAD.EXE**.

Using ActiveX Control Pad

Control Pad is a small application designed specifically to help you place ActiveX objects in your HTML files. The interface is a fairly typical MDI (Multiple Document Interface) that allows you to edit numerous **.htm** files simultaneously. The basic document interface that you get is a little similar to the Windows NotePad application (which some HTML gurus would have you believe is still *the* tool to write Web pages with!).

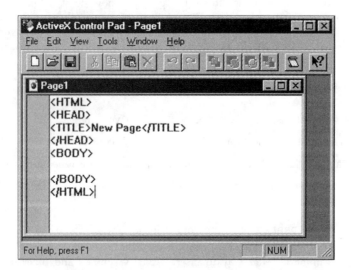

To start a new document, select New HTML from the File menu. You will be presented with a page containing just the bare tags for an HTML document. Modify the title text to something more appropriate than New Page (for example, Objects The Easy Way!), and let's build a page which will calculate the amount of building materials required by a customer. This will be similar to the page featured in the Bob's Builders Supplies application.

The Requirements for the Page

We need to produce a small form which allows the viewer to enter dimensional details of something—for example, a wall. This page will be used to calculate how much material is required. Just to prove that we can, we'll integrate both ActiveX controls and the more traditional HTML `<INPUT>` controls within the same page.

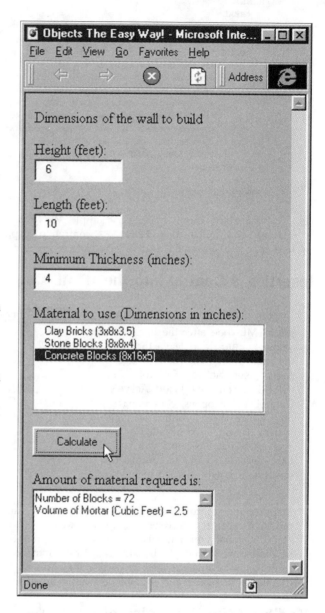

Start by laying out the text of the page, with suitable formatting, in Control Pad (a listing of the code we used is shown overleaf), so that it'll accept the necessary information from the user. We need a few basic items: some text entry controls for the dimensions of the wall, a list box with a selection of the materials available, a button to start the calculation process, and somewhere to display our results. The screenshot shows what we are aiming to produce.

This page can be found at `http://www.wrox.com/books/0448/code/chapter03/BobsWall/FBCalc.htm`

Basic Structure of the HTML code

To create the raw outline of the page, we used the following HTML code:

```
<HTML>
    <HEAD>
        <TITLE>Objects The Easy Way!</TITLE>
    </HEAD>
    <BODY>
        <FORM NAME="Dimensions">
            Dimensions of the wall to build<P>
            <P> Height (feet):<BR> </P>
            <P> Length (feet): <BR> </P>
            <P> Minimum Thickness (inches):<BR> </P>
            <P> Material to use (Dimensions in inches):<BR> </P>
            <P> Amount of material required is: <BR> </P>
            <TEXTAREA NAME="RESULTS" LENGTH=45 HEIGHT=30>
        </FORM>
    </BODY>
</HTML>
```

As you can see, this is really very simple. We've defined an HTML **form** with the name **Dimensions**, and used a **TEXTAREA** control to display the results of our final calculations. The next task is to insert the ActiveX controls where the user will enter the size of the wall.

Inserting a Control into the HTML Code

In Control Pad, insert a blank line in the HTML code after the line **Height (feet):
**, and leave the insertion point (text cursor) there. Select Insert ActiveX Control... from the Edit menu. The Insert ActiveX Control dialog opens, containing a list of every registered control on your system. If you have installed a tool such as Visual Basic this will be quite long, because all of the controls that come with it will also be included.

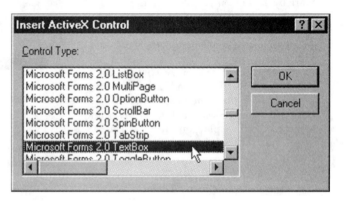

Many of the controls that you find here are not really suitable for Web pages—in fact, they'll probably cause the browser to display a warning about **unsigned code**. This is all part of the security model which has been developed to protect users from unsafe ActiveX controls, and we'll be discussing it in-depth in later chapters. For now, scroll to the Microsoft Forms 2.0 group of controls. These are provided as part of the ActiveX Control Pad itself, and they can also be found in Internet Explorer, and so will be readily available on the user's system.

Modifying the Properties of a Control

Select the Microsoft Forms 2.0 TextBox control, click OK, and two new dialogs open. One is a small form containing the TextBox control, and the other is a Properties dialog. Together these allow you to customize the behavior and appearance of the control. As you set the properties, you actually modify the various attributes of the **<OBJECT>** tag (and the **<PARAM>** tags that are placed within it) for the object definition, which are inserted into the HTML code when you close the Edit ActiveX Control dialog.

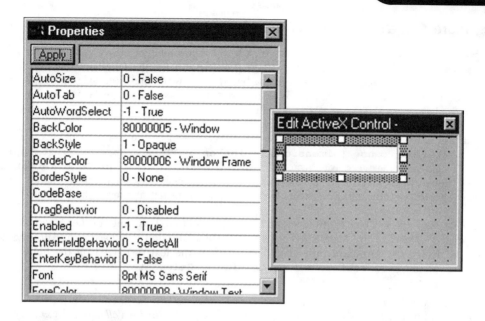

The Edit ActiveX Control dialog is useful for setting the size for the control. The rest of the fine tuning is achieved by modifying the settings in the Properties dialog. For now, the only important property that we need to modify is the **ID** property. For those of you more familiar with Visual Basic or VBA (Visual Basic for Applications), this is the equivalent of the **Name** property normally associated with a control.

Change the **ID** to **txtHeight** and click the Apply button. Then close the two dialogs. Control Pad inserts the appropriate HTML **<OBJECT>** and **<PARAM>** tags for the object directly into your page. This is an easy way of finding the **CLSID** value for a control, or the names and values of all the necessary attributes and properties.

```
...
Height (feet):<BR>
<OBJECT ID="txtHeight" WIDTH=96 HEIGHT=24
 CLASSID="CLSID:8BD21D10-EC42-11CE-9E0D-00AA006002F3">
    <PARAM NAME="VariousPropertyBits" VALUE="746604571">
    <PARAM NAME="Size" VALUE="2540;635">
    <PARAM NAME="FontCharSet" VALUE="0">
    <PARAM NAME="FontPitchAndFamily" VALUE="2">
    <PARAM NAME="FontWeight" VALUE="0">
</OBJECT>
...
```

If you want to modify the control's properties again, once it has been inserted into your page, all you have to do is to click the 'blue box' icon that Control Pad displays in the margin of the HTML document, next to the **<OBJECT>** tag. The Edit ActiveX Control and Properties dialogs open again, and the changes you make are inserted back into the HTML code. These markers also make it easy for you to find out where you have inserted the various controls and other components in your HTML document.

```
Height (feet):<BR>
<OBJECT ID="txtHeight"
CLASSID="CLSID:8BD2
    <PARAM NAME="Vari
    <PARAM NAME="Size
    <PARAM NAME="Font
    <PARAM NAME="Font
    <PARAM NAME="Font
</OBJECT>
```

Adding more Controls to the HTML Code

Now we need to add two more text boxes. We use the same method as we did with the height text box (**txtHeight**), naming these with **ID**s of **txtLength** for the length of the wall, and **txtThickness** for the thickness. Alternatively, because we want the same size and style for these two text boxes, we could just copy and paste the **<OBJECT>** section in the HTML to the appropriate places, and then change the **ID** attributes.

The next task is to add a **list** object and a **button** object. We place the insertion point on a blank line after **Material to use (Dimensions in inches):
, and open the Insert ActiveX Control dialog. This time we select Microsoft Forms 2.0 ListBox and set its **ID to **lstMaterials**. Using the Edit ActiveX Control dialog, we make this a reasonable size, enough for about 30 characters should be sufficient. The other properties should be left at their default values.

Immediately after the list box control, we add a button control. This time, in the Insert ActiveX Control dialog, we select the Microsoft Forms 2.0 CommandButton. We need to modify the **ID** as before, and change the **Caption** property which contains the text displayed on the button. We've changed the **ID** to **cmdCalculate** and the **Caption** to **Calculate**.

> *You may have noticed that we're following a control naming convention here. The first three characters of the control's **ID** property are being used to identify the type of control. The text boxes all start with **txt**, buttons start with **cmd** (for 'command'), and the list box control is prefixed by **lst**. This follows the naming convention recommended in the Visual Basic User manuals.*

If we now save the HTML document and load it into the browser, it appears to be almost identical to our earlier screenshot, although the list box is empty. The page does have one other small drawback—it doesn't do anything! All we have so far are a few controls embedded in a Web page. We can cut and paste text between the text boxes or click the button, but nothing else happens. What we need now is a little script to manipulate the controls, and to give us some useful user interactions.

Enter Script Wizard

Since this book is primarily about VBScript, Script Wizard (a tool designed to help you manage the events, properties and methods of ActiveX objects) is a particular feature of the ActiveX Control Pad that you'll find invaluable. In the same way that a specialized web page tool isn't necessary to create web pages, ActiveX Control Pad and its Script Wizard facility are not actually necessary to produce interactive web pages. However, it does considerably reduce the effort of scripting, as we shall see—and remember, if you find that you don't like it, there's always NotePad!

Adding VBScript to Our Page

Now that the HTML document contains some controls that can be manipulated, we can start to attach code to their events. In Control Pad, select Script Wizard... from the Tools menu, or click the yellow scroll icon on the toolbar. We'll begin by taking a look at the objects and events that are available to us.

Objects and Events in Control Pad

In the upper-left window is a tree view showing the objects in our page. For each object, the tree shows a list of the events that we can attach code to. Script Wizard generally recognizes all of the elements we have placed in the page, as well as a few that we didn't, such as the Window object at the bottom of the list.

The HTML **<FORM>** tags that we inserted in the page are represented by the form's name, **Dimensions**. You may recall that we named it this when we typed in the HTML code. Clicking on the plus symbol next to the Dimensions object icon displays a list of the **objects** and **events** available for our form.

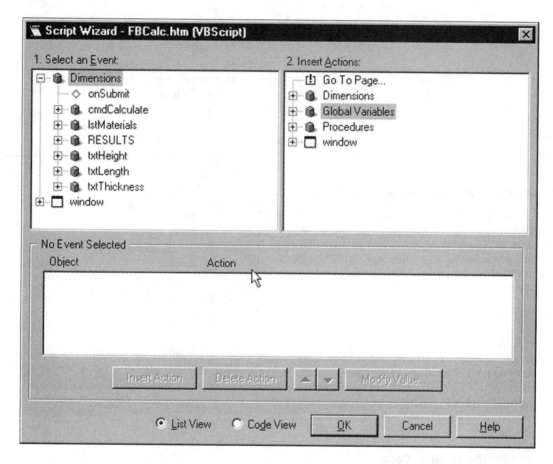

In our example, you can see that the form contains two distinct types of item: other objects, and the events which you can script for. In the case of our form object, there's only one event applicable, and that's **onSubmit**. Events are represented by diamond-shaped icons which are clear when there's no code associated with that particular event, and solid black when some code has been written for it. Notice that the objects contained within **Dimensions** consist of both ActiveX controls that we inserted with **<OBJECT>** tags, and the more traditional HTML form elements such as the **TEXTAREA** control that we called **RESULTS**.

Expanding the tree structure for the button object, **cmdCalculate**, and the **TextArea** control, **Results**, reveals how many more events are available for ActiveX controls as compared to the usual HTML ones. This is one of the benefits of using ActiveX controls. As it happens, we're only going to use a couple of these, but the rich supply of events offers a huge potential for interactive development.

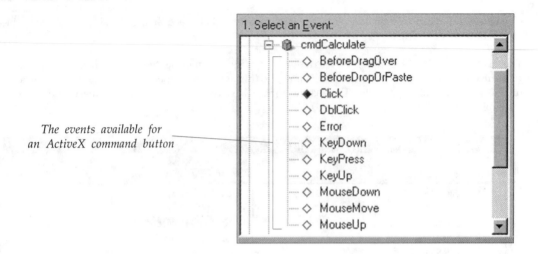

The events available for
an ActiveX command button

Viewing Methods, Properties, and Actions

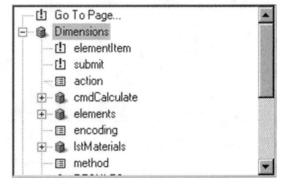

The right-hand tree view provides a list of items similar to those we have just examined, the main difference being that here, all the **methods** and **properties** of all of the objects in the page are listed. Again, take a look at the **Dimensions** object.

As in the events pane, the **Dimension** object contains all of its child objects. While the blue cube represents another object, the two other icons represent the methods and properties of the form. In this case, we see that the **Dimensions** form can itself be **submitted**, and that it has a property of **encoding**. This view is particularly useful because double-clicking on either a property or method icon will paste some code into the code window, helping to avoid bugs due to typos. We'll be using this technique shortly.

Examining the Created Code

The lower pane in Script Wizard is the List or Code View. The default is List, but we'll always be using Code View where you can type your VBScript code.

If we go back and select the Window object's **onLoad** event from the Select an Event: pane, the lower pane changes to an editing window. It already contains the **window_onLoad()** subroutine header, and this subroutine will run whenever the page is loaded. It's connected automatically to the window's **onLoad** event by the name, just as we saw in earlier chapters when we connected a button to its code by using **btnCalculate_onClick()** as the subroutine name. We'll use the **window_onLoad()** event to place our entries in the list box control, **lstMaterials**, when the page is first loaded, by adding this code:

```
Sub window_onLoad()
Dim objLst
set objLst= dimensions.LstMaterials
objLst.AddItem "Clay Bricks (3x8x3.5)"
objLst.AddItem "Stone Blocks (8x8x4)"
objLst.AddItem "Concrete Blocks (8x16x5)"
objLst.ListIndex=0
```

If you are used to VBA then this code should look quite familiar. All we're doing here is creating a variable named **objLst**, and then using the **Set** statement which assigns an **object reference** to the variable, which in this case is the list box **lstMaterials** in the form **Dimensions**. We can then refer to the list box using just this variable rather than the full syntax of **Dimensions.lstMaterials**.

To place some building materials into the list for the user to select, we call the list box's **AddItem** method repeatedly, supplying the text for each item. The final statement is used to programmatically select the first item on the list, and it'll also cause the **Click** event of the list box to fire (although we haven't actually written any code for it yet!).

Clicking OK in the Script Wizard window returns us to the main Control Pad application. Notice that it has inserted a block of script into the **<HEAD>** section of the page:

```
<SCRIPT LANGUAGE="VBScript">
<!--
Sub window_onLoad()
   Dim objLst
   set objLst= dimensions.lstMaterials
   objLst.AddItem "Clay Bricks (3x8x3.5)"
   objLst.AddItem "Stone Blocks (8x8x4)"
   objLst.AddItem "Concrete Blocks (8x16x5)"
   objLst.ListIndex = 0
End Sub
-->
</SCRIPT>
```

*You'll see that Control Pad has automatically added the **End Sub** line to the HTML document, even though we didn't type it ourselves. However, Control Pad isn't intelligent—it'll always add this regardless of whether we type it ourselves or not. You should never type **End Sub** (or **End Function**) in the Script Wizard*

Remember that, in the last chapter, we saw how the placing of a script affects the **context** in which it's available. Script Wizard makes some intelligent guesses as to where each block of script should be positioned. In this case, the **<HEAD>** section of the page has been chosen because the event is for the **Window** object.

One thing you'll find as you examine the code produced by Script Wizard, is that it's not particularly fussy about indenting it, or laying it out neatly. In theory, this isn't important if you always use Script Wizard and Control Pad to maintain your page, but it does make it more difficult to find your way around it 'in the raw'. While Script Wizard places code for the Window events in the **<HEAD>** *section, any event handlers you create for inserted object controls are placed immediately above the respective* **<OBJECT>** *tag. This does mean that, by the time you've created a few event procedures, the body of your HTML page will be littered with* **<SCRIPT>** *tags.*

An Alternative Method of Placing Entries in the List Box

There is another way in which we could have populated the list box. Rather than typing the code for the **AddItem** method calls, we could use the Insert Actions pane and allow Script Wizard to do the work. Open the **Dimensions** form object in this window, and find the list box object **lstMaterials**. Click the plus symbol next to it and a list of its methods and properties appears. Among them is the AddItem method that we've just used.

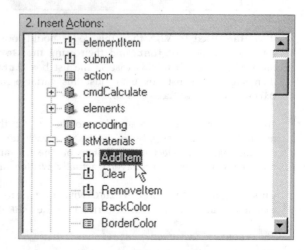

Double-clicking the AddItem method inserts the following code into the lower code editing window, ready for us to add the required argument values:

```
call lstMaterials.AddItem(pvargItem, pvargIndex)
```

However, there are drawbacks to making exclusive use of this particular method, the most significant being that the object for the list has not been fully **qualified**. In other words, it doesn't explicitly define the full 'path' of the object in the hierarchy of the page. The statement should include the name of the form as well, like this:

```
call Dimensions.lstMaterials.AddItem(pvargItem, pvargIndex)
```

If we don't provide this extra qualification then we'll get an error message when we come to execute the script:

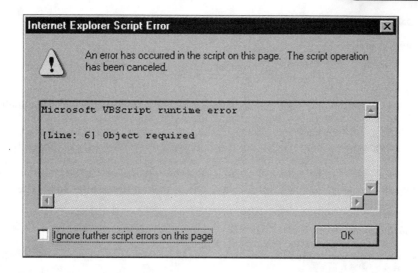

For this reason, we chose to use a reference variable in our own code, as you saw earlier, and **Set** it to reference the object with a fully qualified path. Before we continue with the details of the rest of the script for this page, we should step back and think about what interactions there should be between the user and the page.

The Needs of the Code

Consider what we are trying to achieve with this page. The user needs to enter four iems of data. The dimensions of the wall consist of the length, height, and thickness, and we need to know the type of building material from which to construct it. This last value, the type of material, is easy— all we need to do is to retrieve the user's selection from the list box. As we have already set a default selection, with the code **objLst.ListIndex = 0** in the window's **onLoad** event, there will always be a valid selection. They can only ever change it to one of the other items.

For the dimensional data, however, we have three text box objects. For these we need to ensure that only *valid numeric* data is entered, and that a calculation only takes place when *all three* have valid data

A Generic Function for Input Validation

To meet our first requirement—that only *valid numeric* data is entered in the text boxes—we use the function **IsNumeric()**. However, since we have three text controls, it would be better if we create one generic function which all of these controls can use. To do this, we click the yellow scroll icon on the toolbar to start up Script Wizard and move the mouse over the upper-right pane. Clicking the right button opens a pop-up menu:

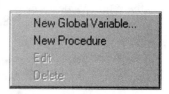

Before we go any further, we need to define the global variables that we'll be using outside of any function or procedure. Select New Global Variable... and do this for each of the following global variables:

 `gflgready`

 `gstrMaterial`

83

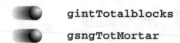

gintTotalblocks

gsngTotMortar

(We'll look at what each of these does in the section where it is first used.)

Now select New Procedure from the same menu to create a new procedure—imaginatively entitled **Procedure1**. In the code window, we highlight the name and replace it with something a little more useful, such as **CheckNumeric**. Also, we need to return a value from this procedure and we must be able to manipulate the text box control that we call it from, so we change the word **Sub** to **Function** and type **objTextBox** between the brackets. The function can now be passed a reference to a text box control, and we'll examine this to make sure that the text it contains is numerical data. If it doesn't then we can prompt the user with a message box. Type the following code for the procedure:

```
Function CheckNumeric(objTextBox)
  If Not IsNumeric(objTextBox.Text) then
    MsgBox "Numbers Only Please"
    objTextBox.SelStart = 0
    objTextBox.SelLength = Len(objTextBox.Text)
    CheckNumeric = False
  Else
    CheckNumeric = True
  End If
End Function 'Added by Control Pad automatically
```

In the case of bad data being entered, we use the **SelStart** and **SelLength** properties of the text box object to highlight the text once the message box has been acknowledged. Click OK and notice once again that the code has been placed in the **<HEAD>** section of the page. Script Wizard also adds the **End Function** line for us.

Text boxes have **SelStart** *and* **SelLength** *properties which define the start position and the number of characters that are highlighted. By setting these properties, you can control which parts of the text are highlighted yourself. Here we have set the start position to zero, the index of the first character, and the length to the whole of the text, so that it's ready for changing.*

The next step is to attach the **Change** events for the text boxes to this new function. Open up Script Wizard once more and, in the Event window under the **Dimensions** branch, select the **txtHeight** text box and click the Change event icon. We'll use the **CheckNumeric** function and the return value to meet our second criteria—that all three text boxes contain valid numerical text. Here's the code for the **Change** event of the **txtHeight** text box:

```
Sub txtHeight_Change()
  If CheckNumeric(Me) = True Then
    gflgReady = gflgReady OR 1      'Set bit 0
  Else
    gflgReady = gflgReady AND 6     'Clear bit 0
  End If
End Sub
```

There are two interesting things to note in this code. One is the call to our new function, **CheckNumeric()**. The argument that we pass is **Me**, which is a reserved word in VBScript which refers to the current object. In this case, the object in question is the text box whose **Change** event we are coding.

84

Secondly, notice how we use the **gflgReady** flag variable. As the user enters values into the text boxes we'll use this variable to reflect the state of their contents. In the case of a numeric value being entered, we'll **OR** the flag variable with a constant—in this case, **1**. This guarantees that the rightmost bit of the flag variable is set to **1**. In the case of an invalid value being entered into the text box, we **AND** the value with **6** which clears the rightmost bit of the variable. We can code similar routines for the **Change** events of the other two text boxes, using the values **2** and **4** when **CheckNumeric()** returns **True**, and **5** and **3** when it returns **False**:

```
Sub txtLength_Change()
   If CheckNumeric(Me) = True Then
      gflgReady = gflgReady OR 2      'Set bit 1
   Else
      gflgReady = gflgReady AND 5     'Clear bit 1
   End If
End Sub

Sub txtThickness_Change()
   If CheckNumeric(Me) = True Then
      gflgReady = gflgReady OR 4      'Set bit 2
   Else
      gflgReady = gflgReady AND 3     'Clear bit 2
   End If
End Sub
```

If you haven't used bit-wise manipulation like this before, or don't see how our example works, read the next section. If it's clear to you after this brief explanation, you can skip to the section on 'Retrieving the Selected Material' from the List Box (and go to the top of the class!).

Using Bit-wise Manipulation in a Flag Variable

The method we've used to ensure that three different controls contain valid data is one which you'll find very useful when writing your own pages. We can store more than one 'value' in a single variable if each value only needs to equate to Yes or No, or **True** or **False**. You'll be aware that computers use binary methods to store data, so any value in memory consists solely of a set of ones and zeros. Here's an example:

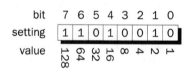

We work from right to left when using bit-wise arithmetic, and in this case, we have bits 1, 4, 6, and 7 set (i.e. they are equal to 1). Adding up the equivalent values, 2 + 16 + 64 + 128, we can see that our 'variable' is storing the value 210. The maximum value that we can store in eight bits is 255—but of course, we can always use more bits.

The trick with bit-wise arithmetic is to think of our variable as storing individual ones and zeros rather than a number like 210. We can set individual bits to 1, and clear them (back to zero) using a selection of special operators as well as by simply adding or subtracting numbers. In our example code, we used the two most popular bit-wise operators, **AND** and **OR**. These take the two values we present them with, and examine them one bit at a time before returning another value based on how the individual bits in the two originals compare.

OR sets the individual bits in the result if the equivalent bits in either one *or* the other of the originals is set. **AND** sets the individual bits in the result only if the equivalent bits in one *and* the other (both) of the originals are set.

So when we set the value in **gflgReady** using the code **gflgReady = gflgReady OR 4**, we effectively just set bit 2, like this:

$$\boxed{0\ 0\ 0\ 0}\ \text{OR}\ \boxed{0\ 1\ 0\ 0}\ =\ \boxed{0\ 1\ 0\ 0}$$

The bonus is that, if any of the other bits were already set, they don't change:

$$\boxed{0\ 0\ 1\ 1}\ \text{OR}\ \boxed{0\ 1\ 0\ 0}\ =\ \boxed{0\ 1\ 1\ 1}$$

We can change individual bits as the values in the three text boxes change. To clear a bit, we use **AND**. This only sets the resulting bit if both of the original bits are set, so the code **gflgReady = gflgReady AND 3** will clear bit 2 without changing the other bits, like this:

$$\boxed{0\ 1\ 1\ 1}\ \text{AND}\ \boxed{0\ 0\ 1\ 1}\ =\ \boxed{0\ 0\ 1\ 1}$$

This is why we used 1, 2, and 4 to set the bits with **OR**, and 6, 5, and 3 to clear them with **AND**. Because we're only concerned with the 'bottom' three bits, to clear bit 0 (value = **1**) we use **6**, because this has bits 1 and 2 set, and bit 0 clear. To clear bit 1 (value = **2**), we use its inverse, which is **5**, because this has bits 0 and 2 set, and bit 1 clear. To clear bit 2 (value = **4**) we use its inverse, **3**, because this has bits 0 and 1 set, and bit 2 clear. Essentially, the **AND OR** pairs that we use are complementary values whose sum is 7. If we were using 8 bits (for eight text boxes say) then the two complementary values would always add up to 255.

Finally, when we come to see if all three controls have valid data in them, we just have to check the value of **gflgReady** to see if it equals **7**. Of course, this only works because we know that the variable started off at zero, and we haven't set any other bits.

Retrieving the Selected Material from the List Box

Now that we have coded the necessary text box events, we're left with just the list box and the command button. We'll consider the list box first. This currently contains details of three types of building material, and it's obviously important for the quantity calculation to determine just which material to use. We have taken a very simple approach to keeping track of the material by using another global variable, **gstrMaterial**. Essentially, the only information we need to store in this string consists of the actual dimensions of the selected building material. To do this, we retrieve the value when the user clicks it just by attaching code to the **Click** event of the list box. To get the currently selected item, we simply read the **Text** property of the control:

```
gstrMaterial = Dimensions.lstMaterials.Text
```

Then we use some of VBScript's string manipulation functions to retrieve the actual dimensions—remember that the list contains a lot more than this: a full description of the material, such as Stone Blocks (8x8x4). We need to use the text between the brackets, so we add the following procedure to the **Click** event of **lstMaterials**:

```
Sub lstMaterials_Click()
  gstrMaterial = Dimensions.lstMaterials.Text
  'Extract the dimensions of the selected material
  'The Text of the Item contains this in a substring
  Dim intDimensionStart
  Dim intDimensionEnd
  intDimensionStart = InStr(gstrMaterial, "(")
  intDimensionEnd = InStr(gstrMaterial, ")")
  If (intDimensionStart = 0) Or (intDimensionEnd = 0) Then
    'There is a problem with the list box Entries
```

```
      MsgBox "Unexpected Error!"
      Exit Sub
   End If
   gstrMaterial = Mid(gstrMaterial, intDimensionStart+1, intDimensionEnd
                                      - intDimensionStart - 1)
   End Sub
```

In brief, **InStr()** returns the starting position of the second string if it's contained within the first one, or zero if it isn't found. We simply look for the opening and closing brackets, and use the position of these to extract the text between them with the aid of the **Mid()** function. The result is then stored in the global variable ready for processing later, when the Calculate button is pressed.

Remember that we set the selection in the list box to the first item in the **window_onLoad** event, and this itself generates a **Click** event which sets the default material in the **gstrMaterial** variable. So, at all times, the global variable **gstrMaterial** holds just the size of the currently selected material, even if the user hasn't clicked in the list box yet.

Calculating the Results

The final work of the page is all done when the Calculate button is actually clicked. Before we launch straight into the calculation itself, it's necessary to check that we have three valid dimensions supplied in the text boxes. As you saw earlier, we do this by checking the value of **gflgReady**. If all is well then we can calculate the results and display them in the text area control (named **Results**) on our **Dimensions** form:

```
Sub cmdCalculate_Click()
   If gflgReady = 7 Then
      Call CalculateMaterial
      Dimensions.Results.Value = "Number of Blocks = " & gintTotalBlocks &
      Chr(13) & Chr(10) & "Volume of Mortar (Cubic Feet) = " & gsngTotMortar
   Else
        MsgBox "You must enter all the dimensions first"
   End If
End Sub
```

You can see from the Calculate button's **Click** event handler that we have called a procedure named **CalculateMaterial**. Assuming that all the necessary data is available, this routine does all of the hard work and stores its results in a couple of global variables, **gsngTotMortar** and **gintTotalBlocks**. We use these to write an appropriate result into the **TEXTAREA** control. Even when using ActiveX controls, there's still a use for the intrinsic HTML controls like the text area.

We need to create a new procedure to do the hard work for us, and clicking the right button in the Insert Actions pane brings up the necessary menu. Let's take a quick look at the code behind this new procedure. First, we define the variables that we're going to use:

```
Sub CalculateMaterial()
   Dim intXPos
   Dim strDimensions
   Dim intLength, intHeight, intThickness
```

Previously, we went to some effort to strip down the list box material description to just the dimension data, and place it in the global variable **gstrMaterial**. We're now going to do some more of the same to get the individual numerical data for the dimensions of a single block:

```
    strDimensions = gstrMaterial

    'First, the get height into intHeight
    intXPos = InStr(gstrMaterial,"x")
    intHeight = CSng(Left(strDimensions, intXPos - 1))

    'now the length into intLength
    strDimensions = Right(strDimensions,len(strDimensions) - intXPos)
    intXPos = InStr(strDimensions,"x")
    intLength = CSng(Left(strDimensions,intXPos - 1))

    'and finally the thickness into intThickness
    strDimensions = Right(strDimensions,len(strDimensions) - intXPos)
    intThickness = CSng(strDimensions)
```

This is really quite straightforward string manipulation. We use **InStr()** to find the 'X marks the spot', cut off the preceding digits with the **Left()** function, and use **CSng()** to convert the data to single precision floating point data. For the next data value, we use the **Right()** function to chop off everything up to and including the next 'X', and repeat the process as before. Then, when we've got the dimensions of each block, we can calculate the total materials required:

```
    'Assume that the mortar between blocks is 1/2 inch thick, and get the
    'number of blocks for each row by adding 1/2 inch for the mortar and
    'then 1 to round up

    Dim intBlocksPerRow, intNoRows, intLayers
    Dim sngLong, sngHigh, sngThick

    sngLong= (CSng(Dimensions.txtLength.Text)*12)          'inches
    intBlocksPerRow = Int(sngLong / (intLength + 0.5)) +1

    sngHigh = CSng(Dimensions.txtHeight.Text) * 12         'inches
    intNoRows = Int(sngHigh / (intHeight + 0.5)) + 1

    sngThick = CSng(Dimensions.txtThickness.Text)          'inches
    If Int(sngThick / intThickness) <> (intThich/intThickness) Then
                                              intLayers = 1  'round up
    intLayers =  intLayers + Int(sngThick / intThickness)

    'Now calculate the total number of blocks required for the job

    gintTotalBlocks = intLayers * intNoRows * intBlocksPerRow

    'Finally, calculate the amount of mortar required. Each block will
    'require a 1/2 inch thick covering on its top surface and one side.

    Dim sngMortarAreaPerBlock   'cubic inches per block
    sngMortarAreaPerBlock = (intLength + intHeight) * intThickness * 0.5

    'Place total volume of mortar in global variable gsngTotMortar

    gsngTotMortar = gintTotalBlocks * sngMortarAreaPerBlock /(12^3) 'cu.ft.
    gsngTotMortar = Int(gsngTotMortar * 10) / 10     'to one decimal place

End sub
```

For the rest of the code, we're just indulging in a spot of number crunching. The only item of particular interest here is the manipulation we do with the `Int()` function. This simply converts an expression to an integer by removing any fractions—hence the 'plus 1' that we use for each part of the calculation. Once we have the number of bricks for a row, the number of rows, and the number of layers to make the wall, we're left with the straightforward task of calculating the end product. Voilà!

Controls Galore

Now that we have seen a couple of the available controls in action, it's time to look at what else we have at our disposal. Open a new HTML document in Control Pad and select Insert ActiveX Control... from the Edit menu. When you used Control Pad before, you may have noticed that there were quite a lot of items in the list. This list represents not only those items provided by Internet Explorer which can be embedded into your HTML pages, but every **registered** ActiveX control (and older OLE controls) found on your system. For instance, if you happen to have Microsoft Access installed on your computer, you may well find that you have an option for a Calendar control. If so, select it and you'll get a control dialog like this:

	August 1996		August ▼	1996 ▼

Sun	Mon	Tue	Wed	Thu	Fri	Sat
28	29	30	31	1	2	3
4	5	6	7	8	9	10
11	12	13	14	15	16	17
18	19	20	21	22	23	24
25	26	27	28	29	30	31
1	2	3	4	5	6	7

Looks pretty good, doesn't it? Just imagine how quickly you can put together great pages when half of the layout is already done for you by `WhateverCoolControl.ocx`. However, there is a catch. If we were to continue developing a page that used this calendar, we would have a nasty surprise in store when the time came to test it. As the page is loading in Internet Explorer, the following dialog will appear:

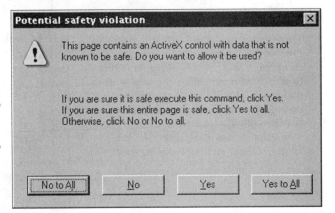

In itself, this isn't actually a major catastrophe. You can always set the options in your browser to ignore potential security risks and get on with loading up the component. However, imagine the impression this could make on the casual user stumbling across your site!

Not only does it look unprofessional, but they can't be sure that the object in your page hasn't been affected with some vicious virus or, even worse, is specially designed to wipe all their valuable data from their hard disk. Any controls or objects which have not been **signed** will present this message to viewers who have their browser set to the normal security levels. So, when it comes to embedding controls in your pages, you should try and keep to those that are supplied with the browser, or are from a trusted source.

> *The issues of software trust, code download and signing are too big for us to give adequate coverage to here. We'll go into this subject in more depth in Chapter 7 of the book.*

So, having decided to only use those controls that are signed and trustworthy, the big question is, which ones in the list offered by Control Pad can you actually use?

What are 'Safe' Controls?

As you have probably guessed, the first trustworthy group of controls are those whose name starts with Microsoft Forms 2.0. These are all to be found as part of the file **FM20.dll**, and were probably installed on your system along with Internet Explorer 3.0. The second grouping of controls that we shall assume are OK are those that start with Microsoft IE 3.0. These are some of the controls that may have found their way onto your system while you were browsing such web sites as the ActiveX gallery. In fact, it's worth your while visiting this site:

        http://microsoft.com/activex/gallery/

By clicking the hyperlinks in the left-hand contents frame, you can see a demonstration of the control in action. At the same time, your browser will automatically download the control for you and store it on your system ready for use in other pages.

These types of control are still likely to give you a warning about the component you are installing, but this time it'll be much more friendly, with a dialog containing a nice certificate stating that the control's software vendor is Microsoft. Do you trust them? Since you want to use these controls, the answer would undoubtedly be yes!

The best way to familiarize yourself with the controls is to use them. Let's take a look at a few small examples using controls that are available from Microsoft. We'll start with a **timer** control.

Using the Timer Control

The page we'll be developing for this example could be part of the main *reception* area of your web site. It might look something like this:

You can find this web page at:

`http://www.wrox.com/books/0448/code/chapter03/timer/company.htm`

It may not represent the 'be all and end all' of creative Web page design, but it does contain two interesting objects. One is a dynamically changing **floating frame**, and, of course, there's the **timer** control itself. This has been embedded in the **<HEAD>** section of the page:

```
<OBJECT ID="timIconChange" WIDTH=39 HEIGHT=39
    CLASSID="CLSID:59CCB4A0-727D-11CF-AC36-00AA00A47DD2"
    CODEBASE="http://activex.microsoft.com/controls/iexplorer/
                                    timer.ocx#Version=4,70,0,1161"
    TYPE="application/x-oleobject">
    <PARAM NAME="Interval" VALUE="2000">
</OBJECT>
```

We've included the **CODEBASE** and **TYPE** attributes in the declaration of the object because this is one of those controls that you can't expect to be present on every computer—unless you are working in the controlled confines of the corporate Intranet.

Availability of controls is something that you'll need to bear in mind as you design pages, because it's likely that you'll have installed a lot more controls than your average viewer, and so their browser will need to download the components the first time they view your page. We'll talk more about this at the end of the chapter.

The timer object has only one parameter that is of interest: its **Interval**. This is the value in milliseconds that elapses between the control firing its one event, **Timer**. In our page, every two seconds (interval = 2000) the **Timer** event causes the graphic displayed in the floating frame to change. The icon displayed in the frame changes from an About icon to a Services icon, to a Software icon, and finally to an Intranet icon. The sequence is then repeated.

Working with Floating Frames

Before we look at the code, let's just take a quick look at how the floating frame itself is created:

```
<IFRAME NAME="fraIcon" WIDTH=101 HEIGHT=66 MARGINHEIGHT=1 MARGINWIDTH=1
   FRAMEBORDER=1 SRC="softwareicon.htm" SCROLLING=no NORESIZE ALIGN=left>
         'A Floating Frame is used here! if you do not see the icons,
            then try downloading MS IE 3.0!
   </IFRAME>
```

A floating frame uses the new **<IFRAME>** tag. You can think of it as a cross between the regular HTML **<FRAME>** tag and an **<IMG>** tag normally used to place graphics in a page. Like normal frames, it has attributes for the margins of the contained text, a source **.htm** file, a **SCROLLING** attribute which controls whether scrollbars are displayed for documents larger that the frame, and a **NORESIZE** attribute to prevent the user from changing the size of the frame and disturbing the layout of the surrounding text.

However, more in common with the **<IMG>** tag, you can specify the **HEIGHT** and **WIDTH** attributes. Normally, the size of a frame will be determined from the **<FRAMESET>** attributes, but since the floating frame can appear anywhere in your document, you will define its dimensions here. The main difference between floating frames and normal frames is the closing **</IFRAME>** tag. This encloses alternative text for browsers that don't support **<IFRAME>**, as you can see from our example above.

Since this is still a frame, it has a **Location.HRef** property that we can manipulate. This defines the **.htm** document (a normal HTML page) that is displayed in the frame. In our case, the documents that we load into the frame contain only the icon that we want to display. For example, the HTML code for **servicesicon.htm** is:

```
<HTML>
   <HEAD> <TITLE>Software Icon</TITLE> </HEAD>
   <BODY> <IMG SRC="Services.gif" ALT="Services"> </BODY>
</HTML>
```

So, changing the icon in the frame every couple of seconds is as easy as changing the **Location.HRef** attribute each time the **Timer** event occurs.

Responding to the Timer Event

To display a series of pages in our floating frame, we need to set up an array of page names. We've done this in the **window_onLoad** event of the main document:

```
Dim gstrIconsURL(3)
Sub window_onLoad()
  'initialize the array of Icon page names
  gstrIconsURL(0)="Servicesicon.htm"
  gstrIconsURL(1)="Intraneticon.htm"
  gstrIconsURL(2)="Abouticon.htm"
  gstrIconsURL(3)="Softwareicon.htm"
  gintIconIndex = 0
End Sub
```

gstrIconsURL(3) is a global array that will hold four page names (remember that the first element of all arrays has a subscript of **0**). **gintIconIndex** is also a global variable, and this is used to reference the different elements of the array. Now we can respond to the **Timer** event by changing the **Location.HRef** property of the floating frame:

```
Sub timIconChange_Timer()
  Document.fraIcon.Location.HRef = gstrIconsURL(gintIconIndex)
  gintIconIndex = gintIconIndex + 1
  If gintIconIndex = 4 Then gintIconIndex = 0    'reset sequence
End Sub
```

Every time the **Timer** fires, we set the source document for the floating frame to **gstrIconsURL(gintIconIndex)**, and then increment **gintIconIndex**. When its value gets to **4**, we reset it to zero.

This isn't exactly what you would call earth-shattering design, but it does the job. If this were a real site then you would probably want to enclose the **<IMG>** tag in **<A HREF="..." TARGET="_parent">** tags, to make your icons actually do something such as navigating to a different page. Notice that setting the **TARGET** attribute when you use a floating frame like this is important. Without it, the new document will be loaded into the floating frame itself, and then be changed again when the timer in the parent updates it with another page.

As you can see, the timer control is potentially very useful. With a little imagination you can create some really interesting effects when it's used in conjunction with other controls.

Using Labels and Scroll Bars

In the previous chapter, you saw an example of the **label** and **scroll bar** controls in use. The label we used was the version 3 control "Microsoft IE 3.0.Label ", rather than version 2 ("Microsoft Forms 2.0.Label"). Again, this label control is one that may not be installed on the user's system, so you should include the **CODEBASE** and **TYPE** attributes in the **<OBJECT>** tag.

```
<OBJECT ID="lblTheText" WIDTH=240 HEIGHT=163
   CLASSID="CLSID:99B42120-6EC7-11CF-A6C7-00AA00A47DD2"
   CODEBASE="http://activex.microsoft.com/controls/iexplorer/
                              ielabel.ocx#Version=4,70,0,1161"
   TYPE="application/x-oleobject">
```

The other controls this example introduced were the scroll bar and command button. The scroll bar object definition we used was:

```
<OBJECT ID="hsbRotation" WIDTH=240 HEIGHT=23
    CLASSID="CLSID:DFD181E0-5E2F-11CE-A449-00AA004A803D">
        <PARAM NAME="Size" VALUE="3545;580">
        <PARAM NAME="Max" VALUE="359">
        <PARAM NAME="SmallChange" VALUE="5">
        <PARAM NAME="LargeChange" VALUE="15">
        <PARAM NAME="Orientation" VALUE="1">
</OBJECT>
```

Because the command button is a standard control, and part of the browser's own repertoire, we didn't include a **CODEBASE** attribute in this case. The **command button** definition was:

```
<OBJECT ID="cmdUp" WIDTH=65 HEIGHT=25
    CLASSID="CLSID:D7053240-CE69-11CD-A777-00DD01143C57">
        <PARAM NAME="Caption" VALUE="Up">
        <PARAM NAME="Size" VALUE="2540;661">
        <PARAM NAME="FontCharSet" VALUE="0">
        <PARAM NAME="FontPitchAndFamily" VALUE="2">
        <PARAM NAME="ParagraphAlign" VALUE="3">
        <PARAM NAME="FontWeight" VALUE="0">
</OBJECT>
```

Using the Spin Button Control

The **spin button** is a control that resembles a scroll bar, but has no slider component. It does have a maximum and minimum range of values which you can use in a similar way to a scroll bar. However, you can continue to click the arrow heads at both ends of the spin button control, even when the **Value** is at an extreme limit, and this still fires an event. To demonstrate the use of spin buttons we have put together the following VBScript application. To try it out for yourself, point your browser at:

`http://www.wrox.com/books/0448/code/chapter03/SpinButton/casino.htm`

As you can see, we've used five spin button controls. The layout of this page uses nested tables and is in fact quite a complex affair—discussing this would distract us from the important aspects of the example. To display the dice, we place two floating frames into the top left cells, and when we want to show a different face we change the **Location.HRef** property of the appropriate frame to a different **URL**—just as we did in the earlier timer example. The **.htm** files we use contain images of the dice faces and are called **D1.htm** to **D6.htm**.

To place your bet, use the spin control in the top right section of the table. The label control next to it, **lblBet**, displays your chosen number. To keep it in synch with the spin button, we only have to update its **Value** parameter every time the value of the spin button changes. The spin button itself is defined in the HTML code as:

```
<OBJECT ID="spbBet" WIDTH=16 HEIGHT=32
    CLASSID="CLSID:79176FB0-B7F2-11CE-97EF-00AA006D2776">
        <PARAM NAME="Size" VALUE="423;846">
        <PARAM NAME="Min" VALUE="2">
        <PARAM NAME="Max" VALUE="12">
        <PARAM NAME="Position" VALUE="7">
</OBJECT>
```

Notice that we have **<PARAM>** tags for the minimum and maximum values that the spin button can represent, just as with a scroll bar. The **Position** parameter is the starting **Value** of the control before the user gets a chance to click on the arrow heads, and in our case, we choose 'lucky' seven. As the user clicks on the arrow heads, the **Value** property of the control is incremented or decremented by the value in the **SmallChange** property. In our case, we haven't specified a value ourselves, and so it remains at the control's default of **1**.

Our code reacts to the spin button's **Change** event, using a subroutine named **spbBet_Change()**. All it has to do is update the label's **Caption** property, like this:

```
Sub spbBet_Change()
    lblBet.Caption = spbBet.Value
end sub
```

Also, in the upper-right hand table cell, we've placed a combo box control which displays a record of each set of dice rolls. Every time the command button is clicked, we build up a string of information and place it in the combo. Here's the code that runs when the Roll! button is clicked:

```
Sub cmdRoll_Click()
  Dim intRoll, strHistory
  Randomize                        'initialize the random number generator
  intRoll = Int(Rnd*6 + 1)         'get the first dice result
  gintResult = intRoll
  Document.D1.Location.HRef = "D" & CStr(intRoll) & ".htm"
  strHistory = CStr(intRoll) & " + "
  intRoll = Int(Rnd*6 + 1)          'get the second dice result
  gintResult = gintResult + intRoll
  Document.D2.Location.HRef = "D" & CStr(intRoll) & ".htm"
  strHistory = strHistory & CStr(intRoll) & " = " & CStr(gintResult)
  cboHistory.AddItem strHistory, 0  'update the combo box
  cboHistory.ListIndex = 0          'and set the index to the first item
  ...
```

Producing Random Numbers

First, we use the **Randomize** statement to prepare the random number generating function, **Rnd**. If we don't do this, the sequence of results will be the same each time the **Rnd** function is used—not very useful for an application relying on some sort of random number! The dice rolls are calculated quite simply as:

```
intRoll = Int(Rnd*6 + 1)        'get the first dice result
```

Rnd produces a floating point number between **0** and **1**, so all we have to do is to multiply it by the largest number we need, add one, and knock off the fractional part to get an integer in the desired range. We then use this to load the correct dice picture into the floating frames, hence the **D1.htm** to **D6.htm** naming convention. We also build up the string to add to the **cboHistory** combo box. Notice that we have an extra argument for the **AddItem** method of the combo box:

```
cboHistory.AddItem strHistory, 0    'update the combo box
cboHistory.ListIndex = 0            'and set the index to the first item
```

This second argument specifies the position in the list where the new item should be added. Setting it to zero means that we always have the most recent roll added to the top of the list rather than the end—which is the default. The final statement sets the index of the combo box to show this new item.

Now all we have to do is to see if you've won! **gintResult** holds the value of the two dice, so we compare it to the value in the label control, **lblBet**.

```
      . . .
      If gintResult = lblBet.Caption Then    'determine if you've won
         Call CalculateWin
      Else
         Call RemoveStake
      End If
End Sub  'end of cmdRoll_Click()
```

Whatever the outcome, win or lose, we have to modify the amount of betting chips represented by the colored labels in the bottom row of the table. To make this event handler easier to read, we have moved the code for this into some of our own subroutines. Before we look specifically at these routines however, we'll take a look at how we have inserted the Bank and Stake labels into the HTML code.

Forms and Element Arrays

To represent the amount of betting chips in the stake and bank, we have two groups of four label controls. Updating all their values after a roll of the dice would mean writing code to change the **Caption** property for four of the eight labels. What we would like to do is to loop through a **control array**, updating each one in turn. If you are familiar with Visual Basic then you may have used control arrays before. Each control is assigned an index number which places it in a control array, and a simple loop allows you to refer to each one in turn. Unfortunately, you can't create control arrays in VBScript! However, we can do something very similar using a form.

Traditionally, forms are used to get the Web server to run a program (or script) when you click a Submit button. The server collects the data from the controls contained between the **<FORM>** and **</FORM>** tags, and produces results which are passed back to the browser. The **Method** and **Action** attributes of the **<FORM>** tag tell the browser how to send the data to the server, and which script or program to execute. We'll be looking into this aspect of forms in Chapter 8. For now, we're going to make use of another feature of forms.

You'll recall from the previous chapter that a hierarchy is created from all the different parts of the browser and the page(s) currently being displayed. We can refer to the elements in this hierarchy using either their name or their index. A form is a **child object** of the **document**, so if a Web page contains two **<FORM>** sections, we can refer to them as **document.forms[0]** and **document.forms[1]**. Alternatively, a form can have a name. In our example we've named the form that contains the Stake labels using:

```
<FORM NAME="Stake">
```

We can now refer to it by name. But the form object has child objects too, including the **controls** (both ActiveX and intrinsic HTML) that appear in it. In our case, the controls are four labels, so we can refer to these as `Stake.Elements[0]`, `Stake.Elements[1]`, `Stake.Elements[2]`, and `Stake.Elements[3]`. This means that we can loop through them using a `For..Next` loop, just as if they were an array of controls in the VB sense of the word.

> *A word of warning here. Looping through the elements on a form like this is fine when you're sure that they are all of the same type, or at least have the same properties. One of the Visual Basic language features that VBScript doesn't support is the* **TypeOf()** *function. This allows you to determine what kind of object you're dealing with. In VBScript, you'll just have to be careful how you design your forms, so that the order in which controls are defined allows this sort of processing to be used when required.*

Updating the Bank and Stake

After a roll of the dice, we need to update the Stake and Bank labels. If you've lost, we remove the existing stake, and if you have no cash left at all, we start over by reloading the page. To the user, the number of each type of chip held is represented by the value displayed in the labels. In the background, though, we have two global arrays, `gintStakeValue()` and `gintBankValue()`, each with four elements (0 to 3), which we're using to mirror the values we want to display in the labels:

```
Sub RemoveStake()
  Dim intLoop
  Dim intCashLeft
  For intLoop = 0 to 3              'loop for each value of chips
    gintStakeValue(intLoop) = 0     'set the curent stake to zero
    intCashLeft = intCashLeft + gintBankValue(intLoop)
  Next
  If intCashLeft = 0 Then           'broke!
    MsgBox "You're Broke! Best make you start over!",32, "Spent Out"
    Call window.navigate("Casino.htm")   'reload the page
  End If
  Call RefreshLabels()              'update the label controls
End Sub
```

The final statement, a call to the `RefreshLabel` routine, is where we actually update the labels themselves. In the casino page, we have **Stake** and **Bank** forms which contain the labels, so we can loop through these and set their **Caption** property to the equivalent value from the global arrays `gintStakeValue()` and `gintBankValue()`:

```
Sub RefreshLabels()
  Dim intLoop
  For intLoop = 0 to 3   'loop for each control
    Stake.Elements(intLoop).Caption = gintStakeValue(intLoop)
    Bank.Elements(intLoop).Caption = gintBankValue(intLoop)
  Next
End Sub
```

If, by some slim chance, you've won, the `CalculateWin` routine is called. It uses a 'chance factor', based on the odds of guessing that number, to increase the values held in the `gintBankValue()` array. Finally, another call to `RefreshLabels` updates the display showing the new Stake and Bank values:

```
Sub CalculateWin()
  Dim intLoop
  Dim intFactor
  Select Case gintResult
    Case 2, 12:
      intFactor = 36
    Case 3, 11:
      intFactor = 18
    Case 4, 10:
      intFactor = 12
    Case 5, 9:
      intFactor = 9
    Case 6, 8:
      intFactor = 7   'a little below odds, the house has to win somehow!
    Case 7:
      intFactor = 6
  End Select
  For intLoop = 0 to 3
    gintBankValue(intLoop) = gintBankValue(intLoop) +
                             gintStakeValue(intLoop) * intFactor
  Next
  Call  RefreshLabels()
End Sub
```

The final thing we need to consider concerns how we actually set the stake for a bet. In our page, we have used spin button controls again. However, the **Change** event of the spin button now becomes inappropriate, because the range of values that should be available will change for each bet—depending on how much is left in the bank or stake. This means that we would need to keep changing the **Maximum** and **Minimum** properties of each spin button.

Finding Different Events to Code For

Let's look elsewhere for a solution. If we embed a spin button control in a page using ActiveX Control Pad, and then examine the events that are available with Script Wizard, we find a **SpinDown** and **SpinUp** event. These fire whenever their respective arrow is clicked, regardless of how the current **Value** of the control compares to its **Maximum** and **Minimum** property settings.

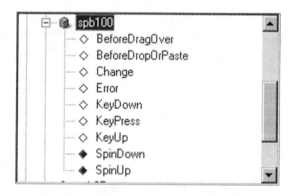

By using the **SpinDown** and **SpinUp** events, we remove the difficulty of managing the range and value of the spin buttons. The only real complexity lies in figuring out which way is up when the controls are orientated horizontally! After some experimentation, we use the following to handle the user's clicks on the controls instead. As you can probably work out from this code, the left arrowhead fires the **SpinUp** event and the right one fires **SpinDown**:

```
Sub spb1_SpinUp()    'need $1 Chip in stake
  If gintBankValue(0) Then       'bank is not zero (False)
    gintBankValue(0) = gintBankValue(0) - 1
```

```
        gintStakeValue(0) = gintStakeValue(0) + 1
        Call RefreshLabels
     End If
  End Sub


  Sub spb1_SpinDown()     'put $1 Chip back in bank
     If gintStakeValue(0) Then        'stake is not zero (False)
        gintStakeValue(0) = gintStakeValue(0) -1
        gintBankValue(0) = gintBankValue(0) + 1
        Call RefreshLabels
     End If
  End Sub
```

One of the great features of the spin button is that the **SpinUp** and **SpinDown** events continue to fire for as long as the mouse button is held down. The rate at which the events occur is set by the **Delay** property, which we've left at its default of **50**ms.

This brings our discussion about the spin button to a close. However, if you take a look at the source code for the page, with its complex nested tables, you'll see the effort that is required to get the layout of the various controls correct. And of course, different browsers will always display it in a slightly different way, especially with the variable font size configuration available to the user of the more modern ones. However, ActiveX offers us another alternative. Before we jump in and explain this, let's consider how the browser's display flexibility could upset your carefully crafted page!

Producing Better Layout

The basic problem with adding controls and objects simply by inserting them directly into the HTML code, is that the overall look will depend upon the actual browser in use. For example, if the viewer resizes their browser window to a narrow width, the controls will be split over two lines, when you had intended them to be alongside each other.

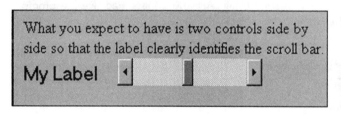

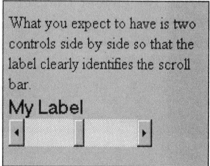

What You Want   *What You Might Get*

This may seem an extreme case, but once you start to use **frames**, you'll find that the working area is significantly smaller than a full browser window. Also, a more complex page is quite likely to have more controls taking up valuable room. The chance of creating confusion increases with the complexity of the pages we want to be able to create. What we need is some way to design our pages so that the end user sees them exactly as we had intended, in a similar manner to when we use Visual Basic or VBA to create screen forms.

Enter the HTML Layout Control

The answer to our layout problem revolves around another control, the HTML **layout control**. This is an ActiveX control just like the other ones we've looked at in this chapter. Its specialization is in the fact that it forms a **container** for other ActiveX controls, in a similar fashion to the way in which the HTML document becomes a container for objects and controls when the **<OBJECT>** tag is used.

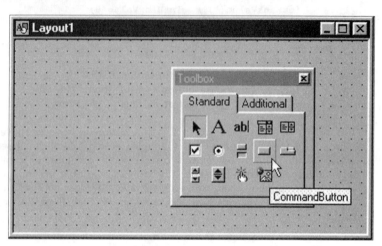

The best way to understand the layout control is to see it in use. In ActiveX Control Pad, select New HTML Layout from the File menu, and a blank form with a grid of dots and a toolbox window appears.

If you have used VBA or Visual Basic, then this will look quite familiar. All we have to do to place a control on the form is select it in the Toolbox and then draw it onto the form by clicking and dragging with the mouse. As in Visual Basic, you can add extra controls to your toolbox. Just right click on it and select Additional Controls... from the menu. We'll be using the layout control to produce a simple calculator, but before this we'll look at how it actually works.

Inside the Layout Control

When we first place a layout control in a web page using ActiveX Control Pad, we are prompted for the name of an **.alx** file. This file contains all the details of the elements included in the layout control. In our HTML page, the control will be defined like this:

```
<OBJECT CLASSID="CLSID:812AE312-8B8E-11CF-93C8-00AA00C08FDF"
    ID="calculator_alx" STYLE="LEFT:0;TOP:0">
    <PARAM NAME="ALXPATH" REF VALUE="calculator.alx">
</OBJECT>
```

The interesting point to note here is that the **<PARAM>** tag is slightly different to the one we would normally see. The **VALUE** attribute for the path to the **.alx** file contains the keyword **REF**, meaning that layout control has a reference its **.alx** file, but you can't change what it points to. In fact, the property **ALXPATH** is unavailable to your VBScript code!

The second thing here is the **ID**. Unlike the other ActiveX controls, whose **ID** (name) we have been able to change with the Properties dialog, changing this option has no effect here. The layout control is given a name based on the file name of the associated **.alx** file. Control Pad even marks the presence of the layout in a different way to other controls. In the margin of your HTML document, we have a new icon to denote a layout control.

Creating a Web Page with the Layout Control

All in all, the layout control is quite a strange beast. To better understand it, we'll create a simple Web page that has a layout control containing just a command button.

In ActiveX Control Pad, select New HTML item from the File menu and type a little descriptive text between the <BODY> tags. Select Insert HTML Layout... from the Edit menu, change to a temporary folder, and type the name Test when prompted for the .alx file. Since it doesn't already exist, it will be created automatically. The HTML document appears with the layout control embedded in it.

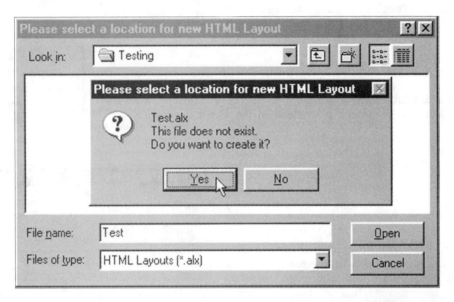

Now edit the control by clicking the layout icon in the margin. This opens the blank layout form, and the Toolbox window containing the various control types available. From the Toolbox select the **command button** tool and draw a button on the form.

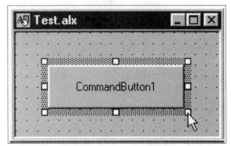

Double-click the blank area of the form to open the Properties dialog, and change the **BackColor** property to white (click on the ellipsis button to get a color dialog).

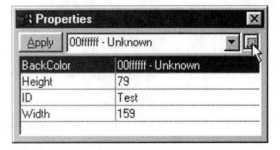

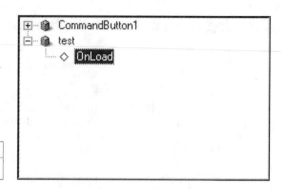

Click the Script Wizard button on the toolbar. Notice that we have two objects to code for. The **Test** object and **CommandButton1**. Place a message box in the **onLoad** event of the **Test** object.

```
Sub test_OnLoad()
  MsgBox "The ALX file has loaded"
```

Click OK and then close the form, saving it when prompted. You should now be back in the normal HTML editing window, and it's time to add a little more script. Click the Script Wizard button on the toolbar, and look at the objects available in the Event window:

Notice that the layout control itself is represented here and that it, too, has an **OnLoad** event. Add a similar message box to this event, save everything, and then load the page into your browser. As you can see, the layout control has a definite area of presence on the page, and its contained control, the command button, appears where we placed it.

Here's what the **test.alx** file looks like when displayed in a text editor:

```
<SCRIPT LANGUAGE="VBScript">
<!--
Sub test_OnLoad()
  MsgBox "The ALX file has loaded"
end sub
-->
</SCRIPT>
<DIV BACKGROUND="#ffffff" ID="Test" STYLE="LAYOUT:FIXED;WIDTH:153pt;HEIGHT:80pt;">
  <OBJECT ID="CommandButton1"
```

102

```
        CLASSID="CLSID:D7053240-CE69-11CD-A777-00DD01143C57"
        STYLE="TOP:10pt;LEFT:10pt;WIDTH:117pt;HEIGHT:39pt;TABINDEX:0;
                                                    ZINDEX:0;">
            <PARAM NAME="Caption" VALUE="CommandButton1">
            <PARAM NAME="Size" VALUE="4128;1376">
            <PARAM NAME="FontCharSet" VALUE="0">
            <PARAM NAME="FontPitchAndFamily" VALUE="2">
            <PARAM NAME="ParagraphAlign" VALUE="3">
            <PARAM NAME="FontWeight" VALUE="0">
        </OBJECT>
    </DIV>
```

The file is just like a regular HTML document. The objects that we draw onto the layout form appear within **<OBJECT>** tags, and the main difference is the extra **STYLE** attribute. This holds the information for the position of the control within the layout. The **form** section of the layout control is defined within **<DIV>** and **</DIV>** tags, which would normally be used in HTML as a document division. However, there are some added attributes here which hold the layout's properties.

That was a whirlwind tour of the structure of the layout control and its **.alx** file, and now, in the best traditions of all good cookery programs, we'll look at a layout control we produced earlier...

A Simple Calculator Layout Control

We've built a page that contains just one object for you to try. It uses a single layout control called **Calculator**—it doesn't need a lot of guesswork to understand the functionality of this page!

The layout control itself contains sixteen command buttons and a text box, and the code behind the buttons allows you to do simple arithmetic. In fact, this could have been done with regular HTML **<INPUT>** controls and some VBScript code, but the really great thing here is that it's basically a **component**. Anytime you feel the need to have a calculator somewhere in your web page, just insert a layout control which points to the **calculator.alx** file and—hey presto—a working calculator.

You can find this page at:

`http://www.wrox.com/books/0448/code/chapter03/calculator/calculator.htm`

This location also holds the **calculator.alx** component file so, if you wish, you can use the browser to download that separately and then just place it in your own Web page.

Calculator Under the Hood

The HTML page, **Calculator.htm**, is deceptively simple. As we suggested earlier, you can use the calculator component (the **.alx** file) by simply embedding it into your own Web pages, just as we've done here:

```
<HTML>
<HEAD>
    <TITLE>A Simple Calculator</TITLE>
</HEAD>
<BODY>
    <OBJECT CLASSID="CLSID:812AE312-8B8E-11CF-93C8-00AA00C08FDF"
        ID="calculator_alx" STYLE="LEFT:0;TOP:0">
        <PARAM NAME="ALXPATH" REF VALUE="calculator.alx">
    </OBJECT>
</BODY>
</HTML>
```

To see the **.alx** layout control, click the icon next to the **<OBJECT>** tag while you're in HTML view in Control Pad. Then right-click on the calculator form background, and select Script Wizard. You'll see the button objects and the other elements that make up the form. For each one, you can open its list of events and see the attached code.

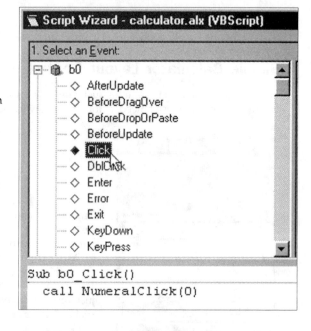

The calculator code itself is built around four main routines, one for the **numeral** buttons called **NumeralClick()**, one for the **operator** buttons called **OperatorClick()**, one for the **equal** button called **cmdCalculate_Click()**, and one for the **decimal point** button called **point_Click()**. The last two are invoked automatically when the appropriate button is clicked, because its name automatically forms the connection between the event and the subroutine.

However, the others are user-defined subroutines which accept an extra argument. We use an argument that is equivalent to the value of the button, and pass it into the routine. So even though it can be called from several buttons, the routine can decipher which button was pressed. For example, the code for the **Click** event of the Zero button, **b0_Click()**, is just **Call NumeralClick(0)**.

We won't be going into a long description of how these routines actually work—it's just a matter of arithmetic and setting the **Text** property of the text box to display the results. The focus of this chapter is on how the layout control allows us to achieve this kind of effect and, as an extra bonus, create a component that can be slotted into other pages.

If you want to examine the code, you can view it (and adapt it as you see fit) in NotePad. Load the file **calculator.alx** into Control Pad, right-click on the form background, and select View Source Code to open it in NotePad (or your default text editor). Alternatively, run up your text editor and open **calculator.alx** directly.

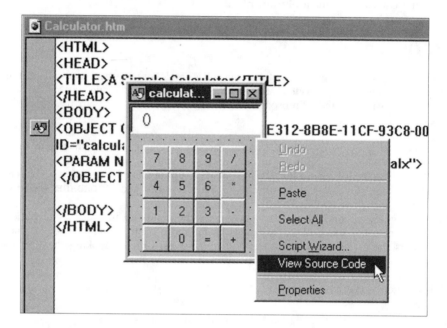

Coping with CODEBASE

On various occasions up to now, we've hinted that you can expect your viewers to have most of the common ActiveX controls already installed on their system, and so you don't have to worry about supplying a **CODEBASE** in the **<OBJECT>** tag when you use ActiveX objects in your pages. Of course, to be absolutely sure that your pages work properly, you should always include it anyway. If the control or other object is already installed, the browser just ignores this.

To make the decision easier, there are some ground rules you can follow. If the user has installed the 'full version' of Internet Explorer 3.0, all the Forms 2.0 controls are automatically installed, including the layout control. However, this won't be the case if they have installed other versions, perhaps by downloading the compact version from Microsoft's own site, or as part of their Internet service provider's software.

To overcome this, Microsoft have an auto-install **.CAB** file at their own Web site which contains all the common ActiveX Internet control objects. All you need to do is to set the **CODEBASE** attribute for your object definition to:

```
CODEBASE="http://activex.microsoft.com/controls/
                    mspert10.cab#version=1,0,4,8020"
```

Internet Explorer will automatically download the object, display the digital certificate, give the user an option to decline the download, and then display the final page. If you want to make installing the controls yourself easier and quicker, you can download the **.CAB** file onto your own machine—an especially useful technique if you're creating pages for your company's Intranet.

The **.CAB** will be updated to reflect new versions of the controls in the future, however, so if you do download it then you should be prepared to keep checking that you still have the latest version. And if you specify a newer version of a control in your pages, which will of course have a different **CLASSID** value, any users with older versions who view your page will have newer versions of the controls automatically downloaded.

Summary

In this chapter, we've seen what an **ActiveX control** is, and how we can manipulate it through VBScript using its **methods**, **properties**, and **events**. We've also seen a selection of the standard controls that are available, and glimpsed some of the things they can help us achieve in our own Web pages.

We also introduced you to the **ActiveX Control Pad**, an excellent tool for managing the creation of HTML pages with embedded controls. In fact, once you start to use it regularly, you'll probably abandon NotePad and all of the other HTML creation utilities—at least until they catch up with object technology and the particular problems of the **CLASSID** and **CODEBASE** attributes.

Arguably, the biggest advance that ActiveX brings is the ability to include Visual Basic style forms in a Web page by using **.alx** files. This gives us far more control over the actual placement of elements, and is the easiest way to ensure that your pages turn out looking the way you want them to, not how the browser decides to interpret them.

So, in this chapter, we've looked at:

- Easier ways of inserting **<OBJECT>** tags into pages.
- How we combine traditional HTML **<INPUT>** controls with ActiveX ones.
- The standard ActiveX controls that are specifically designed for Web pages.
- How we tie together the ActiveX controls and the VBScript on the page.
- A way of exerting more control over the layout of our controls in a page.
- Where the **CODEBASE** attribute comes in, and what values we should use.

Next, we'll move on to look more deeply at the sample application you saw at the beginning of Chapter 1—the Bob's Builders Supplies home page. This uses many of the techniques that you've already seen, and introduces several new ones. In particular, it takes us deeper into the structure and hierarchy of the browser and its documents. This will be the main focus of Chapter 5. It also helps us to start thinking about server interaction, which is another subject that we'll be considering in more detail later in the book.

```vbscript
<HEAD>
    <SCRIPT LANGUAGE="VBScript">

<!--
Sub window_onLoad()
  Dim objLst
  set objLst= dimensions.
                          lstMaterials

  objLst.AddItem "Clay Bricks
                           (3x8x3.5)"

  objLst.AddItem "Stone Blocks
                            (8x8x4)"

  objLst.AddItem "Concrete Blocks
                            (8x16x

  objLst.ListIndex = 0
nd Sub
-->
    </SCRIPT>
```

Bob's Building Supplies

So far in this book, we've been giving you a grounding in the many and varied techniques that go into making your web site interactive. Pages that react to the viewer can help to make your site a lot more user-friendly. Well, now it's time to connect all these techniques together, and you'll see why we have spent time on some aspects of page design that aren't fully VBScript-oriented. In a complex web page, there can be a lot going on, and we need to be sure you have a full grasp of all the basics.

At the very beginning of Chapter 1, we looked briefly at a page from the fictitious site of Bob's Building Supplies. It uses most of the techniques you've seen up to now, and blends them into an attractive and useful page. This is designed to serve Bob's needs as he starts, like so many companies today, to embrace the revolution in communications and consumer expectations that the growth of interest in the Internet is bringing.

The premise that 'your company is dead if it's not on the Web' may be based more on hype than reality at the moment, but there's no doubt that, in the not so distant future, there will be a lot of business done over the Internet. So if you plan to be part of that, you need to start developing some ideas for your site now. Many of the techniques of good web page design are based on artistic flair as well as technical ability. Our aim is to make sure you are fully conversant with the technical part of the task, while we demonstrate both sides in action.

In this chapter, we'll be looking at:

- What the sample application can do, and how it's designed to help customers spend their money more easily.

- The way the application was designed and assembled from a series of components and pages.

- How we can communicate between different parts of the browser window, and dynamically create new pages using VBScript.

- Introducing you to the hierarchy of the browser, as a precursor to the next chapter, where we'll be examining this in more depth.

So first, let's try using Bob's Brick Wall Page to order some bricks for our new garden wall....

Using Bob's Building Supplies Page

Before we go on to see how the sample application, Bob's Building Supplies, actually works under the hood, we'll do two things. First, in this section, we'll 'show you around' so that you can see what it does. Then we'll move on to look at the design behind it, and you can judge how well it meets our (and the user's) requirements. You'll notice that we're referring to it as an **application**. After all, it's more like a specially designed computer program than a normal 'static' web page.

First Impressions

Here's how the application looks when you first fire it up. It uses five frames. Four of them display the same document all the time, but the fifth one, the top right frame, displays different documents as you use the application.

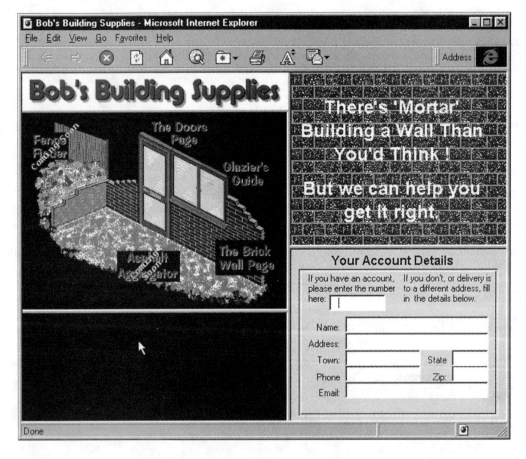

You can open this page yourself from our web site. The address is:

`http://www.wrox.com/books/0448/chapter04/code/BobshomePage.htm`

It's been designed for use in SVGA (800 x 600) resolution or better. If you're using ordinary VGA (640 x 480), switching off display of the browser's toolbar and status bar will enable you to see all of the page.

Even though we refer to Bob's Building Supplies page, remember we are actually dealing with several 'pages' at the same time. Perhaps a better terminology, and one we'll adopt from now on, is to refer to the contents of the main window of the browser as the **page**, and the individual frame contents as **documents**. This will help us to get to grips with the various objects that are part of the browser's hierarchy, especially when we come to the next chapter.

We've used a graphic to draw the user's attention, and make it quite clear exactly what we offer. And, hopefully, the attractive appearance of the page will encourage them to explore further, rather than just surfing past. Notice that the bottom left frame is empty when you first load the page, but after a few seconds a greeting message starts to appear. And, if you watch it, you'll see that Bob makes a typing error, then goes back to correct it. This adds a little extra interest, and may make the visitor more likely to bookmark it for future visits.

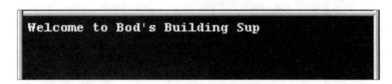

The other frames reinforce the subject of our page, and make it quite clear to visitors that they can actually 'do something' with it, rather than just looking at pictures and reading text.

Filling in the Account Details

The bottom right frame contains a small form with several text boxes. We've arranged for the insertion point cursor to be sitting in the first one, ready for you to type in your account number. If you haven't got an account (and the first time you use it you won't have) then you can type in your name and address instead. If you are trying the page yourself, make sure you fill in all the boxes—you'll see why later.

As we fill in the details, we can *Tab* from one text box to another, and the focus moves from the Town box to the State and Zip boxes, before returning to the Phone and Email boxes. This is something that you can't do using a normal HTML form, which always tabs from top to bottom and left to right.

> *If you are creating complex forms in a web page, you'll find the ability to control the Tab order very useful. Even if you don't actually **need** to use a layout control, you may find that this one aspect makes it worth considering.*

Planning to Build a Wall

Now you've told Bob who you are, it's time to start spending some cash. Click on the Brick Wall Page caption in the graphical menu frame, and Bob's Brick Wall Page appears in the top right frame. Here we can get help to decide on what materials we need to build a wall, which is something that most DIYers will welcome. All we need to do is enter the size of the wall, and select the type of bricks or blocks we want to use. As a bonus, we can get Bob to tell us how much sand and cement we're going to need as well—and, of course, he can supply that too!

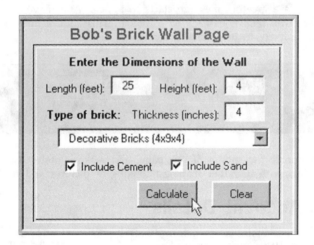

Click the Calculate button, and we get to see how much this project is going to cost. Great value, and all we have to do is click Yes to place the order!

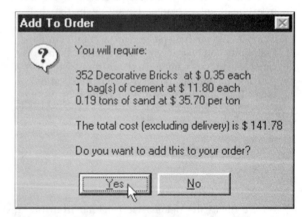

After a brief delay, a new browser window appears containing the order. You can see there's an order number and the current date, plus all the address details we supplied. Underneath that is a neat table containing the details of the order and the total value. Finally, there are two buttons. One will send the order to Bob, and the other allows us to add more items to it first.

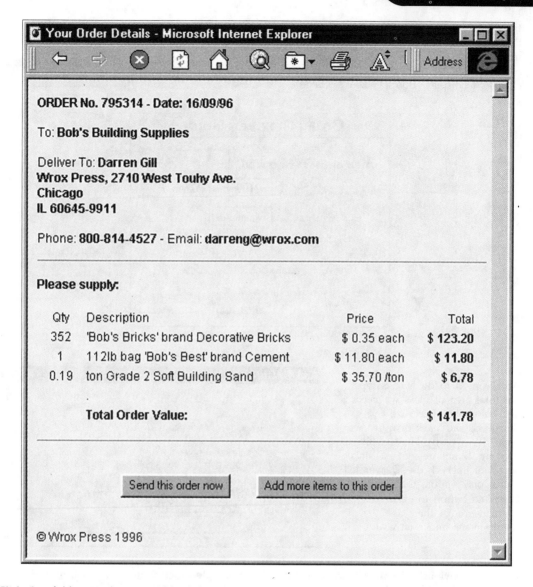

ORDER No. 795314 - Date: 16/09/96

To: **Bob's Building Supplies**

Deliver To: **Darren Gill**
Wrox Press, 2710 West Touhy Ave.
Chicago
IL 60645-9911

Phone: **800-814-4527** - Email: **darreng@wrox.com**

Please supply:

Qty	Description	Price	Total
352	'Bob's Bricks' brand Decorative Bricks	$ 0.35 each	$ 123.20
1	112lb bag 'Bob's Best' brand Cement	$ 11.80 each	$ 11.80
0.19	ton Grade 2 Soft Building Sand	$ 35.70 /ton	$ 6.78
	Total Order Value:		$ 141.78

[Send this order now]   [Add more items to this order]

© Wrox Press 1996

Click the Add more items to this order button, and the new window closes, taking us back to the main application window. Don't just bring the main window to the front—you must click the button. You'll see why later in the chapter, when we come to examine the workings of the application.

Deciding to Reglaze the Sun House

Now we're back in the main window, we should consider what other home improvements we've been neglecting while we were too busy learning about VBScript. Replacing all the broken windows in the sun house is a prime example, and Bob can help here as well.

Instead of clicking the Glazier's Guide caption in the menu graphic, this time click away from all the captions. We get a small pop-up menu, which allows us to select which product we want help with. Select Glazier's Guide in this menu, and the top right hand frame changes to display Bob's Glazier's Guide.

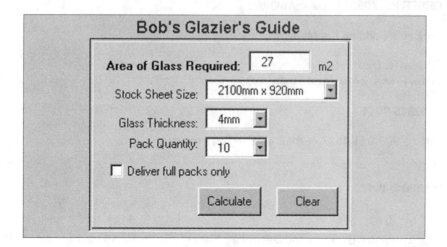

All we need to do here is type the total area of glass we need, and select the sheet size, thickness, and pack quantity we want. It's a pretty big sun house, needing 27 square metres. Make sure you uncheck the Deliver full packs only option, then click the Calculate button to get a confirmation of the glass requirements and total cost.

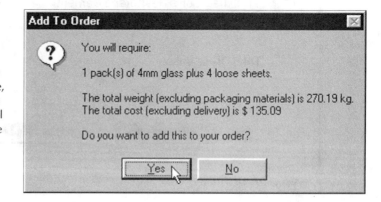

Bob's was obviously the right place to come. He can supply exactly what we need, and at a great price. Click Yes to add the glass to our order. The new order window reopens, and the extra items are added to the bottom of the order.

114

Qty	Description	Price	Total
352	'Bob's Bricks' brand Decorative Bricks	$ 0.35 each	$ 123.20
1	112lb bag 'Bob's Best' brand Cement	$ 11.80 each	$ 11.80
0.19	ton Grade 2 Soft Building Sand	$ 35.70 /ton	$ 6.78
1	Pack (10) 4mm glass 2100mm x 920mm	$ 5.00 /m2	$ 96.50
4	Loose sheets 4mm glass 2100mm x 920mm	$ 5.00 /m2	$ 38.60

Please supply:

Total Order Value: $ 276.88

[Send this order now]   [Add more items to this order]

Placing the Order

All we need to do to place the order is click Send this
order now. Immediately, a message box pops up thanking us
for the order. However, the version of Bob's application we're
using at the moment doesn't actually do anything else. You
can quite safely click the Send this order now button, and
you won't get one of his trucks pulling up outside your
house.

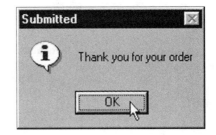

In later chapters, when we come to look in detail at how the browser and server can communicate
and transfer information, you'll see a slightly changed version of Bob's page which does send the
order to our server where it is stored on a database. For the moment, however, you'll need to
reload the main Bob's Building Supplies page if you want to start a new order.

Designing Bob's Page

Now that we've seen what Bob's page can do, we need to consider 'where it came from'. Like all
application development, the *worst* place you can start when you're creating a web site is with the
keyboard. To design an interactive web page which needs to accomplish a task, you need to know
what the task is, and how you can best go about achieving the results you want.

Project management is where the success or failure of a project is decided. Unless the final
application does exactly what's required, and does it within the confines laid down for the cost,

lead time, and accuracy, you may as well not bother. Computing is littered with the corpses of projects, both large and small, which may have been technically feasible or even brilliantly executed but which failed to address the needs of the people who had to use them.

The first step in any project plan is **requirements analysis**, and the best place to find out what's needed is to talk to the people at both ends of the chain. The specifier (in our case Bob) should know what he is expecting from his site, and you need to pin down his requirements in the most detailed way you can. This is especially important, as it's likely that he's the one who will be paying the bill!

At the other end of the spectrum are the users. If they can't understand and work with the end result, you've been wasting your time. The specification for the project needs to include the requirements of the user if it is to stand any chance of being a real success. But of course, behind all this, there's also the need for speed. You can't plan a web site for completion in two years' time, as you can with a new financial database installation. So your plan also has to be able to reach completion within a time-scale where the end result is still applicable. Web styles and technologies tend to change very quickly!

Without going too deep into the subject of application design and requirements analysis, we'll take a look at what our own application has to achieve. We've split this into two sections: planning what it needs to do and how we want it to look. The two are, of course, intertwined, but we'll start with the basic requirements.

Deciding What It Needs to Do

Now that you've seen Bob's application in action, it's pretty easy to see what we designed it to do. But, of course, designing is what you actually do first, and our application only works as smoothly as it does because we took some time early on to plan exactly what was required.

There were obviously two main parts to the process: working out the customer's requirements and then taking the order. To achieve this, we needed to look at the two individual parts of the task, which related more to what **information** we needed, and then what **actions** we had to take using this information.

The basic information we needed to collect was:

- The customer's name, address, phone number, etc.
- The payment details, if they don't already have an account.
- Details of the materials they want to buy.

We decided to help them calculate what materials they'll need for a project, so we also needed to collect information about the project, so that we could perform the calculation.

The actions we needed to carry out were simple enough:

- Calculation of the various materials required.
- Verify we've got all the information we need to create the order.
- Create the order, and then display it for checking.
- Send it off to Bob when the customer clicks the button on the order form.

However, there were other requirements to consider which weren't directly concerned with placing an order. Web pages are like shop windows. They should tempt passers-by to come in and explore. Remember that visitors to a web site may never pass the same way again, and so you should give them a reason to return in the future.

In our case, we realized that there were two things we could do to persuade visitors both to explore the site, and come back again. We can make the initial impression of our site attractive and amusing, and make it obvious that there are things to explore. To persuade people to return, you must offer them something to come back for. This might be catalogs or free samples, or just advice and information that they need. Hopefully, they'll be impressed enough with our site to come back and see more as we add new 'wizards' to it (hence the 'Coming Soon' items on the main menu). And when they actually do need to build a wall, they just might remember where to get help with calculating the material requirements. On top of all this, our database will store their name and address details. We can use this as a base for future promotions, either as email or by more traditional means.

Deciding How It Will Look

The other side of the coin is the 'artistic' element. We needed to decide on a 'look' that would attract the viewer and persuade them to explore our site. Furthermore, it needed to reflect the company's image, and include a corporate color scheme and logo.

When you have several documents in multiple frames, or displayed as separate pages, it's important that they all follow the same style. It is unprofessional to have a site that looks like a mixture of different pages that you've randomly collected together.

If, like Bob, you can't afford to pay a graphic design agency to do the work, you can get plenty of hints from looking at other sites. We opted for the common black background for our menu, and shadowed text for the company logo. These seem to be the trendy design elements at the moment. We then chose a pastel shade for each of the forms used by the viewer, color-matched the titles and added etching to the borders. Well, we like it anyway!

Detailed Planning of Our Page

So, having discovered broadly what our site must achieve, we could pin down the actual tasks more definitely. One of the problems with VBScript, and other programming languages which are (or pretend to be) object-oriented, is that the code gets scattered around in the various objects that you use. In C++, these could be classes, and in VB or Delphi, they might be screen forms. In VBScript, they are the various HTML documents and **.alx** layout control files that make up your project. Right from the start, you must consider how the code within each one will be used, and how you should best encapsulate it within that document while making it available to other objects which need to use it.

Coping with Context during Design

One feature of VBScript is that all the code in all the documents which are loaded into the browser at any one time is in **global context**. In other words, we can always refer to *any* code routine or script-level variable whether it's in the same document as the current one or a document in a different frame.

This had three main influences on our design:

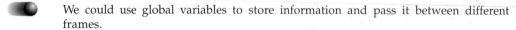

- We could use global variables to store information and pass it between different frames.

- We could create general-purpose subroutines and functions which can be called from different documents.

- We didn't have to put all the code and variables for a document within that document.

> *Notice the term **script-level variable** that we use to mean a variable which is **global** within that script, i.e. declared outside any subroutine or function. **Local** variables, which are declared within a subroutine or function, aren't script-level and, therefore, aren't available from other loaded documents.*

So there are two conflicting requirements. Good sense suggests we should attempt to encapsulate our code to create components, rather like the calculator example you saw in the previous chapter. It acts like an encapsulated object in that you can incorporate it into your page just by using an **<OBJECT>** tag—no other code is required— and you don't need to know how it works to use it.

However, in an application like Bob's page, a lot of the actions we carry out are related. For example, there's some code which is the same for all the Wizards. And tasks such as adding items to an existing order mean that we have to store information and be able to pass it between different frames in the main page. As in life, everything is a compromise in the end. We tried to create stand-alone components where possible, but to keep our design simple we accepted that they needed to operate using global data.

So what were the components we needed? Here's our list:

- An account details form to collect the name and address details

- A 'wizard' form for each of the material types we want to offer

- A menu to allow the viewer to select which wizard they want to use

- An order form which displays the final order ready for sending to Bob

- Something to attract the attention of casual surfers as they pass by

Taking Advantage of the Hierarchy

There's one major component that we haven't mentioned, and that's because it's the one you don't actually see. It's probably the most important, because it ties all the rest together. This is the main document that actually creates the frames and loads the other documents into them. It's also at the top of the hierarchy of items in the browser window, so it has a special place in the design. To understand this, consider how the Bob's Building Supplies page is created. Here's part of **BobsHomePage.htm**, the document you load to start the application:

```
<FRAMESET COLS="355,*">
    <FRAMESET ROWS="50,255,*">
        <FRAME SRC="titlebar.htm" SCROLLING=NO NORESIZE>
        <FRAME SRC="wizmenu.htm" SCROLLING=NO NORESIZE>
        <FRAME SRC="intro.htm" NAME="IntroFrame" SCROLLING=NO >
    </FRAMESET>
```

```
     <FRAMESET ROWS="225,*">
         <FRAME SRC="startwiz.htm" NAME="WizardFrame">
         <FRAME SRC="customer.htm" NAME="CustDetails">
     </FRAMESET>
  </FRAMESET>
```

It first divides the window into two columns, then divides the left column into three rows and the right column into two rows. Into each of these resulting frames, it loads a document. In hierarchy terms, the document **BobsHomePage.htm** is the direct **parent** of all these other pages, as well as being the **top** page.

This means that we can access it from any other document using the code **parent.*object*** or **top.*object***. And because it's always loaded while Bob's page is being viewed, code within it will always be available. If we put our code and variables in **startwiz.htm**, the document which is loaded into the top right frame, we would 'lose' them when we loaded a different wizard document into that frame. So by placing variables and code routines into **BobsHomePage.htm**, we ensure that they will be available as long as the user is at the site.

Laying Out the Final Design

Once we'd established the likely document and frame combination we'd need for our application we could lay out the design in more detail. We also made some assumptions about what code routines were needed, and where they should best be placed. For example, each wizard required different code to carry out its specific task, and this was encapsulated within the wizard itself. But the code that created the new order window was called from all of the wizards, so it was placed at the top level of the hierarchy so that it would be easily available at all times. Here's how the design for Bob's Home Page looked when we started to build it:

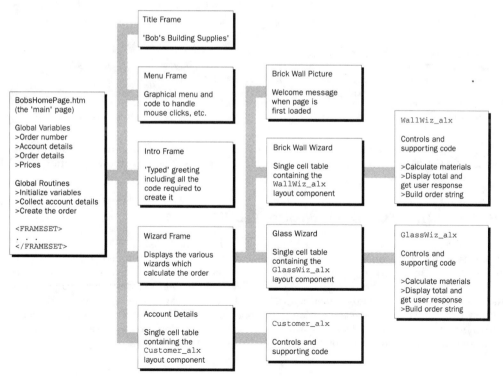

Creating Bob's Page

Now that we've seen how Bob's application fits together, we'll look at some of the techniques that we've used in it. We've already seen how the main document, **BobsHomePage.htm**, creates the five frames and loads the initial documents. These are:

titlebar.htm which just displays the Bob's Building Supplies logo. This is an ordinary image, and we set the **TOPMARGIN** attribute in the page's **<BODY>** tag to **8** to get the logo placed correctly in the frame.

```
<BODY BGCOLOR=WHITE TOPMARGIN=8>
   <CENTER><IMG SRC="picTitle.gif" WIDTH=334 HEIGHT=38></CENTER>
</BODY>
```

wizmenu.htm which holds the menu graphic, and the code which detects mouse clicks and loads the relevant wizard into the top right frame. We'll be looking at this document in detail shortly.

intro.htm is where the 'typing' message appears when the page is first loaded. It contains an ActiveX label control, and a simple routine which places the text in it, as you'll again see in a short while.

startwiz.htm is the 'brick wall' document that appears when the page is first loaded, and where the different wizards appear when you select them in the menu. The frame in which it is displayed is named WizardFrame so that we can refer to it directly in code later on. The document uses a background graphic in the **<BODY>** tag which resembles a brick wall, and some text created in the usual way.

```
<BODY BACKGROUND="bgBrick.gif" TOPMARGIN=30>
   <CENTER><H2>
      There's 'Mortar' Building a Wall Than You'd Think ! <P>
      But we can help you get it right.
   </H2></CENTER>
</BODY>
```

customer.htm is where the Account Details form is displayed. The frame is named CustDetails, so that we can refer to it from elsewhere in the application. We'll look at this in more detail later, as well.

Using an Image as a Main Menu

Many sites use graphical menus, rather than a list of text hotlinks, to make them more attractive. In the past, this has been done either with several small graphics grouped together, with each enclosed in separate **<A>** tags, or by using a **server-side image map** where the browser detects a mouse click and sends the coordinates to the server, which then decides which page to load. Recently the HTML standards widened to allow **client-side image maps** to be used. Here the **<MAP>** section (which defines where the various hot spots are) is an HTML tag in the document itself, and the browser uses it to decide which new page to load. However, VBScript brings with it a new, and more powerful, way of handling graphical menu interaction.

Image Controls and Pop-up Menus

By placing the image in an ActiveX image control, and reacting to the events it produces, we can exert extra control. In our sample application, the page contains two objects, created with the usual **<OBJECT>** tags:

```
<OBJECT ID="imgBob" WIDTH=328 HEIGHT=241
  CLASSID="CLSID:D4A97620-8E8F-11CF-93CD-00AA00C08FDF">
    <PARAM NAME="PicturePath" VALUE="picSMenu.gif">
    <PARAM NAME="BackColor" VALUE="46186496">
    <PARAM NAME="BorderStyle" VALUE="0">
    <PARAM NAME="Size" VALUE="8678;6385">
    <PARAM NAME="PictureAlignment" VALUE="0">
    <PARAM NAME="VariousPropertyBits" VALUE="19">
</OBJECT>

<OBJECT ID="iepopBob" WIDTH=1 HEIGHT=1 TYPE="application/x-oleobject"
  CLASSID="CLSID:7823A620-9DD9-11CF-A662-00AA00C066D2"
  CODEBASE="http://activex.microsoft.com/controls/iexplorer
                              /iemenu.ocx#Version=4,70,0,1161">
    <PARAM NAME="_ExtentX" VALUE="26">
    <PARAM NAME="_ExtentY" VALUE="26">
    <PARAM NAME="Menuitem[0]" VALUE="Brick Wall Page">
    <PARAM NAME="Menuitem[1]" VALUE="Glazier's Guide">
    <PARAM NAME="Menuitem[2]" VALUE="The Doors Page">
</OBJECT>
```

The first is the Microsoft Forms 2.0 Image control. We inserted it into the HTML code using the ActiveX Control Pad, and specified the image it is to display by setting the **PicturePath** property to **picSMenu.gif**. The second control is a Pop-up Menu control, again inserted using the ActiveX Control Pad and, because it isn't one of the standard controls included with the browser, we've also specified the **CODEBASE** for it. Then, we added the entries for the menu itself by typing the **<PARAM>** lines inside the **<OBJECT>** tag afterwards. These are in the form of an array, starting from index zero.

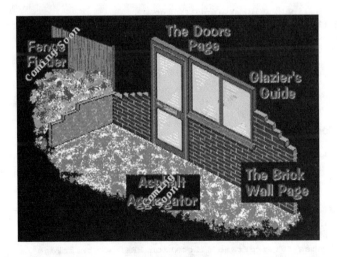

Alternatively, we could have used VBScript code in the **Window_OnLoad** *event of the document to dynamically create them. For example* **iepopBob.Additem("Brick Wall Page",0)**.

The MouseUp Event

The **Image** control has events which are fired when the user clicks the mouse button over the image. We're using the **MouseUp** event, which occurs when the mouse button is released, by writing a subroutine to respond to it. The browser supplies four arguments to the routine automatically:

 Button, which is a number whose value depends on which button was pressed.

 Shift, which reflects the state of the *Shift*, *Alt*, and *Ctrl* keys when the mouse button was clicked.

 X and **Y** coordinates of the mouse pointer within the image.

```
Sub imgBob_MouseUp(Button, Shift, X, Y)
   'runs when the image is clicked. X and Y contain the mouse position
   Dim strWizardPage  'the page to go to
   If Button <> 1  Then Exit Sub          'not the left mouse button
   strWizardPage=""
   If InZone(X,Y, 215,135) Then           'Wall Wizard selected
      strWizardPage="wallwiz.htm"
   ElseIf InZone(X,Y, 215,55) Then        'Glass Wizard selected
      strWizardPage="glasswiz.htm"
   .. etc ..
   Else
      iepopBob.PopUp                       'Pop up the short cut menu
   End If
   GoToPage strWizardPage
End Sub
```

Having checked that the left button was clicked, we just need to know where the mouse pointer is in the image to decide which document to display. We use a separate function **InZone()** for this, sending it the current coordinates of the mouse and the coordinates of the center of the various captions in the graphic, in turn:

```
Function InZone(intMX, intMY, intCX, intCY)
   'check if the click is within a square of size 60 around intCX,intCY
   If (Abs(intCX - intMX) < 30) AND (Abs(intCY - intMY) < 30) Then
      InZone = True
   Else
      InZone = False
   End If
End Function
```

Activating a New Document

If the user clicks in a caption area, the variable **strWizardPage** will contain the name of the new document. To load it, we use a separate routine, **GoToPage**. This checks that the name is OK and then sets the **HRef** property of **WizardFrame**:

```
Sub GoToPage(strThePage)
   If Len(strThePage) Then
      .. etc ..
      Parent.Frames("WizardFrame").Location.HRef = strThePage
   End If
End Sub
```

You can see how we refer to the target frame, as a member of the array of frames in its **parent** document, which is of course **BobsHomePage.htm**. The **HRef** property is actually only part of another object called **Location**, and we'll be looking at this subject in more detail in the next chapter.

If the variable **strWizardPage** is still empty, however, the user clicked outside all the labels. Instead of calling the **GoToPage()** routine, the main code issues a single command:

```
iepopBob.PopUp                          'Pop up the short cut menu
```

This executes the **PopUp** method of the **Pop-up Menu** object, which automatically displays the shortcut menu next to the mouse pointer. Once displayed, nothing else happens until the user selects an entry on the menu, or clicks again outside it (when the menu automatically closes). If they do click on the menu, a **Click** event occurs which receives a value indicating which item was selected:

```
Sub iepopBoB_Click(ByVal x)
  Dim strWizardPage  'the page to go to
  strWizardPage = ""
  Select Case x
    Case 1: strWizardPage = "wallwiz.htm"      'Wall Wizard
    Case 2: strWizardPage = "glasswiz.htm"     'Glass Wizard
    .. etc ..
  End Select
  GoToPage strWizardPage
End Sub
```

All we have to do is set the name of the new document to load, and call our **GoToPage** routine using that name. Easy enough, but notice how the browser tries to catch you out. When we created the items for the menu we had to use indexes **0**, **1**, and **2**. But the **Click** event receives a value of **1**, **2**, or **3**—not what you would call intuitive!

*There are several events for an **Image** control that you can use to liven up a displayed image. For example, you can react to the **MouseMove** event which occurs as the mouse moves over the image. For a list of the events, and help with creating the event handling code, you can always use the ActiveX Control Pad Help menu, or the ActiveX SDK documentation.*

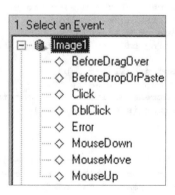

123

The 'Typed Greeting' Frame

To add 'instant interest' to our page we've arranged for a typed greeting message to gradually appear in the lower left frame. This is easy enough to do, but ours is slightly different. It makes an error in the first line and then goes back to correct it, just like using the *Delete* key. All the routine needs is a **label** control and a **timer** object. Here's the HTML code that inserts these into the document:

```
<OBJECT ID="lblOutPut" WIDTH=340 HEIGHT=155
 CLASSID="CLSID:978C9E23-D4B0-11CE-BF2D-00AA003F40D0"
 CODEBASE="http://activex.microsoft.com/controls/
                             mspert10.cab#version=1,0,4,8020">
    <PARAM NAME="ForeColor" VALUE="16777215">
    .. etc ..
</OBJECT>


<OBJECT ID="timTypeWriter" WIDTH=39 HEIGHT=39
 CLASSID="CLSID:59CCB4A0-727D-11CF-AC36-00AA00A47DD2"
 CODEBASE="http://activex.microsoft.com/controls/
                             mspert10.cab#version=1,0,4,8020">
    <PARAM NAME="Interval" VALUE="4000">
</OBJECT>
```

You can see that the **Interval** property of the timer is set to **4** seconds (**4000** ms), and so nothing happens for this period after the document is loaded. Then the first timer event occurs. To handle it, we create a subroutine called **timTypeWriter_Timer**. Here's the complete **<SCRIPT>** section of the document, including the global variables it uses to hold values which would otherwise be lost between individual **Timer** events:

```
Dim gstrMesg1    'first part of the message to print
Dim gstrMesg2    'second part of the message to print
Dim gintTypePos  'current character position
Dim gintErrPos   'position of mistake
Dim gblnDeleting 'True=going back to correct mistake

gstrMesg1 ="Welcome to Bod's Building Sup"      'first part of message
gstrMesg2 ="b's Building Supplies. We're the .." 'rest of message
gintTypePos = 1       'current position, start at first character
gintErrPos = 14       'error is at character 14 in first string
gblnDeleting = False

Sub timTypeWriter_Timer
   If timTypeWriter.Interval > 1000 Then timTypeWriter.Interval = 175
   If (gintTypePos > Len(gstrMesg1)) And ((gintErrPos > 0)) Then
      gblnDeleting = True  'reached end of first string so go back
   End If
   If gblnDeleting Then
      gintTypePos = gintTypePos - 1          'go back one character
```

```
         If gintTypePos = gintErrPos - 1 Then   'reached error position
            'add strings together excluding error character and carry on
            gstrMesg1 = Left(gstrMesg1, gintErrPos - 1) & gstrMesg2
            gintErrPos = 0
            gblnDeleting = False
         End If
      Else
         gintTypePos = gintTypePos + 1          'go to next character
         'if we're at the end of the string disable the timer
         If (gintTypePos = Len(gstrMesg1)) And (gintErrPos = 0) Then
                                         timTypeWriter.Enabled = False
      End If
      lblOutPut.Caption = Left(gstrMesg1, gintTypePos)   'update the label
   End Sub
```

During the first **Timer** event we change the timer's **Interval** property to 175 so that the letters appear at a reasonable 'typing' speed. Then the technique of actually printing the characters is simple enough. We just maintain a pointer to the string in **gintTypePos**, incrementing it with each timer event, and update the label control with the left portion of the string up to **gintTypePos**. Once we reach the end of the first string, we set the **gblnDeleting** flag and decrement **gintTypePos** with each **Timer** event until we reach the error position. Then we combine the two strings, removing the error, and carry on incrementing the pointer and printing the updated string until we reach the end of it, when we disable the timer altogether. By simply changing the two strings and the error position, you can easily achieve this effect in your own pages.

The Account Details Frame

The bottom right of the main window contains the form where the user enters their name, address, and other details. We used an ActiveX **Layout** control to create this form, and enclosed it in a single row, single column table which has the 3D border colors reversed from the usual to give the etched appearance.

```
BODY BGCOLOR="#E0E0FF" TOPMARGIN=5>
  <CENTER><B>Your Account Details</B>
  <TABLE BORDER=1 BORDERCOLORDARK=WHITE BORDERCOLORLIGHT=BLACK>
    <TR><TD>
      <OBJECT CLASSID="CLSID:812AE312-8B8E-11CF-93C8-00AA00C08FDF"
        ID="Customer_alx" STYLE="LEFT:0;TOP:0">
        <PARAM NAME="ALXPATH" REF VALUE="Customer.alx">
      </OBJECT>
    </TD></TR>
```

125

```
        </TABLE></CENTER>
        </BODY>
```

This inserts our **Customer_alx** object, which is the **Layout** control containing the various labels and text boxes. Here, we've succeeded in encapsulating the Account Details form as a reusable object, which can be inserted into any page using just an **<OBJECT>** tag. If you open the **Customer.alx** file in NotePad you can see the objects and the code it contains:

```
Sub SetReadyFlag(intFlagSet, objControl, intNumChars)
  Dim strTheValue
  Dim intTheLength
  strTheValue = objControl.Text        'get the text from the text box
  intTheLength = Len(strTheValue)      'and it's length
  If ((intNumChars > 0) And (intTheLength < intNumChars)) OR
                                        (intTheLength) = 0 Then
    parent.gflgAccReady = parent.gflgAccReady AND (63 - intFlagSet)
  Else
    parent.gflgAccReady = parent.gflgAccReady OR intFlagSet
  End If
End Sub

Sub txtAccount_Change()
  SetReadyFlag 1, Me, 6
End Sub

Sub txtName_Change()
  SetReadyFlag 2, Me, 5
End Sub

.. etc ..
```

It uses a similar technique to that used by **FBCalc.htm** in the previous chapter. Each text box on the form, except for the phone number and email address, has a **Change** event handler which sets or clears the individual bits of a global variable called **gflgAccReady**. This is declared in our main **BobsHomePage.htm** document, so that it is always available to all our code, and therefore we reference it using the syntax **parent.gflgAccReady**.

The **intFlagSet** argument to the **SetReadyFlag** routine is the value of the individual bit for that text box, **objControl** is the text box itself, and **intNumChars** is the minimum number of characters required. To set the bits, we **OR gflgAccReady** with that bit value, and to clear them we **AND** it with the total value, **63**, less the value of that bit. (We covered bitwise arithmetic in detail back in Chapter 3.) So, as the user enters their account details, the global variable **gflgAccReady** always holds a value which reflects which text boxes have valid information.

The Brick Wall Wizard

The final frame we need to look at is the top right, where the different wizards are displayed. These calculate the amount and cost of the various materials required for each project. We've supplied two, and you've already seen how they work in previous chapters. The Glazier's Guide is a modified form of the Glass Load Calculator we introduced in Chapter 2, and the Brick Wall Page works in an identical way to the **FBCalc.htm** page we created at the beginning of Chapter 3. Each is encapsulated in an ActiveX Layout control, and embedded in a normal HTML document. Here's the main document for the Brick Wall Page wizard, showing the **<OBJECT>** tag which inserts the **WallWiz.alx** file:

126

```
<BODY BGCOLOR="#C0FFC0" TOPMARGIN=5>
  <CENTER><B>Bob's Brick Wall Page</B>
  <TABLE BORDER=1 BORDERCOLORDARK=WHITE BORDERCOLORLIGHT=BLACK>
    <TR><TD>
      <OBJECT ID="WallWiz_alx"
        CLASSID="CLSID:812AE312-8B8E-11CF-93C8-00AA00C08FDF">
        <PARAM NAME="ALXPATH" REF VALUE="WallWiz.alx">
      </OBJECT>
    </TD></TR>
  </TABLE></CENTER>
</BODY>
```

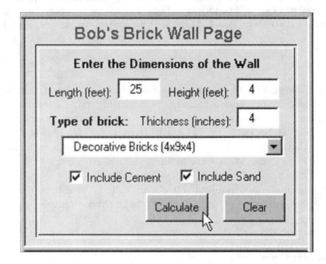

WallWiz.alx contains several code routines. First, when the document is loaded, we need to fill the list box with the types of bricks that are available. This is done in the layout control's **OnLoad** event, and it also sets the current selection in **cboBrick** to the first item, then places the focus (insertion point) in the first control, **txtLength**, on the form:

```
Sub WallWiz_OnLoad()
  cboBrick.AddItem "Clay Bricks (3x8x3.5)"
  cboBrick.AddItem "Stone Blocks (8x8x4)"
  cboBrick.AddItem "Concrete Blocks (8x16x5)"
  cboBrick.AddItem "Screen Blocks (12x12x12)"
  cboBrick.AddItem "Decorative Bricks (4x9x4)"
  cboBrick.ListIndex = 0
  txtLength.SetFocus
End Sub
```

There's also a routine **cmdClear_Click()** *which runs when the* Clear *button is clicked. It clears the current values in the wizard's text boxes, resets the selection in* **cboBrick**, *and places the cursor back in the* **txtLength** *control.*

127

Calculating how many Bricks Are Required

When the Calculate button is clicked, we start the process of adding the materials to the order. First, we execute a subroutine called **SetAccDetail** which collects the current account details in a global string **gstrAccDetail** ready to place this in the order. It's in the main **BobsHomePage.htm** document so, just like a variable, we reference it using the object hierarchy as **parent.SetAccDetail**.

```
Sub cmdCalculate_Click()
   parent.SetAccDetail       'collect the account details
   If Len(parent.gstrAccDetail) Then
     If CalculateMaterials() Then   'calculate material requirements
       BuildOrderString      'add materials into the current order
       parent.CreateOrder    'and display the order in a new window
     End If
   End If
End Sub
```

Now we can check if we've got all the details we need. If the user hasn't supplied enough, **gstrAccDetail** will be empty and a message will already have been displayed by the **SetAccDetail** routine. If all is well we execute the **CalculateMaterials()** function which returns **True** if the user is happy with the result. If they are, we can build the order string and then create the order. You can see that this routine uses several others, including two in the parent document **BobsHomePage.htm**. We'll look at these as we go along.

So, first, calculating the materials required. Here's an edited version of the routine. The missing parts are only those that you saw in the earlier **FBCalc.htm** example:

```
Function CalculateMaterials()

   CalculateMaterials = False

   'calculate the bricks, cement and sand required
   .. etc ..

   'create the output string
   gstrBlockType = Left(cboBrick.Value, InStr(cboBrick.Value, "(") - 1)
   gintBlockIndex = cboBrick.ListIndex + 1
   strOutPut = "You will require:" & parent.CRLF & parent.CRLF _
             & gintTotalBlocks & " " & gstrBlockType & " at $ " _
             & parent.CCurrency(parent.gsngPrices(gintBlockIndex)) _
             & " each" & parent.CRLF
   dblTotPrice = gintTotalBlocks * CDbl(parent.gsngPrices(gintBlockIndex))
   If chkCement.Value Then
     strOutPut = strOutPut & gintTotCement & " " & " bag(s) cement at $ " _
               & parent.CCurrency(parent.gsngPrices(7)) _
               & " each" & parent.CRLF
     dblTotPrice = dblTotPrice + (gintTotCement*CDbl(parent.gsngPrices(7)))
   End If

   .. etc ..

   strOutput = strOutput & "Do you want to add this to your order?"
   If MsgBox(strOutPut,36,"Add To Order")=6 Then CalculateMaterials = True
End Function
```

Once we know the amounts of each material, we can create a string which holds the message asking the user if they are happy with the results. You'll see we've used the VBScript **line continuation character** _ , in several places to keep it neat, although you can place all the code on one line if you wish. To break the code like this, you just type a space, an underscore, and press *Return*. The VBScript interpreter then treats the code as though it was a single line when it runs.

Once the string is complete, we display it using the **MsgBox()** function. The value **36** instructs VBScript to include a question mark icon and Yes and No buttons in the message box. If the user clicks Yes, we get a result of **6**, so we can set **CalculateMaterials** to **True**.

> *To help you out, we've included a table of the values you use with* **MsgBox** *in Appendix B.*

There are a number of things in this routine that are worth noting. We get the name of the brick by using the **Left()** function to truncate the value in the list box at the character before the opening bracket—remember that the list box contains the size as well, in the form Decorative Bricks (4x9x4).

```
gstrBlockType = Left(cboBrick.Value, InStr(cboBrick.Value, "(") - 1)
```

We've stored the prices for the materials in an array called **gsngPrices()**, and so we also need to get the index to this array to find the correct price for the bricks. The line:

```
gintBlockIndex = cboBrick.ListIndex + 1
```

sets the variable **gintBlockIndex** to one more than the index in the list box, and we can then use it to access the prices array. We also use a variable **dblTotPrice** to keep track of the total value of the order, so that we can display it in the message box.

Lastly, notice that we've used a function **parent.CCurrency()** to convert the price into a properly formatted currency format. Unlike Visual Basic, VBScript doesn't contain a **CCur()** function so we've had to design our own. It's again in the main document **BobsHomePage.htm**, so that it's easily available to all the other documents, and we'll take a look at it in a while. Before then, let's see the routine that builds the final order string if the user is happy with the values we calculated earlier:

```
Sub BuildOrderString
   'add the new items to the existing order in HTML table
   Dim strThis          'the order for this item
   Dim dblEachPrice     'the price each item
   Dim dblLineTotal     'the total for that order line

   'first, the block/brick chosen by the user
   dblEachPrice = parent.gsngPrices(gintBlockIndex)
   dblLineTotal = dblEachPrice * gintTotalBlocks
   parent.gdblOrderTotal = parent.gdblOrderTotal + dblLineTotal
   strThis = "<TR><TD ALIGN=CENTER>" & gintTotalBlocks & "</TD>" _
           & "<TD ALIGN=LEFT>'Bob's Bricks' brand " & gstrBlockType _
           & "</TD><TD ALIGN=RIGHT>$ " & parent.CCurrency(dblEachPrice) _
           & " each</TD><TD ALIGN=RIGHT><B>$ " _
           & parent.CCurrency(dblLineTotal) & "</B></TD></TR>"

   If chkCement.Value Then    'now the cement
     strThis = strThis & ..
```

```
          .. etc ..
      End If

      If chkSand.Value Then        'and finally the sand
        strThis = strThis & ..
        .. etc ..
      End If

      parent.gstrOrderDetail = parent.gstrOrderDetail & strThis
    End Sub
```

You can see that it's fundamentally similar to the way we created the string for the message box. However, this time we include the HTML tags required for it to be displayed in a table, rather than just as a text string in a message box. Each line of the order is a separate row, and there are four columns for the quantity, description, price each, and total price. Again, we've used the **gintBlockIndex** block index variable, and the **gstrBlockType** block description in our code, plus calls to our own **CCurrency()** function. To maintain the total price of the current order, we update a global variable **gdblOrderTotal** with the current line total for each material:

```
    parent.gdblOrderTotal = parent.gdblOrderTotal + dblLineTotal
```

Lastly, we add the items on to the end of any existing ones in the global string **gstrOrderDetail**, which is also declared in the main **BobsHomePage.htm** document. This will accumulate all the separate items that the viewer orders. Until we implement the server interaction which accepts and stores the order, which we'll be doing in Chapter 8, you'll have to reload the page to start a fresh order.

The Glazier's Guide Wizard

The Glazier's Guide document, **GlassWiz.htm**, is almost identical to the Brick Wall Page **WallWiz.htm**, though it uses a different layout control object, in this case **GlassWiz.alx**. This is another encapsulated object, which calculates the glass requirements given the total number of square metres required. The structure of the code in **GlassWiz.alx** is almost identical to **WallWiz.alx**, though, of course, the **CalculateMaterials()** function is different.

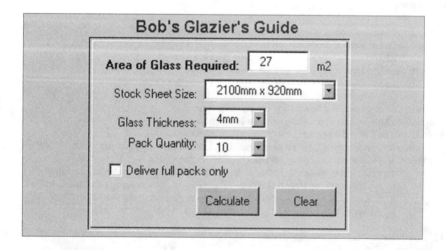

One other difference is the way that we check for acceptable values for the one text input box, **txtArea**. Most Windows applications enable and disable the command buttons as you set values in them, so that only the appropriate ones are available. This is what we've done in **GlassWiz.alx**. When you first open it, the Calculate button is disabled. Only when you've entered a numeric value in the text box does the Calculate button become available. How's it done? Easy, we just write a routine to respond to **Change** events for the text box:

```
Sub txtArea_Change()
  If IsNumeric(txtArea.Text) Then
    cmdCalculate.Enabled = True
  Else
    cmdCalculate.Enabled = False
  End If
End Sub
```

When we create the text box within the layout control, using the ActiveX Control Pad, we make sure we set the **Enabled** property of the button to **No** (**False**). Then it only becomes enabled when the **IsNumeric()** function returns **True**. In fact, if you like to write really efficient code, you could even use:

```
Sub txtArea_Change()
  cmdCalculate.Enabled = IsNumeric(txtArea.Text)
End Sub
```

The Global Variables and Routines

We've mentioned several global variables and routines which are resident in the main document **BobsHomePage.htm**. Because this document is located at the top of the browser's object hierarchy, and so is always loaded when the application is in use, it is a good place to keep them. Here's the variable declarations in **BobsHomePage.htm**:

```
Dim gstrFormHandler   'URL of server form handler for sending order
Dim gsngPrices(7)     'the current material prices array
Dim gobjCustForm      'reference to the account details form
Dim gstrOrderNumber   'customer's order number
Dim gstrAccDetail     'customer's account details
Dim gstrOrderDetail   'order details string
Dim gdblOrderTotal    'total price for all order
Dim CRLF              'newline string constant
Dim gflgAccReady      'flag set if enough customer details entered
                      'bit 0 (value 1) = Account Number
                      'bit 1 (value 2) = Name
                      'bit 2 (value 4) = Address
                      'bit 3 (value 8) = Town
                      'bit 4 (value 16) = State
                      'bit 5 (value 32) = Zip
```

You can see, among other things, the strings which hold the customer's details and the order itself. There's also the total order value, and a variable which we're going to use to refer to the text boxes on the Account Details form.

*One of the accepted coding standards is to use all capital letters for any **constants** that you define. It's a little awkward with VBScript, because it doesn't support real constants as such. However, you can define a variable and give it a value, then just take care not to change it. We've done this with **CRLF**, which we'll be allocating a value to in the **window_onLoad()** event.*

131

When the application first loads, we use the **window_OnLoad** event to set the values of several of these global variables for use later, including the values in the prices array.

```
Sub window_onLoad()
  gstrFormHandler = "nowhere"  'set URL of server form handler
  CRLF = Chr(13) & Chr(10)
  Set gobjCustForm = window.frames("CustDetails").Customer_alx
  gobjCustForm.txtAccount.SetFocus
  gstrAccDetail = ""
  gstrOrderDetail = ""
  gdblOrderTotal = 0
  gsngPrices(0) = 1.25 'glass/m2/mm thick
  gsngPrices(1) = 0.15 'clay bricks each
  gsngPrices(2) = 0.50 'stone blocks each
  gsngPrices(3) = 0.60 'concrete blocks each
  gsngPrices(4) = 0.45 'screen blocks each
  gsngPrices(5) = 0.35 'decorative bricks each
  gsngPrices(6) = 35.7 'sand/ton
  gsngPrices(7) = 11.8 'cement/bag
  Randomize    'create a random order number
  gstrOrderNumber = CStr(Int(Rnd * 1000000))
End Sub
```

The first statement sets the URL of the program which will handle our order (in this version, it's going nowhere till we come to implement the server-side code in Chapter 8). We also create the reference to the Account Details form here, ready for when we want to access the customer's details from it. Following the browser hierarchy, we use the **Set** keyword, and specify the object we want:

```
Set gobjCustForm = window.frames("CustDetails").Customer_alx
```

This sets the variable **gobjCustForm** to refer to the layout control with an **ID** property of **Customer_alx**, which is in the frame which we named **CustDetails** in its **<FRAME>** tag. Then we can place the insertion point in the **txtAccount** control on that layout control by executing its **SetFocus** method:

```
gobjCustForm.txtAccount.SetFocus
```

Finally, we create the random order number, before leaving the routine.

Formatting Currency Values

As we mentioned earlier, VBScript doesn't have either the **CCur()** or **Format()** functions that are used regularly in Visual Basic to format a string so that it displays like a currency value. In **BobsHomePage.htm**, we've included our own, and we can use it to convert any number into a correct string representation. Here's the function we've produced, and you can include it in your own pages by copying it into a **<SCRIPT>** section and calling it with **CCurrency(*number*)**:

```
Function CCurrency(ByVal curVal)
  'VBScript has no currency conversion and formatting - here's our own
  Dim strVal, intDecPos
  If IsNumeric(curVal) Then
    strVal = CStr(Int((CSng(curVal) * 100) + 0.5) / 100)
    'determine location of dec point and pad string appropriately
    intDecPos = InStr(strVal,".")
```

```
          If intDecPos = 1 Then strVal = "0" & strVal        'leading "."
          If (curVal < 0) And (intDecPos = 2) Then           'negative value
             'insert zero between minus sign and leading "."
             strVal = "-0" & Mid(strVal, intDecPos)
          End If
          If intDecPos = 0 Then
             strVal = strVal & ".00"                         'integer value
          ElseIf intDecPos = Len(strVal) - 1 Then
             strVal = strVal & "0"                           '1 decimal place
          Else
             'do nothing                                     'ok as it is
          End If
          If Abs(curVal) >= 1000 Then                        'add a comma
             strVal = Left(strVal, Len(strVal) - 6) & "," & Right(strVal, 6)
          End If
          If Abs(curVal) >= 1000000 Then                     'add another comma
             strVal = Left(strVal, Len(strVal) - 9) & "," & Right(strVal, 9)
          End If
          CCurrency = strVal
       Else
          CCurrency = ""
          Err.description = "Invalid currency data"
          Err.raise
          Exit Function
       End If
    End Function
```

Creating the Order

The two other routines in **BobsHomePage.htm** are concerned with creating the order ready for display in a new browser window. First, the **SetAccDetail** subroutine which we called from the two wizards to collect the customer's account details. Because we intend to display them in a browser window as a web page, rather than as text in a text box, we need to include the relevant HTML tags.

Getting the Account Details

The **SetAccDetail** routine is run when the user clicks a Calculate button in any of the wizards. The first step is to clear any existing details from the global string **gstrAccDetail**, then we can go about collecting the new values. Doing this means that if the user changes the values in the Account Details form before or during creating an order, we'll always get the latest:

```
    Sub SetAccDetail
      Dim strMesg
      gstrAccDetail = ""
      If (gflgAccReady AND 1) Then          'got an account number
        gstrAccDetail = "Customer Account Number: <B>" _
                    & gobjCustForm.txtAccount.Text & "</B>"
      End If
      If gflgAccReady >= 62 Then            'got enough address details
        gstrAccDetail = gstrAccDetail & "<P>Deliver To: <B>" _
                    & gobjCustForm.txtName.Text & "<BR>" _
                    & gobjCustForm.txtAddress.Text & "<BR>" _
                    & gobjCustForm.txtTown.Text & "<BR>" _
                    & UCase(gobjCustForm.txtState.Text) & " " _
```

133

```
                              & gobjCustForm.txtZip.Text & "</B>"
         End If
         If Len(gstrAccDetail) = 0 Then    'not enough details
           strMesg = "You must enter either your six character account" & CRLF _
                   & "number or your full address before placing the order."
           MsgBox strMesg, 48, "Cannot process order"
           Exit Sub     'exit and leave gstrAccDetail empty
         End If
         If Len(gobjCustForm.txtPhone.Text) OR _
            Len(gobjCustForm.txtEmail.Text) Then
             gstrAccDetail = gstrAccDetail & "<P>"
         End If
         If Len(gobjCustForm.txtPhone.Text) Then
           gstrAccDetail = gstrAccDetail & "Phone: <B>" _
                          & gobjCustForm.txtPhone.Text & " </B>"
         End If
         If Len(gobjCustForm.txtEmail.Text) Then
           gstrAccDetail = gstrAccDetail & "- Email: <B>" _
                          & gobjCustForm.txtEmail.Text & "</B>"
         End If
       End Sub
```

You can see that this uses the customer's account number only if bit **0** of the **gflgAccReady** flag variable is set (**gflgAccReady AND 1** is not equal to zero), and the address details only if bits **1** to **5** are set (**gflgAccReady >= 62**). To get the value from a text box, we use the global reference to the Account Details form we created in the **window_OnLoad** event:

```
   gstrAccDetail = " . . . " & gobjCustForm.txtAccount.Text
```

The rest of the routine just formats the string neatly, and adds the phone and email details if these are available. If there isn't enough information, as we saw earlier, the routine displays a message and leaves **gstrAccDetail** as an empty string. This prevents the wizards from progressing with the order.

Building the Order String

If all is well, the currently active wizard will calculate the material requirements, prompt the user to accept them, and then add them to any existing order details in the global variable **gstrOrderDetail**. All we need to do then is incorporate the three global strings, **gstrOrderNumber**, **gstrAccDetail**, and **gstrAccDetail** into a new browser window.

You could do this by writing them out as a new HTML document on disk, then pointing the browser window at the document by changing the **Location.HRef** property, like we did to load a different document into our wizard frame. But VBScript doesn't support any disk access commands, so we have to find another method. Instead, we'll use the **Write** method of the **document** object to place the text directly in the window's document, as we did with the Glass Load Calculator in Chapter 2.

So, first, we build up the string of text for the document, incorporating, of course, the HTML tags we need to format it correctly. Here's the complete routine:

```
   Sub CreateOrder
     'creates the order in new browser window
     Dim objNewWindow      'new window for order
     Dim objOrderDoc       'order window document
```

```
    Dim strNewPage          'the text for the new window

    'create the HTML text for the new window

    'first the head and style section
    strNewPage = "<HTML><HEAD><TITLE>Your Order Details</TITLE>" _
            & "<STYLE>{font-family=Arial; font-size=12}</STYLE>"

    'including the VBScript handler code for the two buttons
    strNewPage = strNewPage & "<SCRIPT LANGUAGE=VBScript>" & CRLF _
            & "Sub btnEdit_OnClick()" & CRLF _
            & "Document.Close" & CRLF _
            & "Window.Close" & CRLF _
            & "End Sub" & CRLF & CRLF _
            & "Sub btnSubmit_OnClick()" & CRLF _
            & "MsgBox ""Thank you for your order"", 64, ""Submitted""" _
            & CRLF & "End Sub" & CRLF _
            & "</" & "SCRIPT></HEAD>"

    'now the body section of the page
    strNewPage = strNewPage & "<BODY BGCOLOR=#FFFFC0><B>ORDER No. " _
            & gstrOrderNumber & " - Date: " & Date() & "</B><P>" _
            & "To: <B>Bob's Building Supplies</B><P>"

    'add the customer's details
    strNewPage = strNewPage & gstrAccDetail

    'then the details of the order - first the table headings
    strNewPage = strNewPage & "<HR><B>Please supply:</B><P>" _
            & "<TABLE WIDTH=100%><TR><TD ALIGN=CENTER>Qty</TD>" _
            & "<TD ALIGN=LEFT>Description</TD>" _
            & "<TD ALIGN=CENTER>Price</TD>" _
            & "<TD ALIGN=RIGHT>Total</TD></TR>"

    'now add the order details to the table
    strNewPage = strNewPage & gstrOrderDetail

    'and add the order value at the end of the table
    strNewPage = strNewPage & "<TR><TD></TD><TD ALIGN=LEFT>.</TD>" _
            & "<TD></TD><TD></TD></TR><TR><TD></TD><TD ALIGN=LEFT>" _
            & "<B>Total Order Value:</B></TD><TD></TD>" _
            & "<TD ALIGN=RIGHT><B>$ " _
            & CCurrency(gdblOrderTotal) & "</B></TD></TR></TABLE><HR>"

    'create a form to send details to the server - here's the <FORM> tag
    strNewPage = strNewPage & "<FORM METHOD=" & Chr(34) & "POST" & Chr(34) _
            & " ACTION=" & Chr(34) & gstrFormHandler & Chr(34) & ">"

    'now a table to hold the two buttons
    strNewPage = strNewPage & "<CENTER><TABLE WIDTH=70%><TR>" _
            & "<TD ALIGN=CENTER><INPUT TYPE=SUBMIT NAME=btnSubmit " _
            & "VALUE=" & Chr(34) & " Send this order now " _
            & Chr(34) & "></TD>" _
            & "<TD ALIGN=CENTER><INPUT TYPE=BUTTON NAME=btnEdit " _
            & "VALUE=" & Chr(34) & " Add more items to this order " _
            & Chr(34) & "></TD></TR></TABLE></CENTER>"

    'then the hidden <INPUT> boxes
```

135

```
        strNewPage = strNewPage & "<INPUT TYPE=HIDDEN NAME=" & Chr(34) _
               & "OrderNo" & Chr(34) & " VALUE=" & Chr(34) _
               & gstrOrderNumber & Chr(34) & ">" _
               & "<INPUT TYPE=HIDDEN NAME=" & Chr(34) & "AccDetails" _
               & Chr(34) & " VALUE=" & Chr(34) & gstrAccDetail _
               & Chr(34) & ">" _
               & "<INPUT TYPE=HIDDEN NAME=" & Chr(34) & "OrderDetails" _
               & Chr(34) & " VALUE=" & Chr(34) & gstrOrderDetail _
               & Chr(34) & "></FORM><BR>&copy Wrox Press 1996"

        'finally add the end of body and head tags
        strNewPage = strNewPage & "</BODY></HTML>"

        'then display the page in a new window
        Set objNewWindow = window.open("", "TheOrder", "Toolbar=Yes", 475, 400)
        Set objOrderDoc = objNewWindow.Document
        objOrderDoc.Write strNewPage
        objOrderDoc.Close
    End Sub
```

Reading through it, you can see that we first declare some variables we're going to need, then start to build up the string. We've included a **<HEAD>** section which specifies the title and the text style. However, you'll also see that we're including VBScript code, within a **<SCRIPT>** tag pair. You will notice that we've broken the closing script tag for the generated document into two pieces. This is just to prevent the browser confusing the closing tag in the document **Write** methods with that of the new document. Not doing this could possibly cause an error in your page.

The order page will contain two push buttons, and we want to be able to react to these by including event handlers. If you check out the code, you can see that it simply writes the VBScript code lines as text into the page, just as you would type it.

> *To include quotation marks (**"**) in a string you have to use one of the two techniques we've included above. The 'correct' way is to specify the ASCII code in a call to the **Chr()** function, which returns a string containing just that character. In our case, **Chr(34)** returns the **"** character we want. The shortcut method that VBScript allows, however, is to just place two quotation marks together. Although this method is quick, you can see that it makes reading the code afterwards rather confusing.*

Once we've completed the VBScript code, we add a **<BODY>** section and the customer's account details from the variable **gstrAccDetail**. Next, its the headings for our order table, and then the actual details of the order which we've already formatted (including HTML codes) in **gstrOrderDetail**. After this, we finish off the table with the total price, and add another table containing the two button controls. These are normal HTML buttons, but we've named them so that the relevant VBScript code routines in the document will run when they are clicked.

To end the string, we add three hidden HTML text controls which have their values set to the three global strings **gstrOrderNumber**, **gstrAccDetail**, and **gstrAccDetail**, then lastly the closing **</BODY>** and **</HTML>** tags.

Displaying the Order in a New Window

Now we've got our string, all we need is a new window to display it in. However, you may come across a few pitfalls as you experiment with this method. It's easy enough to open a new browser window by calling the window's **Open** method:

```
Set objNewWindow = window.open("", "TheOrder", "Toolbar=Yes", 475, 400)
```

This sets the variable **objNewWindow** to refer to the new window, which is 475 pixels wide by 400 pixels high and has a toolbar. The first argument is the URL of the document we want to display, and, of course, we can't supply this because our document is available only as a string. The second argument is the name by which we want to refer to the window when, for example, we're targeting new documents to it from an **<A>** tag.

Because we haven't supplied a source URL, the browser automatically loads its default document— in Internet Explorer this is **BLANK.HTM** and it will probably be in your **Windows\System** folder. In Bob's application, you see this name briefly appear in the title bar when the new order window first opens.

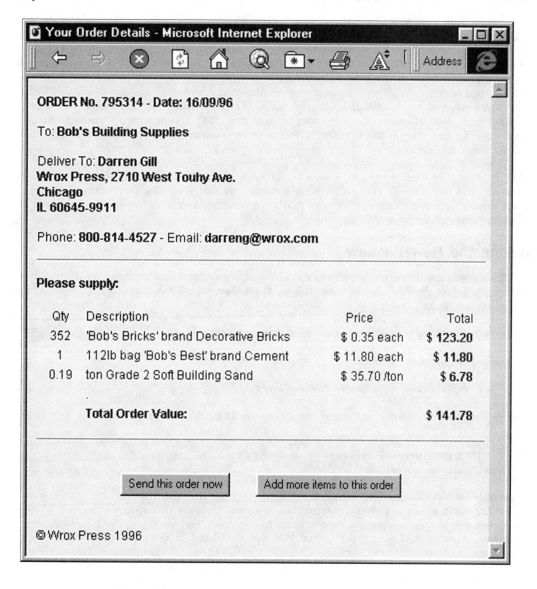

137

Now we can set another variable to refer to the new window's document, and write the string into it, with:

```
Set objOrderDoc = objNewWindow.Document
objOrderDoc.Write strNewPage
objOrderDoc.Close
```

As the string is written to the new window, the HTML codes in it are interpreted by the browser. Then, after we execute the document's **Close** method, the window is updated to display the new document.

'Virtual' HTML and VBScript Code

One interesting aspect of doing things this way is what happens when you right-click on a document and select View Source. All you see is the original **BLANK.HTM**—and not the code and text you've written to it. This only exists 'virtually' until you close the page and then it disappears for good. If you click the Back button, then the Forward button, you'll just get a blank document.

Notice that we've done more than place text in the virtual page. As well as creating HTML-type **<INPUT>** controls, we've included VBScript code. The page works (almost) like it was a real page loaded from disk. However, there are some effects that don't appear to work correctly at present. For example, including a **BACKGROUND** attribute in the **<BODY>** tag, to display a background bitmap, has no effect.

But on the other hand there are exciting possibilities, as you'll see in Chapter 8. One is that the 'virtual' VBScript routines can easily include commands that create another virtual HTML page, and these can include VBScript routines that create another virtual HTML page, and these can include VBScript routines that, etc.

Reusing the New Window

In theory, you can reuse the new window any time you want to, by referring to it with the name you gave it (not the title). In our case, this is **TheOrder**, so we can target a new document to it by using this in an **<A>** tag:

```
<A HREF="http://www.mynewpage.htm" TARGET="TheOrder">
```

We also have an object reference to it, which we created with:

```
Set objOrderDoc = objNewWindow.Document
```

So we can write to it again by calling its **Clear**, **Write**, and **Close** methods:

```
objOrderDoc.Clear
objOrderDoc.Write strNewPage
objOrderDoc.Close
```

The only problem is that this doesn't bring it to the front and make it the active window, which is what we want in our application. Instead we've taken the route that requires the user to close the new window if they want to add more items to the order, and we've supplied a button for that purpose. When clicked it runs the virtual VBScript we placed in the page which closes the document, and then the window:

```
Sub btnEdit_OnClick()
  Document.Close
  Window.Close
End Sub
```

Next time a new window is created, it's displayed in front of the main browser window, in just the way we want. However, if the user brings the main window to the front and tries to add to the existing order while the new window is open we get a problem. A window with the same name already exists, and the browser gets very confused trying to create a new one. Even trying to close the window first, then reopen it, seems to create resource problems in Internet Explorer and should be avoided.

Communicating with the Server

Our final task is to send the order to the server when the user clicks the Send button. This information is in **HIDDEN**-type HTML **<INPUT>** controls in a **<FORM>** section, as well as being neatly displayed in a table. In the version you're using now, all we do is display a message box. However, the button in the order window is a real HTML SUBMIT button, and if you change the line in the **window_OnLoad** event handler to point to a real server the data in these hidden controls will be sent in the normal way.

```
gstrFormHandler = "http://myrealsite/cgi-bin/fh.pl"  'server form handler
```

Our order page also contains a virtual VBScript routine which is connected to the SUBMIT button through the name we gave it when it was created. This displays the message box you see when you click the button:

```
Sub btnSubmit_OnClick()
  MsgBox "Thank you for your order", 64, "Submitted"
End Sub
```

You can quite easily insert code into the events for standard HTML SUBMIT and CANCEL buttons like this, and your code will run to completion before the action specified for the form is executed. In fact, you can add code to many other HTML tags, as you'll see in the next chapter.

The Limitations of Our Design

Before we leave our look at Bob's Building Supplies site, we should consider some of the shortcomings. Obviously, we need to send the details of the user's order to the server and acknowledge them. And there are other things we could do better if we had proper server interaction. We could, for example, download into the page the current list of product descriptions and prices—plus a unique order number rather than a randomly created one.

We could also ask a user to 'log in' to our site, so that we could retrieve their name and address details and automatically display them on the page to save filling them in. Our application doesn't ask for payment details either, but you could display a form asking for their credit card number if they haven't got an account. In fact, you'll see a lot of this functionality added to the application when we come to look at server processing later in the book.

Oh, and you may be wondering what happens when you select The Doors Page in the menu frame. Well, all we can say is, try it and see . . .

Summary

If you've been programming in other languages regularly, you may have recognized something going on in this chapter that's often not part of the process of creating normal web pages using just HTML. Adding objects and scripting to a page increases the complexity a great deal. No longer is it enough to view the result and make sure it *looks* right, you now have to test that it actually *works*.

In the past, if you used CGI scripts, you just had to make sure that these did what was expected of them in response to requests from the browser. Now you have objects whose properties and methods you need to manipulate, and events occurring in the page itself, which have to be linked to the correct code routines.

And, on top of all this, there are often several pages loaded and displayed simultaneously, in different frames. The code in each page now has to be linked together correctly, so that the pages interact to produce the result you want.

All in all, it's a lot more like writing an application than authoring web pages. Hence, as well as showing you how Bob's sample page works, we've spent some time looking at the way we lay down a detailed design plan first. It's much like an engineering project, where you prepare detailed drawings of all the parts you'll need. With the advent of VBScript, ActiveX, and, of course, Java, software engineering has come to be a term which refers just as much to web authoring as creating a new stand-alone application.

In this chapter, we've looked at:

- What the sample application can do.

- How it's designed to promote business and help customers spend their money more easily.

- The way the application was designed and assembled from a series of components and pages.

- How we can communicate between different parts of the browser window, and dynamically create new pages using VBScript.

- Introducing you to the hierarchy of the browser, as a precursor to the next chapter where we'll be examining this in more depth.

So let's get more involved in the browser hierarchy. This is the main subject of the next chapter, and we'll introduce some new techniques and tricks that may well surprise you.

```
<HEAD>
    <SCRIPT LANGUAGE="VBScript">

<!--
Sub window_onLoad()
  Dim objLst
  set objLst= dimensions.
                        lstMaterials

  objLst.AddItem "Clay Bricks
                        (3x8x3.5)"

  objLst.AddItem "Stone Blocks
                        (8x8x4)"

  objLst.AddItem "Concrete Blocks
                        (8x16x

  objLst.ListIndex = 0
nd Sub
->
    </SCRIPT>
```

The Browser Hierarchy

Well, we've had some fun playing with VBScript and ActiveX controls in the last four chapters, and we've discovered just some of the ways these new techniques can make your web pages come alive and interact with your visitors. Now it's time to settle down to some serious study. We've used a lot of the **properties**, **methods**, and **events** of the different objects that are part of your browser, and we've mentioned the **browser hierarchy** many times without really committing ourselves to an in-depth discussion.

We've chosen this approach so that you could actually see VBScript in action early on. Rather than having to wade through pages of theory, when you aren't sure of where it's all going, we've tried to make the journey more exciting. But the time has come when you really ought to have a grasp of the whole picture, so, in this chapter, we're going to concentrate on the browser hierarchy, and the way that the **scripting object model** allows VBScript to manipulate the pages and the controls they contain.

You'll also see a couple of ways of using the browser that may come as a surprise. Microsoft's browser, Internet Explorer, is itself an **object** which we can manipulate using the properties, methods, and events it exposes.

So, in this chapter, we'll be covering:

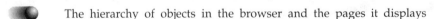

- The hierarchy of objects in the browser and the pages it displays
- An overview of the properties, methods and events for each object
- How you can work with **cookies** using VBScript
- Ways in which you can use Internet Explorer for more than just web pages

We'll start with an overview of the browser object hierarchy...

An Overview of the Browser

Before we do get started, however, there's one important point we should make. Although we have used Microsoft's Internet Explorer browser throughout this book (because at the time of writing it was the only one that natively supported VBScript), the browser hierarchy, and the properties, methods and events of its objects, are actually cross-platform standards. They aren't something that's just there for VBScript, or just available in Internet Explorer.

The Internet is an inherently cross-platform system, where (in most cases) a single document standard is supported by all the different browsers, running on all the different operating systems. Because of this, one browser has to support the same scripting object model as all the others. If it didn't, the scripts and objects in the pages wouldn't work. Equally, the standard object model can just as well be manipulated using JavaScript or any other language, including those that may appear in the future.

This book is about VBScript, so we will be looking at the ways that it can interface with the browser. However, the information itself is general, so it will benefit you whichever scripting language you finally end up using.

Looking at Properties and Methods

So how can we access all these object's properties? To start with, here's a simple example that displays the values of several of the intrinsic properties of the browser and the page it is displaying.

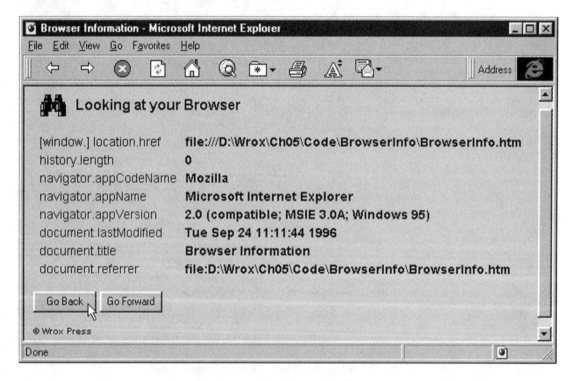

You can open this sample yourself from our web site. The address is:

```
http://www.wrox.com/books/0448/code/chapter05/BrowserInfo/BrowserInfo.htm
```

While Internet Explorer is still in relatively early stages of development, some of the properties, methods and events aren't completely or accurately implemented. In our sample page shown above, for instance, the `history.length` *and* `document.referrer` *properties produce incorrect results.*

The left column shows the syntax of the property, such as **document.title**. You'll recall that in object methodology we use the 'period' notation to link properties (or methods and events) to the object, in the form of *objectname.propertyname*. Looking at the screenshot, you can see the document's title in the title bar of Internet Explorer and the value of the **document.title** property displayed in the page. To produce the list of property values on this page, we used the VBScript code:

```
Dim strInfo

strInfo = "<CENTER><TABLE WIDTH=100%>" _
          & "<TR><TD>[window.] location.HRef</TD>" _
          & "<TD><B>" & window.location.HRef & "</TD></TR>" _
          & "<TR><TD>history.length</TD>" _
          & "<TD><B>" & history.length & "</TD></TR>" _
          & "<TR><TD>navigator.appCodeName</TD>" _
          & "<TD><B>" & navigator.appCodeName & "</TD></TR>" _
          & "<TR><TD>navigator.appName</TD>" _
          & "<TD><B>" & navigator.appName & "</TD></TR>" _
          & "<TR><TD>navigator.appVersion</TD>" _
          & "<TD><B>" & navigator.appVersion & "</TD></TR>" _
          & "<TR><TD>document.lastModified</TD>" _
          & "<TD><B>" & document.lastModified & "</TD></TR>" _
          & "<TR><TD>document.title</TD>" _
          & "<TD><B>" & document.title & "</TD></TR>" _
          & "<TR><TD>document.referrer</TD>" _
          & "<TD><B>" & document.referrer & "</TD></TR>" _
          & "</TABLE></CENTER><P>"
document.write strInfo
document.close
```

As you can see, this creates a string which contains a two-column table, then writes it into the document. The first column contains a 'text version' of the code that will retrieve the value of the property, and in the second column, we actually retrieve it. For example, our **document.title** property is created with:

```
          & "<TR><TD>document.title</TD>" _          'column one
          & "<TD><B>" & document.title & "</TD></TR>" _    'column two
```

We'll assume that, from earlier chapters, you have grasped the way VBScript can create tables in strings and print them to a document. In this chapter, we're concentrating on the objects themselves rather than the way the code that produces these sample applications works.

The first thing you'll notice from the page is that we're accessing the properties of several different objects. The address of the page that's being displayed is held in the **HRef** property of the **location** object, and because this is a child of the **window** object itself, we really ought to use the full syntax **window.location.HRef** to retrieve it. However, **window** is the default object for your VBScript, so it can be omitted. The shortened version **location.HRef** works fine. Below that are properties taken from the **history**, **navigator**, and **document** objects. Again, these are all child objects of the **window**, but we can safely omit the **window** object when we access them, provided that we are referring to the current window.

There are also two buttons in the page, which when clicked will take you a random number of places either backwards or forwards through your **history** list. This list is maintained by the browser and is a record of all the pages you've visited during the current session. Here's the code for these two buttons:

145

```
Sub cmdBack_OnClick()
   Dim intPlaces
   Randomize
   intPlaces = CInt((Rnd() * 3) + 1)
   MsgBox "Trying to go back " & intPlaces & " places."
   history.back intPlaces
End Sub

Sub cmdForward_OnClick()
   Dim intPlaces
   Randomize
   intPlaces = CInt((Rnd() * 3) + 1)
   MsgBox "Trying to go forward " & intPlaces & " places."
   history.forward intPlaces
End Sub
```

All the code does is create a random number then pass this to the **back** or **forward** method of the **history** object.

The Main Object Structure

It should be obvious from the previous example that there are several objects lurking in the browser, and that they have very different properties, methods and events. At the top of the hierarchy is the **window** object, and all these other objects are children of this. So in its simplest form, the object hierarchy looks like this:

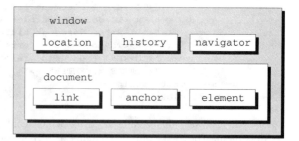

The **window** object is a **container** which can hold other objects, and within it are two different types of object. One of these types is also a container, while the other type is just a simple 'single-level' object. In our case, the containers are the top level **window** object and the **document** object. The others (**location**, **history**, **navigator**, **link**, **anchor**, and **element**) are simple objects which cannot contain other objects.

Notice that in this first example there's only one **document**, and it's displayed in the single browser **window**. But as well as holding the normal **links**, **anchors**, and **elements** (or controls), a document can also contain **forms**. These forms are themselves container objects, which can contain their own **elements**. Here's how we can illustrate this:

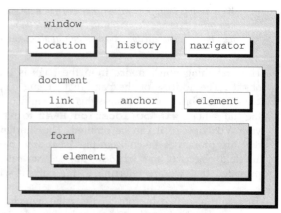

146

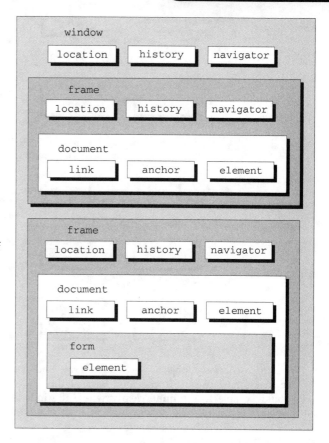

And bear in mind that we aren't limited to displaying just a single document. By using **frames**, we can have more than one document loaded into the browser window. To accommodate these, the browser hierarchy defines a **frames** collection, which is really just an array of windows. Each frame in the array can hold one **document** object, as seen here:

In earlier chapters, though, you've seen how we can **nest** frames to create more complex pages. Each frame can itself be divided up into separate frames, rather than displaying a single document. And each of these nested frames can hold a document or another set of frames. Remember, also, that we can create new windows—as you saw in the Bob's Builder's Supplies application. There, we displayed the completed order in a separate browser window rather than in a frame in the main window.

Because each frame or window can display a different document, each has its own set of **location**, **history**, and **navigator** objects, which reflect the values for that window. When you divide a window up into separate frames, each one of these becomes, in effect, a **window** object in its own right.

So the hierarchy needs to be complex to manage the many different ways you can create complex pages. And there is another object that we haven't mentioned yet. The browser defines a **script** object which holds all the scripts defined in each window. (Remember that all scripts are accessible from all documents in that window.) To help make things clearer, here's a diagram that shows all the objects and the relationships between them.

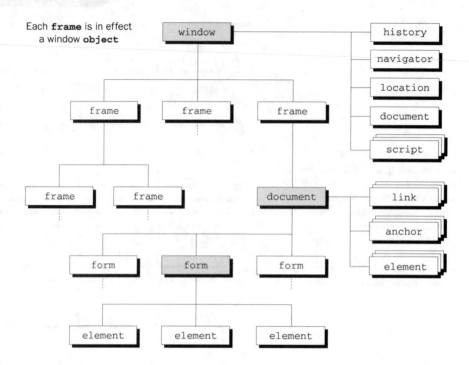

Each **frame** is in effect a window **object**

The main container objects are shaded gray, and it's these whose properties, methods, and events we make most use of. If you look back at the Browser Information example we showed earlier, you should be able to see quite clearly where the individual objects we used are situated in the browser hierarchy. We'll take a look at each of the main objects next, starting with the easy ones!

The History Object

This object stores the URL of all the pages you have visited with the current window (but not necessarily all those you've got stored in your History folder). The total number is given in **history.length**, and there are just three methods which allow you to move backwards or forwards through the history list.

Property	Description
length	Returns the length of the history list.

Method	Description
back *n*	Jumps back in the history *n* steps, like clicking back button *n* times.
forward *n*	Jumps forward in the history *n* steps, like clicking forward *n* times.
go *n*	Goes to the *n*th item in the history list.

The Navigator Object

The **navigator** object holds the details of the browser itself, and exists for each **window** you create. You've seen in the first sample of this chapter how we can retrieve and display the values of its properties. There are no methods or events associated with this object.

Property	Description
appCodeName	Returns the code name of the application.
appName	Returns the actual name of the application.
appVersion	Returns the version of the application.
userAgent	Returns the user agent of the application.

One particular use of the properties of the **navigator** object is to decide exactly which browser the user is running. Instead of writing web pages that are broadly suitable for all browsers, you can create a different set for each of the popular browsers, taking full advantage of the capabilities of each one. Then, using the **appName** and **appVersion** properties of the browser, you can decide which set of pages to display.

The Location Object

The **location** object stores details of the document currently being displayed in the window. Remember that, in a page that uses frames, each frame has its own **location** object because each frame can (and probably will) be displaying a different document. You can retrieve or set all the properties, as we've done in earlier chapters. For example, to display a different document in a window we just changed its **location.HRef** property like this:

```
location.HRef = "http://mysite.com/index.htm"
```

There are no methods or events associated with the **location** object.

Property	Description
HRef	Gets or sets the compete URL for the location.
Protocol	Gets or sets the protocol portion of the URL.
Host	Gets or sets the host and port portion of the URL.
Hostname	Gets or sets just the host portion of the URL.
Port	Gets or sets just the port portion of the URL.
Pathname	Gets or sets the path name in the URL.
Search	Gets or sets the search portion of the URL, if specified.
Hash	Gets or sets the hash portion of the URL, if specified.

The Window Object

The properties of the **window** object are primarily concerned with providing references to other objects in the hierarchy. In particular, we can use the properties to reference other windows or frames when we want to work with objects in them. There are also two main events, **onLoad** and **onUnload**, that we regularly use to initialize variables in our scripts, or perform 'cleaning up' operations. You've seen the **window_onLoad()** event used regularly in our previous sample applications.

The **window** object also provides a set of methods which mirror the **MsgBox** and **InputBox** functions we've been using in our code. These are used mainly in other scripting languages, such as JavaScript, and aren't as flexible as the VBScript ones.

Property	Description
name	Returns the name of the current window.
parent	Returns the window object of the window's parent.
self	Returns the window object of the current window.
top	Returns the window object of the topmost window.
location	Returns the location object for the current window.
defaultStatus	Gets or sets the default text for the left portion of the status bar.
status	Gets or sets the status text in the left of the status bar.
frames	Returns the collection of frames for the current window.
history	Returns the history object of the current window.
navigator	Returns the navigator object of the current window.
document	Returns the document object of the current window.

Method	Description
alert	Displays an alert message box.
confirm	Displays a message box with OK and Cancel buttons, returns **TRUE** or **FALSE**.
prompt	Prompts the user for input.
open	Creates a new window.
close	Closes the window.
setTimeout	Sets a timer to call a function after a specific number of milliseconds.
clearTimeout	Clears the timer having a particular ID.
navigate	Navigates the window to a new URL.

Event	Description
`onLoad`	Fired when the contents of the window are loaded.
`onUnload`	Fired when the contents of the window are unloaded.

Notice also the **setTimeout** and **clearTimeout** methods. These allow you to define a control event which will occur a preset time after the document has been loaded. In our examples, we've tended to use the ActiveX **Timer** control instead, because this continues to fire rather than being a 'one-shot' event.

Other methods allow you to create a new window (using the **open** method) and **close** a window. Again, we saw these in use in our sample Bob's Builder Supplies application:

```
'display the page in a new window
Set objNewWindow = window.open("", "TheOrder", "Toolbar=Yes", 475, 400)
```

```
Sub btnEdit_onClick()     'close the window when the Edit button is clicked
   document.close          'close the document
   window.close            'then close the window
End Sub
```

Collections of Objects

Several of the **window** object's properties return a **collection** of other objects. A collection is like an array, but, in most cases, you can access its members with their name as well as with their index. Some other object's properties are also collections, as you'll see later on. In the window object, we have a **frames** collection.

The **frames collection** contains all the frames defined for the current document, which, in the case of nested frames, may itself be displayed within a frame created by a different document. We can access individual frames by their index, starting from zero and going up to **frames.count - 1**, or with their name. Both these lines of code give the same result if the second frame is named **fraSecondFrame**:

```
Set objMyDoc = frames(1).document        'access document in the 2nd frame
```

```
Set objMyDoc = frames("fraSecondFrame").document       'and again
```

Because a **frame** is in fact a **window**, we can access the document it is displaying using the **document** property just as we would with a **window** object.

Reaching across Frames

Of course, when we do have nested frames in a page, things get a little more complicated. Here's an example that shows how you can reach across from one frame to another, using the various properties of the **window** object. You can load this sample yourself from our web site. The address is:

```
http://www.wrox.com/books/0448/code/chapter.05/Frames/Frames.htm
```

151

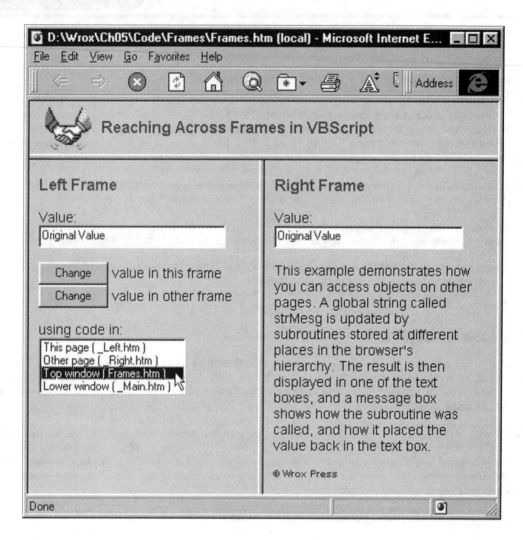

```
<FRAMESET ROWS="57,*">
  <FRAME SRC="_Title.htm" NAME="TopFrame" SCROLLING=NO NORESIZE>
  <FRAME SRC="_Main.htm" NAME="MainFrame">
</FRAMESET>
```

The top frame is loaded with just the page title, as **_Title.htm**. However, the bottom frame loads the document **_Main.htm**, which itself defines another frame set, like this:

```
<FRAMESET COLS="50%,*">
  <FRAME SRC="_Left.htm" NAME="LeftFrame">
  <FRAME SRC="_Right.htm" NAME="RightFrame">
</FRAMESET>
```

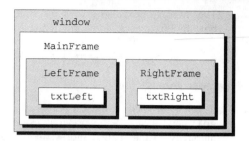

So the two documents, **_Left.htm** and **_Right.htm**, are child objects of the frame we've named **MainFrame** (in **Frames.htm**). However, **MainFrame** is itself a child window object of the top-level browser window object. Each of the lowest-level documents has (among other controls) a text box, named **txtLeft** and **txtRight**. To refer to the **Value** property of **txtRight** from the main window we have to use:

```
strTheValue = frames("MainFrame").frames("RightFrame").txtRight.Value
```

This works because we've named the frames. If we hadn't, we would have to use the index of the frame, like this:

```
strTheValue = frames(0).frames(1).txtRight.Value
```

Conversely, we use the **parent** property of the lower-level frames to get back to the higher-level ones. To get at **txtRight**'s value using code within the left-hand frame, using the frame indexes, we go back up the hierarchy to the first object that contains them both (in this case **MainFrame**) then down the other side again, like this:

```
strTheValue = parent.frames(1).txtRight.Value
```

And, of course, we can use the frame name instead, like this:

```
strTheValue = parent.frames("RightFrame").txtRight.Value
```

Running Code at other Hierarchy Levels

Our sample goes a bit further than just retrieving values in text boxes. The documents at each level of the hierarchy (**LeftFrame**, **RightFrame**, **MainFrame**, and the **top** window), contain a subroutine called **SetNewValue** which sets the value of one of the text boxes. Which one of these routines actually gets executed depends on the selection you make in the list below the buttons. Here, we've selected the Top window (the document **Frames.htm**) and you can see that we have to call the routine using

```
parent.parent.SetNewValue
```

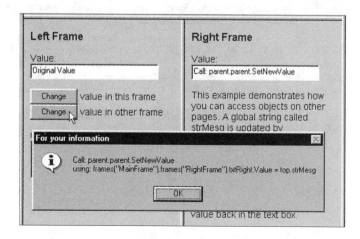

The message box also shows the statement it used to place the new value in the respective text box. In this case it went down the hierarchy through **MainFrame** and **RightFrame** using:

```
frames("MainFrame").frames("RightFrame").txtRight.Value = top.strMesg
```

'parent' versus 'top'

If you look back at the properties of the **window** object, you'll see that they include **parent**, **self**, and **top**. In the previous example, we've used **parent.parent** to go back up the hierarchy to the main window, and **top** to reference a global variable stored there. However, using **top** is dangerous, and, in some cases, will break your pages altogether. You'll see an example of this in the next chapter, when we look at a tool called Document Analyzer. In the meantime, be warned. In some circles, use of **top** is classed as a mortal sin!

Why is it so dangerous? Well, if your page is actually being displayed inside *someone else's* frame set, what your code calls **top** is not actually **top** at all. Calling a VBScript code routine which is in your **top** page won't work when the **top** page is actually someone else's, but it will only break *your* page. However, if your page loads a new document into **top**, it will remove all the frames, including the other person's, and you probably won't get invited to their next cocktail party.

> **self** *just refers to the window from which the code is running. It's normally used only if you want to override a default* **TARGET** *set in the* **BASE** *attribute of a page's* **<BODY>** *tag.*

Using Object Variable References

To avoid the awkward syntax requirements when working with complex pages, where you have several levels of the hierarchy to traverse, you can define **object variables** to refer to objects in other places in the hierarchy. When you have to refer to an object repeatedly in your script, this method can save you a lot of typing, and as a by-product it will reduce the overall size of your document. It also helps if you redesign your site, so that pages are loaded into different frames. Then you only have to change the line that creates the reference, instead of every line where it is used. For example, instead of the following statement:

```
strTheValue = frames("MainFrame").frames("RightFrame").txtRight.Value
```

we could define an object variable, **objRightFrame**, and set it to refer to the frame in which the text box resides, like this:

```
Set objRightFrame = frames("MainFrame").frames("RightFrame")
strTheValue = objRightFrame.txtRight.Value
```

We can even **Set** a variable to refer to the control itself, for example:

```
Set objRightTextBox = frames("MainFrame").frames("RightFrame").txtRight
txtTheValue = objRightTextBox.Value
```

While it doesn't seem like much, if used consistently, it can dramatically reduce the size of large, complex scripts, thus reducing download time.

The Document Object

After the **window** object, the properties, methods, and events that you are most likely to use are those of the **document** object. You can retrieve and set the values for several of the document's properties which affect how the page appears.

Changing the Colors in a Document

As an example of some of the properties, here's a page which allows you to change the color of various items dynamically while it is loaded. You can open this sample yourself from our web site. The address is:

`http://www.wrox.com/books/0448/code/chapter05/DocObject/DocObject.htm`

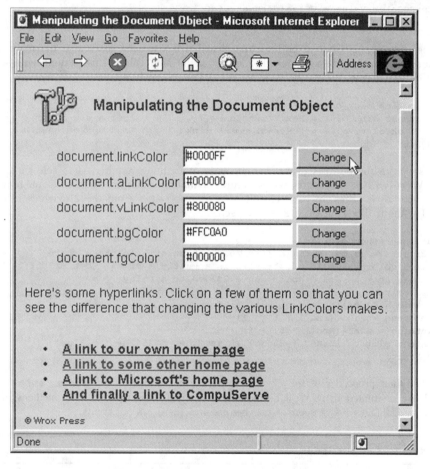

As you click the Change buttons, the VBScript code in the page creates a random color and assigns it to the respective document property. So that you can see the way the changes affect *visited* links, you'll need to click on one or two of these first. Notice that the color of the page heading doesn't change because it's set up with a **<STYLE>** tag in the HTML that creates the page. However, all the other text, which doesn't have a specified foreground color, changes when you click the button.

In Internet Explorer, you'll find that changing the **aLinkColor** *has no effect. This is the color of the* *active links in a document, and is used only when the mouse button is actually depressed over that link.* *Internet Explorer doesn't provide active links.*

The VBScript that carries out the work itself is pretty simple. In the **onLoad** event of the **window** object, we assign the current colors for each item to their respective text boxes. The properties hold the values as hexadecimal RGB triplets (as we saw in Chapter 1), so we just force them into uppercase using the **UCase** function, to tidy up the display.

```
Sub window_onLoad()
  txtLinkColor.Value = UCase(document.linkColor)
  txtALinkColor.Value = UCase(document.aLinkColor)
  txtVLinkColor.Value = UCase(document.vLinkColor)
  txtBGColor.Value = UCase(document.bgColor)
  txtFGColor.Value = UCase(document.fgColor)
End Sub
```

Then, when any of the Change buttons are clicked, we just need to change the relevant property of the document, and update the text box to show the new value. This is done with a separate routine for each button. Here's the code for the **linkcolor** button:

```
Sub cmdLinkColor_onClick()
  document.linkColor = Hex(RandomColor())        'get a new color
  txtLinkColor.Value = UCase(document.linkColor)  'and update text box
End Sub
```

You can see from the button's event that the only other thing required is to select a new color at random. We've written a function which returns a random color number, and you may find this useful in your own pages. In particular, it only returns values from the 216 which can always be displayed without dithering on a 256 color screen.

```
Function RandomColor()
  'creates a solid random color. The best colors are those where
  'each color value in the triplet is a multiple of #33 (decimal 51).
  'These show as solid colors on a 256 color display.
  Randomize
  intRed = CInt((Rnd() * 5) + 1) * 51
  intGreen = CInt((Rnd() * 5) + 1) * 51
  intBlue = CInt((Rnd() * 5) + 1) * 51
  RandomColor = (intRed * 65536) + (intGreen * 256) + (intBlue)
End Function
```

Among the other **properties** of the document are the collections of the **forms**, **anchors** and **links** that are situated in it. We'll be looking at each of these in turn. The **methods** of the document are all ones we've seen in use before, and there are no **events**.

Property	Description
linkColor	Gets or sets the color of the links in a document.
aLinkColor	Gets or sets the color of the active links in a document.
vLinkColor	Gets or sets the color of the visited links in a document.
bgColor	Gets or sets the background color of a document.

Table continued on next page

156

Property	Description
fgColor	Gets or sets the foreground color.
anchors	Returns the collection of anchors in a document.
links	Returns the collection of links for the current document.
forms	Returns the collection of forms for the current document.
location	Returns a read-only representation of the location object.
lastModified	Returns the last modified date of the current page.
title	Returns a read-only representation of the document's title.
cookie	Gets or sets the cookie for the current document.
referrer	Gets the URL of the referring document.

Method	Description
write	Places a string into the current document.
writeLn	Places a string plus new-line character into the current document.
open	Opens the document stream for output.
close	Updates the screen showing the text written since last **open** call.
clear	Closes the document output stream and clears the document.

One of the properties that deserves a little extra attention is the **cookie** property. Cookies are a form of client-server interaction, between your browser and the server you are connected to. They are generally used to preserve information between connections, something VBScript can't do because each time you load (or reload) a page, the variables in it are reinitialized.

A **cookie** is the quaint name for a string of characters which is specific to a particular page (or URL), and which is sent from the server and stored on the client system's hard drive. When the server next connects to that client, it can query that specific stored string to obtain the information it contains.

Sharing Your Cookies

While VBScript and ActiveX controls are very good at creating an interactive experience, there's one aspect that they can't assist you with. The Web is basically an anonymous protocol system where, when you load a page, you don't have to log in as a 'known' user unless the WebMaster there has specially implemented this requirement. And you only remain connected to the server for the period it takes to transfer the HTML page or the file you've requested.

After that the server disconnects, and it's only when your browser asks for the other components of the page (graphics, controls, objects, etc.), or another page, that you connect to the server again. So, while you are reading the page, the server goes off and forgets about you.

OK, that's not a problem most of the time. But what happens if the server wants to remember some details about visitors? For example, it could ask you to enter your name, then greet you personally on later visits. Or you may select your preferences for background color or even page contents, and expect them to be the same throughout the site, and when you next visit the site. (Remember that your next 'visit' could be as close as clicking the Refresh button.)

The easiest way to maintain values between page reloads, or between visits from the same person that could be seconds or weeks apart, is with cookies. Here's an example that demonstrates how cookies can store values, then reload them on a later visit. You can load this sample page yourself from this address:

```
http://www.wrox.com/books/0448/code/chapter05/Cookies/Cookies.htm
```

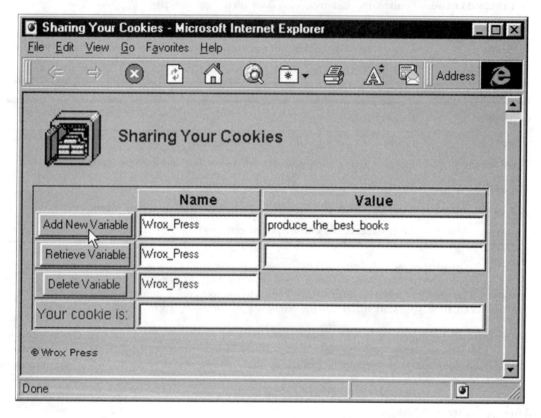

To see this example working, you must load the page over the Web. The cookie information is transmitted to the browser within the HTTP protocol packets. It won't work if you are running it from a local drive, where your browser loads it directly as a file.

The page suggests some values to start with, though of course you can change these. Clicking Add New Variable sends the value to the server which then sends back a cookie containing this. If you've got your browser set up to warn you before accepting cookies (in Internet Explorer this setting is in the Advanced page of the Options window), you'll see the warning dialog. Clicking Yes allows the browser to process the cookie, and it gets added to your document's **cookie** property.

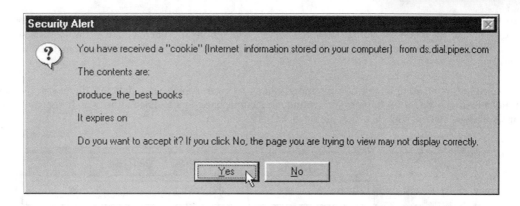

Basically, the document's cookie is a **value pair string** which contains the name of the variable and its value, separated by an equals sign. Even though it's stored in your browser's cache, you normally don't see the cookie, and only the server can access it. In our example, we're using VBScript to retrieve the **cookie** property, and display it in the lower text box on the page:

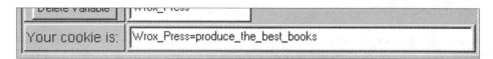

You can retrieve information from your document's **cookie** property by processing it locally in VBScript, within your browser. In our example, entering a name for the variable and clicking the Retrieve Variable button displays the current value of that variable.

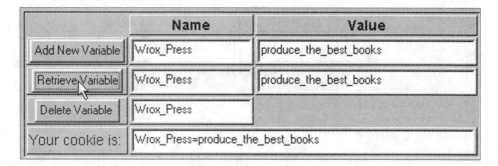

The **cookie** property can hold more than one value, though, plus other information. For example, you can set the date that the cookie expires, the domain and path for which it applies, and the security to be used for transmitting it.

Here's a cookie called **MyValue**, which is valid for all documents in the current domain (http: address), and which expires at tea-time on October 17th:

```
MyValue=VBScript_Is_Great;expires 17-Oct-97 17:30:00 GMT; path="/"
```

Appending the date when the cookie should no longer be valid to the end of the string, effectively expires it on that date. Adding the path to the string means that the server will only use it for pages stored within that area of the server.

To delete a value from your cookie, all you need to do is set its **expires** date to some time in the past, and its value to **NULL**. Then the server will ignore it. When you use the expires section of a cookie, you should make sure it contains the date and time in the correct format, as shown above.

To complete our example, try adding more values to your cookie, and deleting them. At the same time reload the page, or have a surf round and come back again. Each time, you'll see the values are still there when you click the Retrieve Variable button.

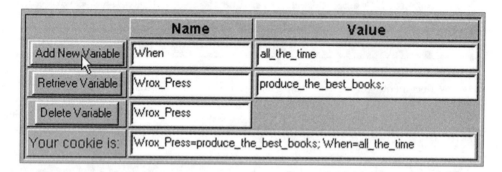

Your document's **cookie** property can be up to several kilobytes in size, so you can store lots of information in it. The main limitation is that you can only use normal characters that are legal for HTML text. In some cases, problems can also arise using spaces. In our example, we've used underline characters instead, and prevented the use of spaces in either the name or value. If you try it, a message warns you that this isn't possible:

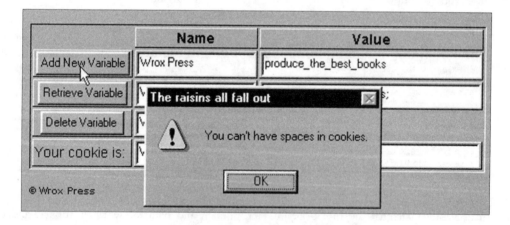

How It Works

How does it work? Well, all we have to do is modify the document's **cookie** property. In fact, for adding new values, it's even easier than that. After checking for spaces in the name and value, we just assign them to our cookie property, separated by an equals sign. The browser looks after the details of appending it to any values already stored there. If there's already a value with that name, it's updated with the new value:

```
Sub cmdAdd_OnClick()
  If Instr(txtAddName.Value & txtAddValue.Value, " ") Then
    SpacesMessage                     'no spaces allowed
    Exit Sub
  End If
  document.cookie = txtAddName.Value & "=" & txtAddValue.Value
  txtCookie.Value = document.cookie      'display whole cookie on page
End Sub
```

Retrieving a value is a little more complicated because when we retrieve the document's **cookie**
property, we get the whole shooting match—all the currently stored name-value pairs plus the
expiry date, path, etc. We need a subroutine which, given the name of the variable, parses the
cookie string and returns the matching value. If it's not there, the function returns an empty string.
Although it looks complicated, it's really just a matter of string searching. The most difficult part is
protecting against finding our variable name within the cookie as a substring of another cookie's
name or a value. To do this, we check that the character after the name is an equals sign, if it isn't
we continue the search from the next character:

```
Function FindValue(strName)  'get the value of a cookie named strName
  Dim intStart, intEnd, intLength
  Dim strCookie, strValue
  strValue = ""
  strCookie = document.cookie                'get cookie string
  intStart = Instr(strCookie, strName)       'starting position of name
  While intStart > 0                         'found if > zero
    strCookie = Mid(strCookie, intStart)     'remove left part of string
    If Mid(strCookie, Len(strName) + 1, 1) = "=" Then
      intStart = Len(strName) + 2            'starting position of value
      intEnd = Instr(intStart, strCookie, ";") 'look for end of value
      If intEnd = 0 Then                     'last value in cookie
        strValue = Mid(strCookie, intStart)  'so use rest of string
        intStart = 0                         'set start position to 0
      ElseIf intEnd > (intStart + 1) Then    'value in middle of string
        intLength = intEnd - intStart        'find the length and get
        strValue = Mid(strCookie, intStart, intLength) 'the value
        intStart = 0                         'set start position to 0
      Else
        intStart = Instr(2, strCookie, strName) 'is it in rest of string?
      End If
    Else
      intStart = Instr(2, strCookie, strName)   'is it in rest of string?
    End If
  Wend
  FindValue = strValue
End Function
```

Once we've got this function, which does all the hard work, retrieving a value from the cookie is
as easy as this:

```
Sub cmdGet_OnClick()
  If Instr(txtGetName.Value, " ") Then
    SpacesMessage  'no spaces allowed in name
    Exit Sub
  End If
  txtGetValue.Value = FindValue(txtGetName.Value)
  If Len(txtGetValue.Value) = 0 Then
```

```
        MsgBox "This value was not found.", 64, "Sorry"
     End If
End Sub
```

To delete a cookie, we just set a new value for the **expires** date. However, to be tidy, we first check to see if it's already there, again using our new function:

```
Sub cmdKill_OnClick()
   If Instr(txtKillName.Value, " ") Then
      SpacesMessage  'no spaces allowed in name
      Exit Sub
   End If
   If Len(FindValue(txtKillName.Value)) Then
      document.cookie = txtKillName.Value & "=NULL;expires 01-Jan-90 00:00:00GMT"
      txtCookie.Value = document.cookie
   Else
      MsgBox "This value was not found.", 64, "Sorry"
   End If
End Sub
```

The Form Object

Each **<FORM>** section in a document has its own **form** object. This allows you to retrieve or set the form's properties, react to the events, and carry out the methods appropriate for a form. For example, you can write code which runs when the **onSubmit** event occurs, and changes the **TARGET** (the name of the window which will display the page that comes back from the server) so that it is displayed in a different window:

```
Sub frmQueryServer_onSubmit()
  If strControl = "JohnF" Then
     document.forms("frmQueryServer").target = "JohnsFrame"
  End If
End Sub
```

Property	Description
action	Gets or sets the address for the **ACTION** of the form.
encoding	Gets or sets the encoding for the form.
method	Gets or sets the **METHOD** for how the data should be sent to the server.
target	Gets or sets the **TARGET** window name for displaying the form results.
elements	Returns the collection of elements contained in the form.

Method	Description
submit	Submits the form, just like clicking a SUBMIT button.

Event	Description
onSubmit	Fired when the form is submitted.

The Link Object

This object stores details of all the hyperlinks in the current document. Of course, if your page uses frames to display several documents, there's a separate **link** object for each one. The properties are very similar to those of the **location** object, containing the various parts of the address that the link points to. However, unlike the **location** object, there are also events that you can react to. (Two of these, **mouseMove** and **onMouseOver**, are similar and are included for compatibility between different browsers and scripting languages.) Here's an example that shows how you can use the **link** object. You can find it at this address:

        http://www.wrox.com/books/0448/code/chapter05/Links/Links.htm

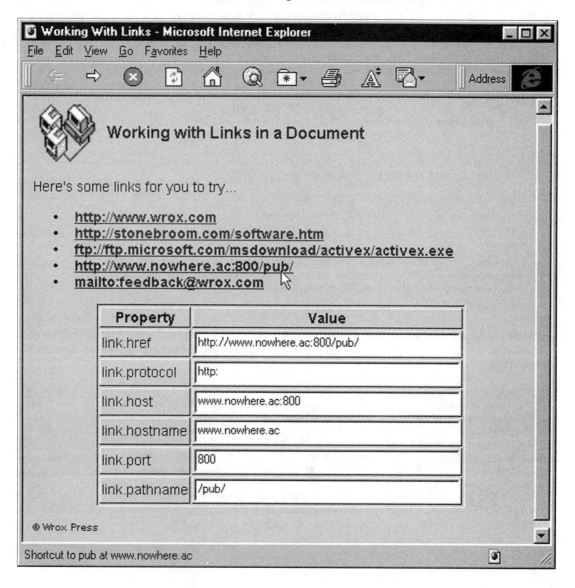

There are five predefined links for you to try. As the mouse moves over them, the various properties are displayed in the text boxes below. When you click on the fourth link, to www.nowhere.ac, a message box pops up with a sarcastic comment. And when you click OK, you're sent to a different location.

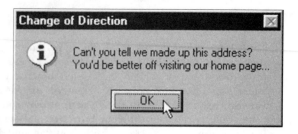

The table and its text boxes are created in normal HTML code, and it's the various VBScript routines that do all the work. We haven't printed all of them, because many are similar and you can view them in the sample page. First, the routine that updates the values in the text boxes:

```
Sub SetValues(intLink)   'intLink is the index to the Link's collection
  txtHRef.Value = document.links(intLink).HRef
  txtProtocol.Value = document.links(intLink).protocol
  txtHost.Value = document.links(intLink).host
  txtHostname.Value = document.links(intLink).hostname
  txtPort.Value = document.links(intLink).port
  txtPathname.Value = document.links(intLink).pathname
End Sub
```

Each link defines a **mouseMove** event routine, which calls the **SetValues** routine with the index of that particular link. Here's the first of them:

```
Sub Wrox_mouseMove(shift, button, x, y)
  SetValues 0  'the first link in the page
End Sub
```

To connect your code to the links in the document, you have to give each one a name. This is something new, because in normal HTML there was never any reason to name links, as you couldn't refer to them. Here's how we named the Wrox link in the HTML part of the code:

```
<A HREF="http://www.wrox.com" NAME="Wrox">http://www.wrox.com</A>
```

Changing the address a link points to is also easy. When the user clicks the link we've named **Nowhere**, the following subroutine runs automatically, before the browser makes the jump to the new page:

```
Sub Nowhere_onClick()
  Dim strMesg
  strMesg = "Can't you tell we made up this address?" & Chr(13) _
            & "You'd be better off visiting our home page..."
  MsgBox strMesg, 64, "Change of Direction"
  location.HRef = "http://www.wrox.com"
End Sub
```

By changing the **HRef** property of the window's **location** object, we force a different document to be loaded instead of the fictitious one defined in the link. Notice that, unlike the **location** object, the properties in the **link** can't be changed—they are read-only.

Property	Description
HRef	Returns the compete URL for the link.
protocol	Returns the protocol portion of the URL.
host	Returns both the host and port portion of the URL (hostname:port).
hostname	Returns just the host portion of the URL.
port	Returns just the port portion of the URL.
pathname	Returns the path name in the URL.
search	Returns the search portion of the URL, if specified.
hash	Returns the hash portion of the URL, if specified.
target	Returns the name of target window for the link, if specified.

Event	Description
mouseMove	Fires an event any time the pointer moves over a link.
onMouseOver	Fires an event any time the pointer moves over a link.

The Anchor Object

An anchor is just a location in your document that you can jump *to* (not to be confused with a link, which is where you jump *from*). It's defined using the usual **<A>** tag, but with a **NAME** rather than an **HREF** attribute:

```
<A NAME="MyAnchor">
```

The anchor object just stores these tags in a collection so that you can reference them. The only property is the name you assigned to the anchor.

Property	Description
name	Gets or sets the name of the anchor.

The Element Object

The final object on the hierarchy that we need to consider is the **element** object. This encapsulates all the different types of HTML control that you normally use in your pages. We used most of these properties, methods and events in Chapter 2, where we designed and built the Glass Load Calculator application.

Property	Description
`form`	Gets the form object containing the element.
`name`	Gets or sets the name of the element.
`value`	Gets or sets the value of the element.
`defaultValue`	Gets or sets the default value of the element.
`checked`	Gets or sets the checked state of a check box or a radio button.
`defaultChecked`	Gets or sets the default checked property of a check box.
`enabled`	Gets or sets whether the control is enabled.
`listCount`	Gets the count of elements in the list.
`multiSelect`	Gets or sets whether a combo is multiselect or not.
`listIndex`	Gets or sets the list index.
`length`	Gets the number of options in a `select` element.
`selectedIndex`	Gets the index of the selected option, or the first one selected when there is more than one selected.
`options`	Gets the `<options>` tags for a `select` element, with these properties:

`defaultSelected`	The currently selected items
`index`	The index of an item
`length`	The number of items in the list
`name`	The name attribute of the object
`selected`	Used to programmatically select an item
`selectedIndex`	The index of the selected item
`text`	The text of the item
`value`	The value attribute

Method	Description
`click`	Clicks the element.
`focus`	Sets the focus to the element.
`blur`	Clears the focus from the element.
`select`	Selects the contents of the element.
`removeItem`	Removes the item at index from the element.
`addItem`	Adds the item to the element before the item at index.
`clear`	Clears the contents of the element.

166

Event	Description
onClick	Fired when the element is clicked.
onFocus	Fired when the element gets the focus.
onBlur	Fired when the element loses the focus.
onChange	Fired when the element has changed.
onSelect	Fired when the contents of the element are selected.

HTML versus ActiveX Events

It's important to point out that the properties, methods, and events of the **element** object *do not* represent those for ActiveX controls or other objects. These all have different properties, methods and events depending on the actual control. And just to confuse you, the same events often have different names. For example, an HTML button has an **onClick** event, while the Forms 2.0 ActiveX command button object has a **Click** event instead. Remember that we're looking at the structure of the browser itself, and the **element** object it contains is there to allow manipulation of the standard HTML controls.

> *The easiest way to manage ActiveX controls is to insert them into a page using the ActiveX Control Pad, then view the properties, methods, and events that are available there. In Chapter 3, we showed you just how easy this is. If you want more information on standard controls take a look at Control Pad's help file.*

Reaching Out to Elements

Often, the hardest part of managing controls on your pages is getting the syntax of the reference to them correct. Generally, they are at the bottom of a multilayer hierarchy, and the reference you need becomes quite complicated. We've supplied a sample page which contains a mixture of forms and controls, plus a few links and anchors. You can load and run this example from our web site, at this address:

    http://www.wrox.com/books/0448/code/chapter05/Elements/Elements.htm

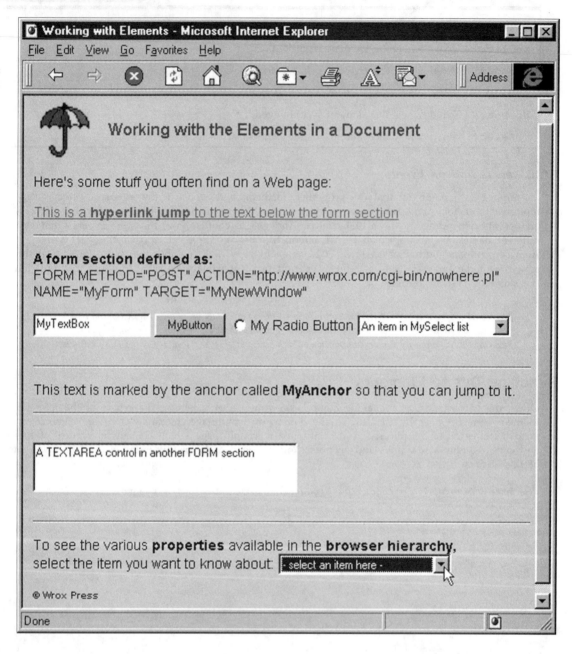

At the bottom of the page is a drop-down list box, which contains a selection of the properties that you may want to access from the various items in the page. Selecting a property produces a message box which shows the syntax of the statement needed to retrieve the value, and the value itself.

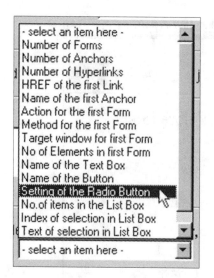

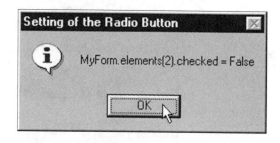

The VBScript on the page is very basic, using a **Select Case** construct to fill the message box. If you want to see how the example page works, just right-click on it and select View Source from the pop-up menu.

Browsing other Document Types

In the fully object-oriented future of computing, whenever it finally does arrive, one of the cornerstones will be the **document-centric** approach. Instead of deciding to open Microsoft Word to write your letter, and Excel to insert a column of figures into it, you'll just create the document itself. The operating system will automatically select the correct application, and look after streaming the data into a file which stores each application's data in an object-oriented way.

We're part way there now in Windows, because selecting a file will load the correct application for you automatically. For example, double-clicking a file with the **.htm** extension starts your web browser and loads the file. However, the future sees the browser merging into your desktop, and becoming the default container in which all documents are loaded and edited. This is going to be a whole new experience for most people, but if you're on the road to an Intranet in your company, it really does offer some exciting possibilities.

A Sample Local Document Browser

Here's an example page which loads local files and displays them in your browser. You can open it from our web site. The address is:

```
http://www.wrox.com/books/0448/code/chapter05/FileList/FileList.htm
```

As you can see, all the links except one are to local documents stored on your own drive or elsewhere on your network. Because we don't know what you've got stored on your computer, you'll have to edit the HTML source to change it to point to suitable documents on your own system.

This is the code that creates the links in the sample page:

```
<TABLE WIDTH=75%>
  <TR><TD><IMG SRC="Explore.gif" ALIGN=MIDDLE>
    <B><A HREF="file:C:\">Root of drive C:</A></TD></TR>
  <TR><TD><IMG SRC="Explore.gif" ALIGN=MIDDLE>
    <B><A HREF="file:C:\My Documents\">My Documents folder</A></TD></TR>
  <TR><TD><IMG SRC="Explore.gif" ALIGN=MIDDLE>
    <B><A HREF="file:Explore.gif">A picture of the world</A></TD></TR>
  <TR><TD><IMG SRC="Explore.gif" ALIGN=MIDDLE>
    <B><A HREF="file:C:\My Documents\Std_loan.xls">An Excel spreadsheet
    </A></TD></TR>
  <TR><TD><IMG SRC="Explore.gif" ALIGN=MIDDLE>
    <B><A HREF="file:C:\My Documents\Symbols.doc">A Word document
    </A></TD></TR>
</TABLE>
```

Clicking each link gives a different effect. The first displays a view of your hard drive, just like a normal Explorer window, and from it you can open real Explorer windows for any of the subfolders. You can also double-click on a file here, and your browser will attempt to load it.

The same effect occurs if you select a file directly from the sample page. The third link is to the graphic on our server that's used as the bullet-point graphic on the page. Your browser loads it like it would any other graphic, because it knows that a **.gif** file is a picture.

The two final links are to local files. What happens when you select one of these depends on which browser you are using. Internet Explorer will treat an **.xls** or **.doc** file in a proper document-centric way by loading it into the browser. However, to do this, it uses what was OLE, and is now 'ActiveX Documents'. With the Excel spreadsheet, for example, the browser actually starts its own copy of the Microsoft Excel **object**, embedding it in the browser window.

The process is called **in-place activation**, and you can see that Excel's screen furniture (toolbars, etc.) appear within Internet Explorer. The file is then loaded into this, and you can freely edit and save any changes to it—all from within your browser.

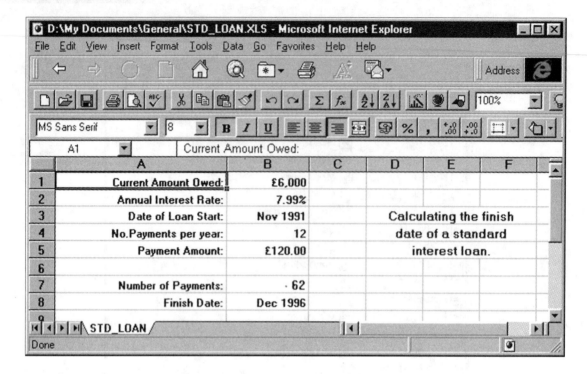

The only problem is that we can't guarantee that your system will behave exactly like this. The whole process is controlled by the settings in your Registry, and there are so many possible setup configurations that you could get totally different results (just as we sometimes do!). However, the technology is stabilizing, and this kind of operation will probably become the main way you work with files on your system in the not-so-distant future.

The Browser as just another Object

Lastly, in this chapter, we'll step back and take a look at the browser itself from an object-based point of view. The file that you run to start Internet Explorer, **IExplore.exe** isn't the whole application. It's just a wrapper which starts an instance of the **InternetExplorer** object. We can work with this object ourselves. Rather than creating an Excel object within the web browser, as we did in the previous example, we could create a web browser object within an Excel spreadsheet page.

Here's a similar idea, but using Microsoft Access. You can download it from our site and run it yourself if you've got a copy of Access 95 installed on your machine. The address is:

```
http://www.wrox.com/books/0448/code/chapter05/SiteSelect/SiteSelect.mdb
```

All we've done is create a small database containing a few web site addresses and descriptions. You can scroll through these in Access using the record selectors at the bottom of the window:

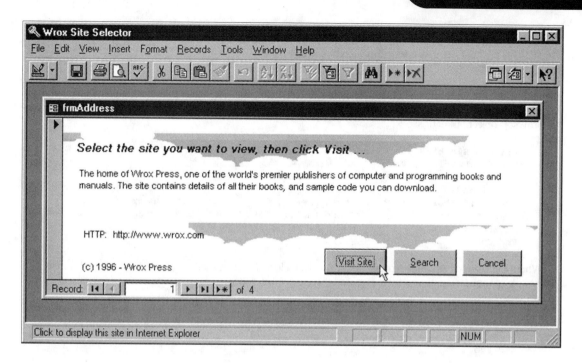

Clicking the Visit Site button starts up a new instance of Internet Explorer and displays that page. This instance of the web browser object is created with VBA code in Access. It belongs to Access, which can then control it through the properties, methods, and events it exposes. Of course, the language we use is Visual Basic for Applications, but it's very similar to VBScript. (VBScript is, in fact, a subset of VBA.) We've defined two global variables to hold the reference to the browser object, and a flag to indicate if it's been initialized (loaded) the first time:

```
Dim TheBrowser
Dim Loaded As Boolean
```

To load the browser, we use the **CreateObject()** function. (This is one of the Visual Basic functions that isn't available in VBScript for security reasons, because it could be used to create objects and then manipulate them to damage your system.) If **CreateObject()** is successful, it returns a pointer which we can use to refer to the object, and the first thing we do is set its **Visible** property to **True**, so that it's displayed.

```
Function LoadBrowser()              'load Internet Explorer as an object
   Set TheBrowser = CreateObject("InternetExplorer.Application")
   TheBrowser.Visible = True        'make it visible
   LoadBrowser = True
End Function
```

Once we've got Internet Explorer running, we can specify the page we want it to display. The code that runs when you click the Search button first checks that the browser is loaded, and if not starts it using our **LoadBrowser()** function. Once that's done, we can manipulate it just like we do with objects in VBScript:

```
Sub btnSearch_Click()
   If Not Loaded Then Loaded = LoadBrowser()
```

```
        'Call the browser's GoSearch method, just like clicking
        'the Search button in the browser's tool bar.
        If Loaded Then TheBrowser.GoSearch
    End Sub
```

The Visit Site button uses a similar routine, but this time we have to retrieve the address of the site from the text box on our Access form. Then we just use it in the **Navigate** method of the browser object, like this:

```
    Private Sub btnVisit_Click()
        Dim TheForm As Form
        If Not Loaded Then Loaded = LoadBrowser()
        If Loaded Then
            Set TheForm = Forms("frmAddress")       'just like VBScript!
            TheBrowser.Navigate URL:= TheForm.HTTP  'call the Navigate method
        End If
    End Sub
```

When the user closes the Access form, we can close the browser as well. All we need to do is execute its **Quit** method, then remove the object reference to it:

```
    Private Sub Form_Unload(Cancel As Integer)
        TheBrowser.Quit                 'call the browser's Quit method
        Set TheBrowser = Nothing        'remove the object variable link
    End Sub
```

We make no apologies for including VBA code in a book about VBScript. First, the two are so similar that you can generally grasp VBA without having to learn it separately. Second, true integration of the different Office-based applications with the operating system and your web browser will mean you are going to meet more and more of it as you go along. Besides, it should help you appreciate just how different types of object can be manipulated using the properties, methods, and events they expose to the outside world.

Properties and Methods of the InternetExplorer Object

Here's some of the common properties and methods that the **InternetExplorer** object supports:

Property	Description
LocationName	Returns the short name of the current document.
LocationURL	Returns the URL of the current document.
MenuBar	Sets or returns the display state of the menu bar.
StatusBar	Sets or returns the display state of the window's status bar.
StatusText	Sets or returns the text content of the window's status bar.
ToolBar	Sets or returns the display state of the tool bar.
Visible	Displays or hides the application.
Left	Sets or returns the left position of the application window.
Top	Sets or returns the top position of the application window.

Table continued on next page

Property	Description
`Width`	Sets or returns the width of the application window.
`Height`	Sets or returns the height position of the application window.
`FullScreen`	Displays the application using the whole screen.

Method	Description
`GoBack`	Equivalent to clicking the Back button.
`GoForward`	Equivalent to clicking the Forward button.
`GoHome`	Equivalent to clicking the Home button.
`GoSearch`	Equivalent to clicking the Search button.
`Navigate`	Sets the URL of the file to display.
`Quit`	Quits the application.
`Refresh`	Equivalent to clicking the Refresh button.
`Stop`	Equivalent to clicking the Stop button.

So you can use this method to add browsing abilities to the applications on your own system. With a little imagination, it's not hard to see how your Intranet can use web pages which include VBScript functionality, linked to your company's existing document resources.

If you want to experiment, you might like to try controlling the browser directly from VBScript in a web page, using its properties and methods. For example, `Explorer.FullScreen = True` *will turn on 'kiosk' mode, where the document fills the whole screen.*

Summary

In this chapter, we've taken some time to look in depth at the structure of the **browser hierarchy**, and the **properties**, **methods**, and **events** of the different objects that are part of it. Being able to manage the many different types of document that you display, while allowing full access from a scripting language, means that the **scripting object model** has to be quite complicated. But we've supplied you with some examples which make this easier to follow, and by now you should be feeling pretty confident about creating your own VBScript code.

However, bear in mind that the object structure of the browser isn't there just for VBScript. Other scripting languages use it in exactly the same way, so if you decide to go off now and learn JavaScript, or any other new scripting languages that appear in the future, you're already halfway there!

We've also looked at a couple of ways that the browser behaves outside its normal environment. Microsoft's browser, Internet Explorer, is itself an **object**, and we've seen how it can be manipulated using the properties, methods and events it exposes. We even went as far as to look at some Visual Basic for Application code in Microsoft Access!

So, in this chapter, we've seen:

- The hierarchy of objects in the browser and the pages it displays.
- An overview of the properties, methods, and events for each main object.
- How you can work with **cookies** using VBScript.
- Ways in which you can use Internet Explorer for more than just web pages.

In the next chapter, we start to look at what happens when things don't go as smoothly as our carefully-crafted samples might suggest. While we like you to think that they all worked fine first time, that's usually not the case! It's time to look more closely at the types of errors that can creep into your pages, and your web site as a whole, and how you can make finding and curing them a great deal easier.

```
<HEAD>
    <SCRIPT LANGUAGE="VBScript">

<!--
Sub window_onLoad()
  Dim objLst
  set objLst= dimensions.
                          lstMaterials

  objLst.AddItem "Clay Bricks
                           (3x8x3.5)"

  objLst.AddItem "Stone Blocks
                           (8x8x4)"

  objLst.AddItem "Concrete Blocks
                           (8x16x

  objLst.ListIndex = 0
nd Sub
-->
    </SCRIPT>
```

Analyzing and Debugging Your Pages

So far in this book, we've looked at how VBScript and ActiveX controls provide us with huge potential for interactive web page design. What we haven't really covered is how you can reduce the effort (and headache) that will often be needed to turn the design into actual pages on your server. Once you have taken the time to properly design your latest creation, you are left with the small task of implementing it. However, in the real world, you'll end up adding some extra features (or to be more accurate, bugs!) into your pages. What should have been a simple chore, now looks like a major undertaking!

Along with the normal bugs that you should always expect when programming in any language, there's another dimension to consider when you're working with the Web. Since we're merging two technologies, HTML and scripting, we have to consider not only the more usual types of code bugs, but also the flow of the actual HTML pages at the web site you're creating, and the links and references between them.

In this chapter, we'll be discussing some of the issues, and ways that you can track and remedy errors in your pages. We'll also look at a tool designed to help you manage your site. It enables you to document complex pages and generally helps you to identify why they may not be working as expected. This tool is created with a little VBScript programming of the browser, and helps to reinforce the techniques of managing the browser's hierarchy.

So in this chapter, you'll see:

- How different kinds of errors can arise in your VBScript code
- Ways of tracking down bugs, and killing them for good
- How we use the **Err** object to cope with different run-time errors
- Building a debug logging object, to make error detection easier
- A tool to analyze your web pages and to help you manage your site

We'll start by examining how you should go about looking for those potential bugs that creep into your code while you're not looking...

Where Do Bugs Come from?

No one ever wants to admit to creating functionally challenged code! However, bugs are an inevitable side effect of programming. The fact is, you will need to debug your code at some point. The question is, what types of bug do you have, and how should you deal with them?

Different Types of Error

The simplest types of bug in your code are **syntactical** errors, where you have inadvertently missed some code necessary for the smooth running of your program. This is possibly the simplest type of error to solve, since your program stops dead. Hopefully, it becomes immediately obvious, from the error message you receive, what action you should take.

Errors when typing variable names can be a little more tricky since VBScript allows **implicit variable declaration**. That's to say, a new variable will be implicitly created when the misspelled name appears in your code. It will have a value of zero, or an empty string, which is probably not what you intended. This type of error comes into the realm of **logical** errors where your code functions, but just not in the manner you intended!

The third general category of errors are those that occur at **run time**. These errors can appear if you have coded a loop that will run indefinitely, or when a user enters non-numeric input that your program tries to use in a calculation. However, at the end of the day, it's up to you to prevent the user from breaking your page. Code defensively, and assume the user will throw something unexpected at your program. If you allow for every case then there should be no problems. The trick is in finding every case.

Finding and Killing Bugs

It's important that we have a good strategy for debugging our web pages, and to identify and solve any problems that may be lurking there. Different types of bugs require different techniques to hunt them down. Once you find the location of a bug, you then have to modify your code to fix it. This in itself may introduce more bugs! Be prepared for this, and keep copies of your pages as you develop and fix them. Alternatively, you might even consider some source code control system to allow you to easily manage the different versions of your files. There are many such products on the market that could be useful for you to keep control of large and complex web sites.

Finding

Some bugs are easier to find than others. If the nature of the problem is syntactical, then the message you get from the browser itself will help identify it. You'll get an explanation of the error and a line number telling you exactly where your page finally failed, but not necessarily where the syntax error is located. Typical problems include forgetting to add an **End If** statement to an **If** block. If the code that's being run is in a regular document, and not inside a layout control, then the number will be a simple count of the line number in the HTML file itself. However, if the erroneous code is part of a layout control **.alx** file then the line number that you're given is actually a count of the number of lines after the opening comment in the **<SCRIPT>** block.

```
<HTML> <!-- This is Line 1 in a normal scripted page-->
<HEAD> ... ...
```

```
<SCRIPT LANGUAGE="VBScript">
<!--
'This is line 1 in a layout control
```

Rather than have many such blocks of script in a layout control, it's far better to have one block. If, for example, you have separate blocks of script for every object in the layout control, and an error is occurring after a button is clicked, it's likely to be in the event code for that button. You could probably trace through the code by eye, although this isn't a pleasant prospect.

One of the hardest types of bugs to find are those hidden in infinite loops. If you were to have the following:

```
Sub MySub()
  Dim intX
  Do Until(intX)
    If SomeCondition Then
      inttX = 0
    End If
  Loop
End Sub
```

then because of the typing error (**inttX** rather than **intX**), this code would run forever. However, the VBScript run-time DLL will eventually time-out after deciding that it has executed the code for an excessive amount of time. A warning dialog is displayed:

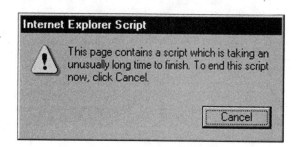

The big problem with this is that you don't get a line number for where the error occurs, and so you won't have an initial starting point for your bug hunting. This is because, as far as the script interpreter is concerned, no one line is responsible for the problem.

The Minimum Protection

The very least you can do to help protect the validity of your code is to use the **Option Explicit** statement, as was pointed out in Chapter 1. If this statement is found at the top of a script block, it means any variable you use, that has *not* been declared with a **Dim** statement within the block, will cause an error to be generated. This is subtly different from what you may be familiar with in Visual Basic or VBA. In those languages, the appearance of this **Option Explicit** statement at the beginning of the code module meant that every variable in that module had to be declared. With VBScript, it only applies to those procedures that lie within the same **<SCRIPT>** block as the **Option Explicit** statement.

```
<SCRIPT LANGUAGE="VBScript">
<!--
Option Explicit
  ...
```

If you're using Script Wizard to write a lot of your code, then you'll have to add **Option Explicit** to each and every block of script by hand. This can be quite tiresome, especially as

Script Wizard has a tendency to litter your HTML page with lots of small blocks of code. Also, the `Option Explicit` statement should be the very first statement after the opening HTML `<!--` comment tag. Placing it anywhere else in the block will cause a run-time error.

Tracking Information

If you have spelt all your variable names correctly, and you are still confronted with some erroneous code, you'll have to either read through your script carefully, or try and track the problem in a more scientific way. Currently, VBScript doesn't offer a robust mechanism for debugging code. The `Option Explicit` statement is only useful against typos, not in tracking **logical** errors. What you have to do is to add extra code to your scripts for the specific job of bug hunting. The simplest code you can add is the good old message box.

The addition of **MsgBox** statements to your code gives practical benefits, by demonstrating that a piece of code is actually reached in your script execution. They can also display the values of any variables that you need to examine at that point, for example:

```
Sub DubiousControl_SomeEvent()
  MsgBox "Some global variable = " & gintMyVal
  ' Code here
End Sub
```

You can use this kind of technique to watch just about anything in your programs. Because VBScript is interpreted, you can actually use the message boxes to determine how far through your code the interpreter got before a run-time error broke your code. This tends to encourage you to have a whole host of message box statements littering your code when you're trying to discover a particularly elusive bug. However, continually clicking the OK button can be a little painful; there are also a couple of real drawbacks to this technique. For one thing it breaks up the flow of what is going on, and worse still, it can actually change the nature of the bug that you're trying to observe!

> Don't be tempted to place a message box in a **timer** event for the IETimer control. If the **interval** is small then you'll find that message boxes are appearing faster than you can click OK!

The Heisen-bug Principle

If you ever studied any quantum physics at college then you can't have failed to meet 'The Heisenburg Principle' which essentially states:

 Observing something will actually change it.

This can also be applied to programming code as:

 Observing code for bugs can actually change the bugs.

We have categorized three types of debugging problems that can be introduced when you are attempting a debug session of your code.

 Actively looking for a bug will make it *apparently* disappear.

 Adding debugging code introduces new bugs.

Looking at the code with debugging statements modifies old bugs.

The best way to understand this is to actually examine a situation where it applies. We have put together a small sample that boasts an example of buggy code through the use of **focus**.

The following example can be found at:

http://www.wrox.com/books/0448/code/chapter06/errors/focus1.htm

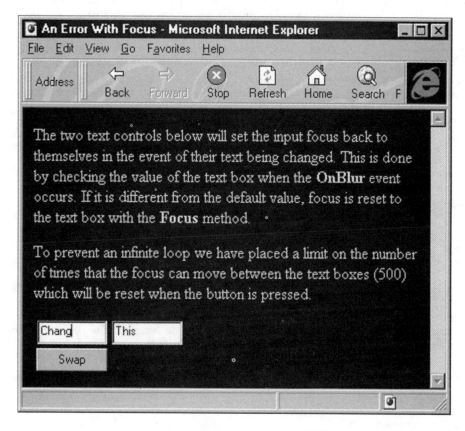

This small example demonstrates how some perfectly correct code can cause a bug to appear in your program, in the right (or wrong) circumstances. First of all, try the code so that it works as originally intended. Load the page, and modify the text in either text box from the default values of Change and This, respectively. Then attempt to move the input focus away from the text control. The **onBlur** event of the text control will call a routine, **LostFocus**, which sets the input focus back to the text box.

A bug will occur when you attempt to move focus between the two text controls, when both of them contain invalid data. This is where the Swap button comes in. It swaps the values of the text controls around without having the **onBlur** event check the data, so that they both contain incorrect data. It's now possible for an infinite loop to occur with the input passing back from one text control to the other. Actually, it won't be quite infinite in this particular case, since we don't want users' machines to hang. To prevent this, we've added some code to count the iterations of the loop and exit after more than 500.

183

Try this, move the focus to the first text control (now having the value This), and then try to move to the second control (with the value Change). You can now watch the input cursor flicker between the two boxes 500 times. This particular sort of infinite loop is even worse than that described above with the misspelled variable. Because each routine runs to completion before the next pass through from the other text box, the VBScript interpreter will never realize that your code is taking too long to complete and, therefore, will not stop the execution itself. In fact, you'll be left with just the one option of closing down Internet Explorer from the task list.

There's nothing wrong with the technique of checking input data with **onBlur**, but you do have to be careful about how you move the focus around where this sort of situation can occur. The code for the **LostFocus** routine is:

```
Dim gintCounter
Sub LostFocus(intBox)
 If gintCounter > 500 Then Exit Sub
  gintCounter = gintCounter +1
  Select Case intBox
   Case 1:
     If txt1.Value <> "Change" Then
       txt1.Focus
     End If
   Case 2:
     If txt2.Value <> "This" Then
       txt2.Focus
     End If
   Case Else:
      'Should never get here!
  End Select
End Sub
```

Obviously, the bug we've introduced is completely contrived, and we know exactly what's happening. However, if we were trying to genuinely debug some code, we might want to drop in some message boxes to see what's happening. We've provided another version of this page (**Focus2.htm**), which has some debugging message box code inserted. The only difference in this page is in the **Case** statement, where we've added a couple of message boxes:

```
Sub LostFocus(intBox)
  ...
   Case 1:
     If txt1.Value <> "Change" Then
       txt1.Focus
       MsgBox "Box 1 set focus"
     End If
   Case 2:
     If txt2.Value <> "This" Then
       txt2.Focus
       MsgBox "Box 2 set focus"
     End If
  ...
End Sub
```

If you swap the text of the two boxes over with the Swap button, and then attempt to move the input cursor between them, you again trigger the error. However, this time, there's a difference. You might expect to have to click the OK button 500 times to finally get out of the routine, but, in fact, three clicks will suffice.

184

What has happened here is that the message box is altering the states of focus in the page. This is an effect of observing something, and so changing its nature. The message box is very intrusive to the code's operation. What you need is some method of looking at your code, and the values of the variables in it, without moving the focus around so aggressively. To achieve this, we have put together a little tool that you can use to display strings of information about your program.

Building a Debug Information Viewer

Visual Basic, which is where the origins of VBScript are found, makes available the **debug window**. This is a window where you can **Print** information about various elements of your program, while it's running in the design environment of Visual Basic. The debug window is actually the screen representation of the **Debug** object inherent to VB, which allows your application to output information while you're developing and testing it. This is an incredibly flexible and powerful way to help you trace errors in your Visual Basic code, and would be a welcome addition to any tool sets that are released to help you with your VBScript code. Unfortunately, there is no help of this nature currently available, so you'll just have to do the best you can with the limited tools that are available, i.e. VBScript itself and the browser.

Requirements

The tool that we're producing should simply allow the VBScript to output data while it's running. It should not halt the code of the program like a message box would, and should have as little impact on the design of the page as possible; also, the data it's going to be reporting on could be in any format, such as floating point, integer, or plain text. Therefore, the tool needs to be data-type independent. Fortunately, VBScript only has the **Variant** data type anyway, so this is looked after automatically. The second issue we need to cover is where to place this data we produce.

Writing to a Text Area

There are a couple of places where you could have your debug information appearing. The first is in an extra control on your page. This is perhaps the easiest to implement. All you would need to do is place a **<TEXTAREA>** tag to the bottom of your page and simply add strings of information to its value property. So, if you have a web page that ends like this:

```
<!-- End of Text →
<TEXTAREA ROWS=60 COLS=10 NAME="Debug">
</BODY>
</HTML>
```

you could use this to report on anything in your program script:

```
<SCRIPT LANGUAGE="VBScript">
<!--
Function DivideCalculation(dblNum1, dblNum2)
  Dim dblResult
'Start a new line in the debug control
  Debug.Value = Debug.Value & Chr(13) & Chr(10)
  Debug.Value = Debug.Value &  CStr(dblNum1) & " \ " & CStr(dblNum2)
'Add calculation details to the Debug information
  dblResult = dblNum1 \ dblNum2
  Debug.Value = Debug.Value & " = " & CStr(dblResult)
'The debug text area now contains details of the sum!
```

```
      DivideCalcualtion = dblResult
   End Function
   -->
   </SCRIPT>
```

This may not seem particularly useful, but if you were quite reasonably expecting a result which contained a fractional element, and had not realized that your function was using integer division (the \ operator), then the information in the text box may well help you track down awkward logic errors.

Adding an HTML **<TEXTAREA>** is quite a useful technique, but it isn't always the approach that you want to take. If you have quite a large page that can't all be on the screen at the same time, this will require you to scroll about a lot. By doing that, of course, you might miss something else. Instead, there is another technique that's very useful.

Writing to a New Window

We can make use of the **Window.Open** method of the browser to actually produce a new blank window, which we can then write information to. This simulates the debug window of Visual Basic more closely than a simple **TEXTAREA** addition does.

We have encapsulated all the details of this debugging tool into a single subroutine that you can place into the head of any page:

```
   Dim gstrStaticInfo

   Sub DebugPrint(Line)
     Dim win
     gstrStaticInfo =CStr(Line) & "<BR>" & gstrStaticInfo
     set win = window.open(0, "Debug", 0, 300, 200)
     win.document.write "<HTML><HEAD><TITLE>Debug Information</TITLE>"
     win.document.write "</HEAD><BODY>"
     win.document.Write "<H1>DEBUG:</H1>"
     win.document.writeln gstrStaticInfo
     win.document.Write "</BODY></HTML>"
     win.document.close
   End Sub
```

How It Works

The first thing you probably notice is that we have declared a global variable **gstrStaticInfo**. This is actually a bit of a hack. We use it to hold the previous information that was written to the debug window. What we basically want is some way to either add new lines to the document in the new debug window, or to have a variable declared within the routine that isn't destroyed at the **End Sub** statement. In other words, we need a **Static** variable declaration. Unfortunately, VBScript doesn't currently support **Static** variables, and so we have to use a carefully named global variable.

The routine itself is straightforward. We declare an object variable, **win**, which is used to represent our new Debug Information window. The actual assignment statement:

```
   set win = window.open("", "Debug", 0, 300, 200)
```

requires five pieces of information. From the left, they are:

- The URL of the document to display in the window. We're writing the document ourselves, and so this isn't required here for us.

- The name of the window. This can be used to access the document, but we are setting a reference to the whole thing anyway.

- A string which describes what features of the browser window to implement, such as the toolbar, status bar, etc. We don't want any of the other options, so we just leave it with its defaults. However, we could easily add the toolbar to the window placing the string **"Toolbar=Yes"** for this argument.

- The last two arguments are the width and height of the new window specified in pixels.

Once the window is created, we take the latest bit of information to be displayed and add it to the front of all the old stuff held in **gstrStaticInfo**, then separate them with a **
** tag. All this information is then rendered to the window display through the use of a few document **Write** method calls. That's basically all there is to it. You can keep on adding lines of text to the window, so long as the overall character length doesn't exceed the maximum length for a string variable.

Once you have this code pasted into the **<HEAD>** section of your HTML document, it's available for use throughout your script. The routine can be called from anywhere, but you will have to remember where exactly the code resides. If you are using a document which is composed of three frames, for example, any routines in one of the child frame's documents would need to call **DebugPrint** with the qualifier for the parent document, like this:

```
Call Parent.DebugPrint("Some Debug Information")
```

This also applies for script inside a layout control, since the routine will be contained within its parent document and not its own **.alx** *file.*

This isn't the 'be all and end all' of debugging VBScript, but it's certainly an aid in helping you find those elusive code errors. There are some features to using this technique that you should remember:

- VBScript processes its code in the order it finds it. This may sound obvious, but what it really means is that a quick call to the **DebugPrint** routine will be significantly slower than displaying a message box. This is especially true if you have closed the Debug Information window.

- You will have to wait for the printing to be done before the next line of code will run. You will probably only notice this slowness when the window is first being created, so most of the time things will appear fairly quick.

Reacting to Errors

All of the above is fine as far as detecting errors in your code, but there are some situations that you just can't predict. These come under the general umbrella of **run-time errors**.

A run-time error is one that occurs during the execution of the program. With VBScript, this will often be some sort of data entry fault, such as taking the contents of two text boxes and trying to

187

divide them when one contains non-numeric data. At this point, you get the dreaded Type Mismatch error dialog.

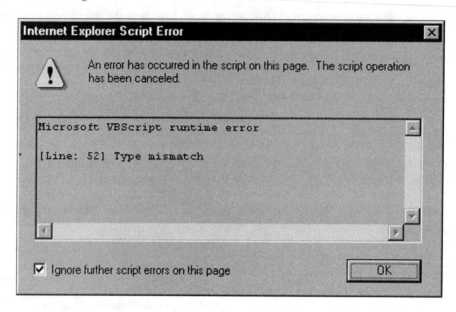

The result is that you leave your user feeling they've reached a broken and unprofessional page. Even though the fault was quite likely to have been generated by the *user* (probably a typo when they entered the values in the text boxes), it's generally accepted that telling them they are dumb is not a good strategy. So what can you do? Earlier, with the Brick Wall Page in Chapter 3, we bullet-proofed data input by using the **Change** event of the text boxes to make sure that the user entered numeric data. This is one way you can prevent a fatal error cropping up in your programs, but there is also another method: VBScript can be instructed to ignore run-time errors with the **On Error Resume Next** statement.

On Error Do What?

If you place the statement:

```
Sub MyRoutine()
  On Error Resume Next
  . . .
```

then the VBScript interpreter will simply ignore any errors it comes across, and continue execution with the next line.

This isn't necessarily a good thing. All that happens is that the user doesn't get the failure dialog shown above. The error has occurred, but we have done nothing about it, and so any resulting information generated by the program will almost certainly be invalid in some way. Using this statement will also override the effect of **Option Explicit**. After all, this simply throws an error at you when you attempt to use an undeclared variable, and **On Error Resume Next** tells the browser to ignore any errors!

You may be left wondering, then, just what *is* the point? The point is that, although you have ignored the error and skipped over it, the error has happened and something knows about it. That something is the **Err** object.

The Err Object

The **Err** object is a feature that's available for you to use at all levels of your script. It holds information about the last error that occurred. Its properties are:

Property	Comment
Description	A textual description of the error.
Number	A integer representing the VBScript error number or an ActiveX control Status Code (SCODE) number.
Source	String describing where the error occurred. If the error has occurred in an object then it will probably be its programmatic ID name (for example, **Forms.Tabstrip.1**).

The **Err** object also has two methods:

Method	Use
Clear	Removes all the information about any previously encountered errors. This is called automatically whenever an **Exit** or an **On Error Resume Next** statement is encountered.
Raise	To explicitly cause an error in your code. It takes arguments for the error number, the description.

Returning a Value from the Err Object

We generally use **Err.Number** to detect the occurrence of an error, and we've put together the following sample to illustrate the technique. This page can be found at the following address:

> `http://www.wrox.com/BOOKS/0448/Chapter06/Code/errObject.htm`

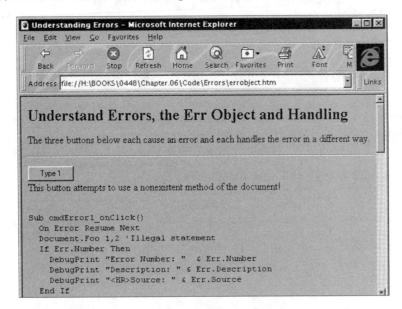

The sample page contains three HTML buttons that each cause an error in a different way. The first is shown above. When clicked, the handling routine will attempt to use an illegal method of the **Document** object. Since **Foo** isn't valid, an error will occur. However, we're ignoring all errors with the **On Error Resume Next** statement, so the only way we can tell that something has gone awry is by examining the **Err** object. **Err.Number** will only be zero if no error has occurred. In our case, there *is* an error, so the **DebugPrint** routine we created earlier is used to output some information for us.

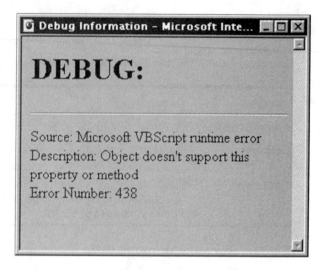

As you can see, we now have access to the actual error number (438 in this case), and also the description and source that Internet Explorer would normally display in an unhandled error dialog.

Knowing what problem these error numbers actually relate to is valuable. With it, you can create more elegant error handlers than the simple 'information blaster' we have here. For instance, while developing a page you may inadvertently misspell the name of a method for an object. As part of your debugging code, you could add something like this:

```
Sub MySub()
  On Error Resume Next
.... ...
  If Err Then
    Select Case Err.Number
    Case 438:
        DebugPrint "Check Method/Property spelling in MySub!"
    Case Else:
        DebugPrint "<HR>Number: "& Err.Number
    End Select
  End If
  ... ...
End Sub
```

Another use of this technique would be to re-enable the use of **Option Explicit**. Currently, **Option Explicit** is countered by the **On Error Resume Next** statement. However, by using the **Err** object in the way we've shown above, you can at least have a warning displayed in the Debug Information window. The error number for an undeclared variable is 500, so by adding a **Case 500** part to the code above, you would know that this was the reason for the error. (You'll find a comprehensive listing of all error codes in Appendix B.)

Of course, the reporting of an error to you, the developer, is not the only use of the **Err** object. You can use it to help the user at run time. Suppose that you have to carry out a calculation with data that they supply. If they have accidentally entered data that will cause a type mismatch error, you can trap it neatly and exit from the procedure, like this:

```
Sub SumCalculation()
  On Error Resume Next
  Dim intResult
  'Take data from text boxes
  intResult = Int(txtBox1.Value + txtBox2.Value)
  If Err.Number Then
    'We probably had a data entry error
    MsgBox "Check that you have given valid numbers.", 48, "Invalid Input"
    Exit Sub
  End If
  ... ...
End Sub
```

With this style of error handling, you don't actually prevent an error, but you do stop it in its tracks before the code runs on, giving some faulty information later. You can also, in some cases, get the user to correct their mistakes.

> *Note that when the **Exit Sub** (or **Exit Function**) statement is used in this sort of an error handler, it has the effect of clearing the error information, just as though we had placed a call to the **Err.Clear** method in the code. This has quite important consequences, which we'll look at after we've considered the call chain.*

Understanding the Call Chain

In the example above, we produced an error in the click procedure itself. Much of the time, you will have built your own functions and subroutines that also require error handling. In fact, you will often find that you have functions that have been called by subroutines, that have been called by an event handler, and so on. The exact placing of **On Error Resume Next**, and the use of the **Err** object, can have significant impact on the way that your code runs. To help you fully appreciate this, take a look at the sample page we saw earlier.

The Type 2 button has code attached that uses a call chain which contains an error. The code for the button and the called procedure is:

```
Option Explicit
Sub cmdError2_onClick()
  On Error Resume Next
  Call Faulty2 ("An Argument")
  If Err Then
    DebugPrint "Error Number: "  & Err.Number
    DebugPrint "Description: " & Err.Description
    DebugPrint "<HR>Source: " & Err.Source
  End If
End Sub
```

```
Sub Faulty2(strSomeText)
  strCopyOfText = strSomeText
  'Attempted to use an uninitialized variable when we have Option Explicit
  MsgBox "This will never display because of an error above!"
End Sub
```

When this code is run, you don't get a message box from the **Faulty2** subroutine. The **On Error Resume Next** statement in the calling procedure is still active, so the error generated from the undeclared variable **strCopyOfText** is sent back up the call chain. In this case, it's a very small call chain and the error is thrown up to **cmdError_onClick**. This event handler routine does have an enabled error trap, and so execution continues with *its* next statement, *not* the next statement in the erroneous routine! In this case, we have an **If Err.Number** block which displays the error information:

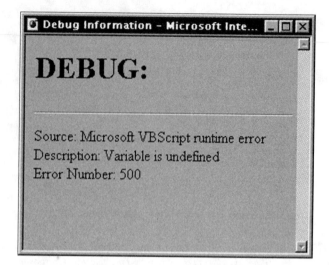

Having the error information displayed from a higher point in the call chain is all very well, but it doesn't make for easy debugging. You may find yourself looking for the error in the routine where it was reported, rather than where it actually occurred.

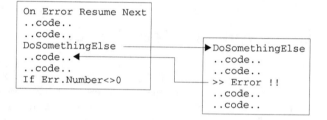

Handle Errors Everywhere

The solution, of course, is to handle errors in every procedure where they could conceivably occur. We won't pretend that this is a trivial task, but in a large project, you will appreciate the effort in the long run. With a great deal of the error handling code you create, you won't necessarily know the sort of bug that is going to occur. Because of this, much of the error handling is, in fact, going to be just some reporting for yourself. While the page is in development, you can place the code into the various routines, and remove it when you're happy with the result.

```
Sub ErrorCheck()
If Err Then
    DebugPrint "Error Number: "  & Err.Number
    DebugPrint "Description: " & Err.Description
    DebugPrint "<HR>Source: " & Err.Source
    Err.Clear
  End If
End Sub
```

Just paste this routine into the head section of your page and use it liberally; though obviously you will also need the main **DebugPrint** routine in the same place. Assuming a dodgy procedure has an error trap enabled, then a simple call tb **ErrorCheck** at the end will give you information about it in the Debug Information window. Notice the use of the **Clear** method. This is important, because, if you don't explicitly clear the error, you may find that you handle it in the wrong place, or worse still, more than once! To illustrate this type of situation we have the third button in the Understanding Errors page.

Pass Along the Chain and the Raise Method

This example illustrates an error that occurs in one procedure, is handled there, and is then handled again, more thoroughly, further up the call chain.

```
Sub cmdError3_onClick()
    'Note the lack of On Error here
    Call Faulty3 ("An Argument")
    If Err Then
        DebugPrint "Error Number: " & Err.Number
        DebugPrint "Description: " & Err.Description
        DebugPrint "<HR>Source: " & Err.Source
    End If
End Sub
```

```
Sub Faulty3(strSomeText)
    On Error Resume Next
    Dim dblBigNumber
    dblBigNumber = strSomeText * 10
    'Attempted to use a double floating point variable
    'with a string for multiplication!
    If Err Then
        DebugPrint "There was an error in the subroutine"
    End If
End Sub
```

The output that you get from this is:

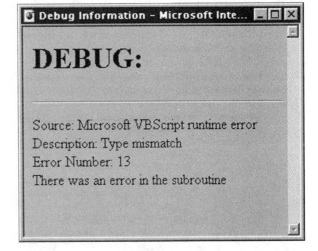

The bottom line of output shows that we have detected the error in the **Faulty3** procedure and have reported it. However, we did not **Clear** the error and, at the end of the routine, control is passed back up to the calling procedure, **cmdError3_onClick**. This procedure goes through the usual error check and report code again, and so we get the rest of the output. The reason that the code behaves like this is that an error is persistent, and you have to explicitly clear out the information about it if you don't want to repeatedly handle it. The obvious way to do this is by placing a call to the **Clear** method of the **Err** object immediately after you have handled it. Alternatively, if you handle the error by **Exit**ing the procedure, then this automatically invokes the **clear** method. VBScript assumes that by such an exit you must have handled the error, and so it is cleared.

There is one other occasion when an error will be cleared for you, and that is when an error trap is enabled with the **On Error Resume Next** statement. This automatically prevents a subprocedure that has error handling enabled, from handling an uncleared error that occurred in the procedure that called it. This does have some impact on the placement of error handling code. Consider the following code sample:

```
Sub SomeRoutine
  On Error Resume Next
  Document.Opn ' A mispelled method
  Call AnotherRoutine()
  ...
  If Err Then
      'Error handling code will not react to typo in method name!
  ...
  End If
End Sub
```

```
Sub AnotherRoutine()
  On Error Resume Next  'The previous error from above is cleared here
  ' Statements for the routine
  If Err Then
    'Error handling for this routine as normal
      ...
    Err.Clear
  End If
End Sub
```

There's a moral behind this little sample: you can't easily pass an error down the call chain. In fact, the only time that it's sensible to do so would be in a specific error handling routine, like **ErrorCheck** that we described above. In any other case, the error handling destroys the information about the error.

So, passing an error down the call chain is a 'bad thing', but you might want to pass an error up. Look at the following code sample:

```
Sub cmdCalculate_onClick()
  On Error Resume Next
  Call DoTheArithmetic()
  Call ErrorCheck
End Sub
```

```
Sub DoTheArithmetic()
  On Error Resume Next
  Dim dblResult
  dblResult = txtLeftSide.Value / txtRightSide.Value
  'If we have non numeric input then
  'dblResult would contain invalid information
  If Err Then
    Select Case Err.Number
       Case 13: 'type Mismatch
       'modify the error accordingly
       If IsNumeric(txtLeftSide.Value) Then
         Err.Raise 13, ,"Right hand side of sum invalid"
       Else
         Err.Raise 13, ,"Left hand  side of sum invalid"
       End if
```

```
            Case Else: ' Some unexpected error so leave it as is!
        End Select
    End If
End Sub
```

What we have done here is to allow the error to pass up to the calling procedure whatever happens. However, if it is a Type Mismatch error then it occurred because of non-numeric input from one of the controls. We can examine these controls and modify the error description appropriately through the **Raise** method. This allows us to set the properties of the error object, and can also be useful in procedures that do not have their own error-handling code. In this case, it can throw an error back up the call chain with custom information. The syntax of the **Raise** method is:

```
Err.Raise number, source, description, helpfile, helpcontext
```

The number and description arguments are somewhat self-explanatory. However, the description is optional, and if you omit it then VBScript will supply the text from its own list. The source argument is used to give the location of the error, and this will generally be Microsoft VBScript Runtime Error, although you can change this detail yourself. It is meant to be used within an ActiveX control and you supply the **Programmatic ID** string for this. The last two arguments are only useful if there is a Help file on the local system which can be used to give more information about the error. Again, these are generally used more with ActiveX controls than they are with your VBScript.

We have spent some time looking at the various cases of bugs in your code, and what you can do to protect yourself from their sudden appearances. It's time we showed you how useful VBScript can be in helping you look at the overall structure of your page by creating your own VBScript tool.

A Tool to Analyze Your Pages

To give you some idea of how you can build your own tools, which can help when you develop your own site, we've created the **Document Analyzer**. A web page can be a complex affair, containing not only VBScript and various objects, but also the more familiar links and anchors that we looked at in the previous chapter. When it doesn't work, you can spend a lot of time checking out all the links and references to find the error.

But what's even worse is that you may not even know a fault is there. Only when your visitors complain that they're getting messages about documents not being found, or missing graphics, are you aware there is a problem. Not only bad publicity, but another job you could have done without!

What the Document Analyzer Does

The tool that we've built allows you to load a web page into it, and it builds a report detailing its various elements—the forms, controls, links, anchors, etc. Once you've got this information on hand, checking that your site is working properly, and fixing errors, is much easier. The **Document Analyzer** uses the features provided by the **object model** of Internet Explorer, that we examined in the last chapter, to get this information from any web page. The finished product can be found at this address:

```
http://www.wrox.com/books/0448/code/chapter06/analysis/analysis.htm
```

195

and it looks something like this:

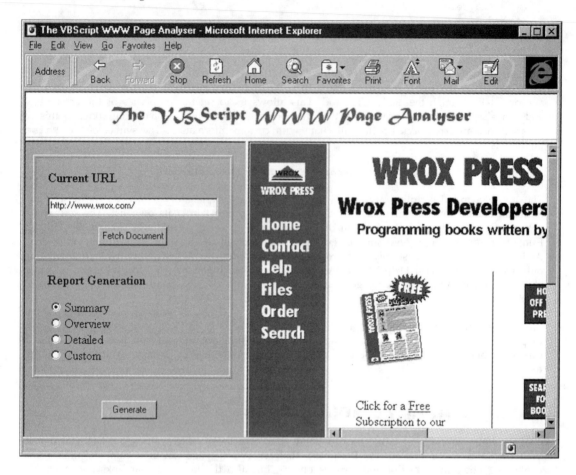

As you can see, there are three frames in the main analysis page. The top frame contains a simple banner graphic, included purely for aesthetic reasons. The lower right frame contains the web page (or document) that we wish to analyze. We're using our own home page in this example, but it could be *any* HTML document. The lower left frame is where most of the code for the tool resides. The report itself is created as a 'virtual' document using a new browser window. Part of a report on the Wrox web site is shown on the next page.

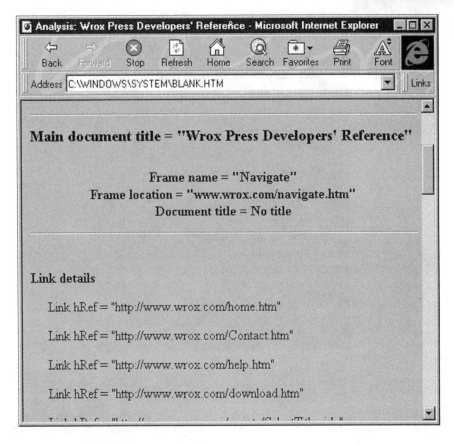

You'll notice that the address of this virtual page is, as we've seen in earlier chapters, the default document **BLANK.HTM** (or similar) which comes from your local drive. If you view the source code for this page, by right-clicking and selecting View Source, all you get is the contents of this file. This is because the page was generated using a few VBScript **Document.Write** statements within the browser, and not really downloaded at all. If you wanted to keep a copy of these details, there's always the ability to copy the contents to the Clipboard, or even print the page!

Before we dive into the code used to create the report we should consider just what we are trying to achieve with the tool.

How the Document Analyzer Works

To actually query the contents of another page with VBScript, that page needs to be loaded into the browser simultaneously with the Analyzer page. We can achieve this using the **<FRAMESET>** tag. Since we need an overall parent (top) document to hold the **<FRAMESET>** and **<FRAME>** tags, this will also be a convenient place to store some global variables and other procedures.

The left hand frame, where you control the Analyzer, has just three essential parts. The top part of the page allows you to select a web document to be analyzed, and load it into the right hand frame. Below this is the section where you can select the type of report you want, and finally there's the button that starts the process. This page also contains the VBScript code which actually carries out the analysis. We've named this frame **Control** in the HTML code that creates it.

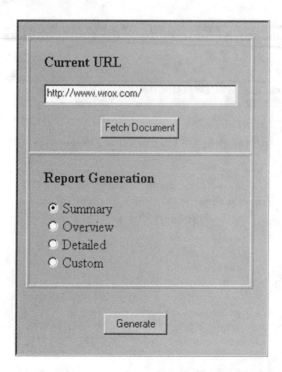

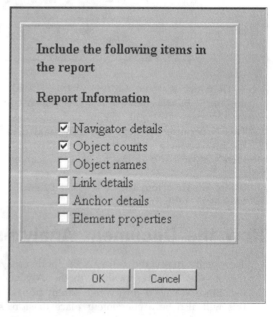

Additionally, we want to allow some customization of the details that the report will contain. This page gives general options describing how detailed the report will be, but it doesn't give the user any control over which actual elements of the page are included. To do this, we use the Custom option which gives you the following page.

We could have put these six check boxes into the original page, but it would have made the analyzer look a lot more intimidating, and left the page very cluttered. Instead, we have used a completely different page to allow different components to be selected. This is loaded into the left hand frame when the Custom option button is clicked.

This certainly looks better, and the benefit of this approach is that we have a couple of pages that are, in effect, **modules** of our complete tool and can be worked upon separately.

The Report Components

The report itself is composed of individual text entries describing the elements of the analyzed page. Precisely which of these are included depends on the options mentioned above that the user selects. The URL location is included in every report, and we have chosen to include six other basic elements in the analysis process:

Component	Description
Navigator details	The navigator object provides four properties. These are actually independent of the page, but may be considered useful if you run the analyzer from another browser.
Object counts	The number of each type of object contained in the page.
Object names	The names of the frames, forms, controls, etc.
Details on links	A listing of all the hyperlinks in the page and their **Href** attributes.
Details on anchors	Similar to the links, this will list all of the anchor tags in the document. This could be useful when checking that your link **Href**'s actually reference valid anchors.
Properties of elements	The HTML form elements that proliferate the web have a small set of properties. We shall use this component to report on each form element's property values.

Different combinations of these will be included, depending on the **reporting level** selected in the main left hand page. The options are Summary, Overview, Detailed, or Custom. The component usage is summarized here:

Reporting Requirement	Summary	Overview	Detailed	Custom
URL location	✓	✓	✓	?
Navigator details	✓	✓	✓	?
Object counts	✓	✓	✓	?
Object names		✓	✓	?
Details on links			✓	?
Details on anchors			✓	?
Properties of elements			✓	?

Interscript Communication

Using two different pages in the left hand frame, for selecting the actual level of report detail, does introduce an extra level of complexity. What we need is some way to communicate between these modules, since only one of them will be loaded at any one time. We mentioned earlier that the main document containing the **<FRAMESET>** would be a good place to store global variables. This is the same as the method we used in Bob's Builders Supplies application in Chapter 4:

```
<HTML>
<!-- GLOBAL CODE AND VARIABLES -->
<SCRIPT LANGUAGE="VBScript">
<!--
Option Explicit

'Analyzer tool global variables

Dim gstrRepLevel
Dim gstrDefaultDoc
Dim gblnNavigatorDetails, gblnObjectCounts,
Dim gblnObjectNames, gblnLinkDetails
Dim gblnAnchorDetails, gblnElementProperties

  gstrRepLevel = "Summary" 'Initialize
  gstrDefaultDoc = "http://www.wrox.com/books/0448/code/" _
      & "chapter06/analysis/default.htm"
  gblnNavigatorDetails = True
  gblnObjectCounts = True
-->
</SCRIPT>
<HEAD>
<TITLE>The VBScript WWW Page Analyser</TITLE>
</HEAD>
<BODY BGCOLOR=#FFFFFF TEXT=#000000 LINK=#006600 VLINK=#330099 ALINK=#FFFFFF>
<FRAMESET ROWS="60,*">
   <FRAME SRC="title.htm" NAME="Title" SCROLLING="no" NORESIZE>
   <FRAMESET COLS="42%,58%">
        <FRAME SRC="control.htm" NAME="Control" NORESIZE>
        <FRAME SRC="default.htm" NAME="View" NORESIZE>
   </FRAMESET>
   </FRAMESET>
</BODY>
</HTML>
```

As you can see, we have declared six Boolean variables to represent the state of each of the elements that can be included in the report. We also have a couple of strings. The first holds the reporting level description, and the second is used to display the URL of the page being analyzed in the control panel's text box. At any time, and no matter which page is loaded in the left hand window, we can always set and retrieve the values in these global variables.

Implementing the Main Control Panel

The control panel displayed in the left hand window when you start the Analyzer is really where everything comes together. The page contains an HTML **<FORM>** section named **ControlPanel**, which contains all of the controls on the page. This page also makes use of global variables. Here they are used as object references throughout the script to refer to things such as the option buttons and the new browser window, that we intend to create for the actual report:

```
Dim ref_RepLevel_Summary
Dim ref_RepLevel_Overview
Dim ref_RepLevel_Detailed
Dim ref_RepLevel_Custom
Dim ref_OutputLocation

Set ref_RepLevel_Summary = Document.ControlPanel.Elements(2)
Set ref_RepLevel_Overview = Document.ControlPanel.Elements(3)
Set ref_RepLevel_Detailed = Document.ControlPanel.Elements(4)
Set ref_RepLevel_Custom = Document.ControlPanel.Elements(5)
```

In the **onLoad** event of the left hand window, we check the global variables for the required reporting level. All of the option buttons are set to false by default, and if this is the initial loading of the page, the reporting level in **gstrRepLevel** will be **"Summary"**. We also update the text box holding the URL of the page to be analyzed:

```
Sub Window_onLoad()
    If Parent.gstrDefaultDoc <> "" Then
      Document.ControlPanel.txtURL.Value = Parent.gstrDefaultDoc
    End If

    Select Case parent.gstrRepLevel
    Case "Summary"
      ref_RepLevel_Summary.Checked = TRUE
    Case "Overview"
      ref_RepLevel_Overview.Checked = TRUE
    Case "Detailed"
      ref_RepLevel_Detailed.Checked = TRUE
    Case "Custom"
      ref_RepLevel_Custom.Checked = TRUE
    End Select
End Sub
```

The variables **gstrDefaultDoc** and **gstrRepLevel** are global variables, declared in the parent document (the main one containing the **<FRAMESET>** tags). Notice, that even though we refer to them as *global*, we still have to qualify their location with the **Parent** reference.

The code for the Fetch button isn't particularly interesting. It simply modifies the **Href** property of the right hand frame to that of the text boxes' contents:

```
Sub cmdFetchDoc_onClick()
    Parent.Frames(2).Location.Href = Parent.Frames(1).ControlPanel.txtURL.Value
End Sub
```

Changing the Reporting Level

The **OnClick** event of each of the option buttons in the Control Panel page is connected to a single subroutine called **SetRepLevel**. However, we supply a different argument to it, depending on which option button was chosen. For example, here's the HTML tag that creates the Custom button:

```
<INPUT TYPE=RADIO ONCLICK="SetRepLevel('Custom')" NAME="opt_RepLevel"">
```

The code for the **SetRepLevel** subroutine just updates the global variable **gstrRepLevel**:

```
Sub SetRepLevel(strLevel)
   Parent.gstrRepLevel = strLevel
   If strLevel = "Custom" Then
         Parent.gstrDefaultDoc = Document.ControlPanel.txtURL.Value
         Location.Href = "options.htm"
   End If
End Sub
```

Selecting the Custom button allows you to modify which items will be included in the report. When it's pressed, we load the report details selector page, called **options.htm** in place of the control panel. Notice that we save the value of the selected document in the **gstrDefaultDic** variable in the parent window.

Assuming that the current setting is Custom, we store the URL from the text box in the global variable ready for when the user leaves the option screen again.

The Report Details Selector

Selecting the Custom reporting level loads the other control panel into the left hand window. Here the user can actually specify the individual elements they want to include in the report. Again, since we only need to do simple setting and reading of control values within this page, we've used HTML **<INPUT>** tags to create the controls rather than ActiveX objects:

```
<HTML><HEAD><TITLE>Options</TITLE></HEAD>
<BODY BGCOLOR=#AAAAAA TEXT=#000000 LINK=#006600 VLINK=#330099 ALINK=#FFFFFF>
<FORM NAME="ReportOptions">

<TABLE COLUMNS=1 WIDTH=100% BORDER=1 CELLPADDING=15>
  <TR>
  <TD>
   <H4>Include the following items in the report</H4>
    <H4>Report Information</H4>
   <UL>
      <INPUT TYPE=CHECKBOX NAME="chkNavigatorDetails"> Navigator details<BR>
      <INPUT TYPE=CHECKBOX NAME="chkObjectCounts"> Object counts<BR>
      <INPUT TYPE=CHECKBOX NAME="chkObjectNames"> Object names<BR>
      <INPUT TYPE=CHECKBOX NAME="chkLinkDetails"> Link details<BR>
      <INPUT TYPE=CHECKBOX NAME="chkAnchorDetails"> Anchor details<BR>
      <INPUT TYPE=CHECKBOX NAME="chkElementProperties"> Element properties<BR>
   </UL>
  </TD>
  </TR>
</TABLE><BR><BR>
<CENTER>
    <INPUT TYPE="BUTTON" VALUE="OK" NAME="cmdOK">
    <INPUT TYPE="BUTTON" VALUE="Cancel" NAME="cmdCancel">
</CENTER>
</FORM>
```

Since we want the check box settings to represent our selected reporting level, we use the **onLoad** event of the window object to set all of the values. These are the values currently set in the global variables in the main page:

```
Sub Window_onLoad()
    Document.ReportOptions.chkNavigatorDetails.Checked = _
```

```
              Parent.gblnNavigatorDetails
         Document.ReportOptions.chkObjectCounts.Checked = _
             Parent.gblnObjectCounts
         Document.ReportOptions.chkObjectNames.Checked = Parent.gblnObjectNames
         Document.ReportOptions.chkLinkDetails.Checked = Parent.gblnLinkDetails
         Document.ReportOptions.chkAnchorDetails.Checked = _
             Parent.gblnAnchorDetails
         Document.ReportOptions.chkElementProperties.Checked = _
             Parent.gblnElementProperties
    End Sub
```

No prizes for guessing that the code for the OK button just reverses all of this to update the global variables with values selected in the check boxes:

```
Sub cmdOK_onClick()
    Parent.gblnNavigatorDetails = _
      Document.ReportOptions.chkNavigatorDetails.Checked
    Parent.gblnObjectCounts = _
      Document.ReportOptions.chkObjectCounts.Checked
    Parent.gblnObjectNames = Document.ReportOptions.chkObjectNames.Checked
    Parent.gblnLinkDetails = _
      Document.ReportOptions.chkLinkDetails.Checked
    Parent.gblnAnchorDetails = _
      Document.ReportOptions.chkAnchorDetails.Checked
    Parent.gblnElementProperties = _
      Document.ReportOptions.chkElementProperties.Checked
    Parent.Frames(1).History.Back 1
End Sub
```

Notice here, how the final statement makes use of the **History** object of the frame, executing its **Back** method to return you to the Control Panel page.

Preparing the Page

Now we come to the last button, Generate, which generates the report itself. This is where it all happens. As you can probably guess, there is a fair amount of looping through collections of the browser's objects, and much HTML formatting. But, before we dive into details of the implementation, we'll take a look at another generic function that we have created to make the task easier—**IIF()**.

If Not One then the Other

If you are at all familiar with Visual Basic, then you may well have come across the **IIF()** function, also known as the **Immediate If**. This returns one of two values, depending on the Boolean result of an expression passed to it. For example, the following code would give a message box with **True** as the text:

```
Dim strResult
strResult = IIF( 1 < 2, "True", "False")
MsgBox strResult
```

The first argument is the expression to evaluate, the second is what will be returned if the expression is **True** and the third argument is what will be returned if the expression is **False**. This function doesn't exist in VBScript, so we have created our own version because it's so useful:

```
Function IIf(boolValue, strIfTrue, strIfFalse)
   If boolValue Then
      IIf = strIfTrue
   Else
      IIf = strIfFalse
   End If
End Function
```

It's pretty simple, but allows for the code in our report generation to be made that much more elegant.

Creating a New Window

As you've already seen in several samples in this book, we are going to open a new browser window in which to write the report. We have already declared the reference variable we will be using for this new window. Actually creating the window takes place when the Generate button is pressed:

```
Sub cmd_GenerateReport_onClick()
    Set ref_OutputLocation = Window.Open ("", "RPT", "Toolbar=Yes")

    ref_OutputLocation.Document.Clear
    ref_OutputLocation.Document.Write "<HTML><HEAD><TITLE>Analysis: " _
        & parent.Frames(2).Document.Title &   "</TITLE></HEAD><BODY>"

    ref_OutputLocation.Document.Write GenerateReportBody()

    ref_OutputLocation.Document.Write "</BODY></HTML>"
    ref_OutputLocation.Document.Close

End Sub
```

The window that we create has no source document and so your system will use its default document for the URL. We have named the new window **RPT**, and set the toolbar option to **True**, so that we have a printer button available in case a hard copy of the report is required. In fact, this is the only way that you can save the contents of the report, since the whole thing is produced with **Write** statements. The **GenerateReportBody()** is where all the work is done, and we'll concentrate on the various facets of the code as we go along:

```
Function GenerateReportBody()
    'Variables used to determine level of reporting
    Dim blnNavigatorDetails, blnObjectCounts
    Dim blnObjectNames, blnLinkDetails
    Dim blnAnchorDetails, blnElementProperties

    'The report textvariable
    Dim strRepText
    Dim Crlf
    Dim Sep

    'Variables for documents objects etc.
    Dim DocumentCount, LinkCount, AnchorCount, FormCount, FormElementCount

    Dim IndexFrame, IndexForm, IndexElements, IndexLinks, IndexAnchors

    On Error Resume Next
```

204

```
    'Initialize Booleans
    blnNavigatorDetails = False : blnObjectCounts = False
    blnObjectNames = False : blnLinkDetails = False
    blnAnchorDetails = False : blnElementProperties = False

Select case Parent.gstrRepLevel
Case "Summary"
  blnNavigatorDetails = True
  blnObjectCounts = True

Case "Overview"
  blnNavigatorDetails = True
  blnObjectCounts = True
  blnObjectNames = True
Case "Detailed"
  blnNavigatorDetails = True
  blnObjectCounts = True
  blnObjectNames = True
  blnLinkDetails = True
  blnAnchorDetails = True
  blnElementProperties = True

Case "Custom"
  blnNavigatorDetails = Parent.gblnNavigatorDetails
  blnObjectCounts = Parent.gblnObjectCounts
  blnObjectNames = Parent.gblnObjectNames
  blnLinkDetails = Parent.gblnLinkDetails
  blnAnchorDetails = Parent.gblnAnchorDetails
  blnElementProperties = Parent.gblnElementProperties
End Select

Crlf = "<BR>"
Sep = "<HR>"              'Define ourselves some useful constants
```

The reporting level is used to specify which of the components of the page to report on. This information is assigned to the local Boolean variables used in the function. In the case of **"Custom"** being set, we just check which options to use by looking at the global variables in the parent document. These will have already been set by the code in the report details selector page.

Notice that, at the end of the code, we've defined ourselves a couple of strings which we will be using extensively for the formatting of the report. **Sep** gives a horizontal ruled line, and **Crlf** provides a line break in HTML.

Next, the code starts the report by creating a variable, **strRepText**, which will hold the text of the report. First, the URL of the analyzed page is added, then, if **blnNavigatorDetails** is **True**, the details of the user's browser are added:

```
strRepText = Crlf & "URL = """ & Parent.Frames(2).Location.HostName &_
    Parent.Frames(2).Location.PathName & """"

If blnNavigatorDetails Then
  strRepText = strRepText & Sep & _
    "<DL><DT><B>Navigator properties</B></DT>" & Crlf _& _
    "<DD>appName = """ & Navigator.appName & """" & Crlf  & _
    "appCodeName = """ & Navigator.appCodeName & """" & Crlf & _
    "appVersion = """ & Navigator.appVersion & """" & Crlf & _
```

```
      "userAgent = """ & Navigator.userAgent & """</DD></DL>"
   End If
   DocumentCount = 0 : LinkCount = 0
   AnchorCount = 0 : FormCount = 0 : FormElementCount = 0
```

Next, if the user has indicated that they want object names included in the report, this code gives the title of the main document enclosed in **<H3>** tags:

```
   If blnObjectNames Then
      strRepText = strRepText & Sep & "<H3>Main document title = " _
         & IIf(Parent.Frames(2).Document.Title = "", "No title", """" & _
         Parent.Frames(2).Document.Title & """</H3>")  & Crlf
   End If
```

Now we need to consider how to handle a document containing more than one frame. The following code gets a count of the number of frames, then sets up the **For...Next** loop so that the analysis is carried out on each frame in turn. We'll refer to this as the **main** loop from here onwards, and within it we'll be looping through each of the appropriate object collections, such as the links and anchors collection of the document object in that frame:

```
   DocumentCount = Parent.Frames(2).Frames.Length + 1
   For IndexFrame = 0 To Parent.Frames(2).Frames.Length
     If Parent.Frames(2).Frames.Length = 0 Or _
        IndexFrame < Parent.Frames(2).Frames.Length Then
        Dim FrameLevel
        Dim DocLevel
        If Parent.Frames(2).Frames.Length = 0 Then
          Set FrameLevel = Parent.Frames(2)
        Else
          Set FrameLevel = Parent.Frames(2).Frames(IndexFrame)
        End If
        Set DocLevel = FrameLevel.Document
```

We use the **FrameLevel** and **DocLevel** variables to reference the appropriate browser hierarchy objects in the main loop. Where you have a simple (no frames) document to analyze, **FrameLevel** will refer to the left hand Analyzer frame itself. Otherwise, it will represent one of the frames of the document being analyzed.

In the same way as we retrieved the main document title if Object Names is selected, we collect the names of the documents in the individual frames. Notice here, the use of our generic **IIF(DocLevel.Title, ...)** to determine what should be used when there is no title for the frame's document:

```
      If blnObjectNames Then
        strRepText = strRepText &_
        "<CENTER><STRONG>Frame name = """ & FrameLevel.Name & """" &_
        Crlf & "Frame location = """ & FrameLevel.Location.HostName & _
        FrameLevel.Location.PathName & """" & Crlf &_
        "Document title = " & IIf(DocLevel.Title = "",  "No title", _
           """" & DocLevel.Title & """") & CrLf
        strRepText = strRepText & "</STRONG></CENTER>"
      End If
```

The code for collecting information about the links and anchors in each page is really quite similar, and so we'll discuss them together. First, the count of each type of object is updated, then, inside the **If <blnObjectType>** construct for that object's collection, we set up another loop to iterate through the members. To format the report, we've chosen to use a definition list style created with the **<DL>** and **<DT>** tags. Again, we use the **IIF()** function to ensure that we always have something to report for each of the links and anchors that we find:

```
        LinkCount = LinkCount + DocLevel.Links.Length
        If blnLinkDetails Then
          If DocLevel.Links.Length > 0 Then
            strRepText = strRepText & Sep & _
              "<DL><DT><B>Link details</B></DT><DD>"
            For IndexLink = 0 To DocLevel.Links.Length - 1
              strRepText = strRepText  & "<BR>Link hRef = " & _
            IIf(DocLevel.Links(IndexLink).hRef = "", "No hRef", """" & _
              DocLevel.Links(IndexLink).href & """")
              If IndexLink < DocLevel.Links.Length - 1 Then
                strRepText = strRepText & Crlf
              End If
            Next
            strRepText = strRepText & "</DD></DL>"
          Else
            strRepText = strRepText & Sep & _
              "<DL><DT><B>Link details</B></DT><DD>No links found</DD></DL>"
          End If
        End If

        AnchorCount = AnchorCount + DocLevel.Anchors.Length
        If blnAnchorDetails Then
          If DocLevel.Anchors.Length > 0 Then
            strRepText = strRepText & Sep & _
              "<DL><DT><B>Anchor details</B></DT>"
            For IndexAnchor = 0 To DocLevel.Anchors.Length - 1
              strRepText = strRepText &  "<DD>Anchor name = " & _
              IIf(Len(DocLevel.Anchors(IndexAnchor).Name) = 1, _
      "No Anchor Name", """" & Left(DocLevel.Anchors(IndexAnchor).Name, _
    Len(DocLevel.Anchors(IndexAnchor).Name) - 1) & """")
            Next
            strRepText = strRepText & "</DD></DL>"
          Else
            strRepText = strRepText & Sep & "<DL><DT><B>Anchor details</B></
    DT><DD>No anchors found</DD></DL>"
          End If
          strRepText = strRepText & Sep
        End If
```

The **Form** objects are in themselves no more difficult, or interesting, than the anchors or links. However, since they contain a collection of elements which aren't necessarily of the same type (text boxes, buttons, etc.), they require some effort to get all the details we need. We created another function, **GenElementPropsReport**, to make this task easier, and we use it to analyze each of the forms we find in the document:

```
        FormCount = FormCount + DocLevel.Forms.Length
        For IndexForm = 0 To DocLevel.Forms.Length - 1
          Dim FormLevel
          Set FormLevel = DocLevel.Forms(IndexForm)

          On Error Resume Next 'Expect an error with ActiveX object names
          If blnObjectNames Then
            strRepText = strRepText & Sep & _
```

207

```
                        "<DL><DT><B>Form</B></DT><DD> action = " & _
                         IIf(FormLevel.Action = "","None", """" & _
                        FormLevel.Action & """") & Crlf &_
                         " method = " & IIF(FormLevel.Method = "", "None", """" & _
                        FormLevel.Method & """") & Crlf & " target = " & _
                         IIF(FormLevel.Target = "", "None", """" & _
                        FormLevel.Target & """") & "</DD></DL>"
                    End If


              If blnObjectNames And bln_ElementProperties Then
                  strRepText = strRepText & Sep & "<H5>Object names and Element
properties</H5>"
              ElseIf blnObjectNames Then
                  strRepText = strRepText & Sep & "<H5>Object names</H5>"
              ElseIf blnElementProperties Then
                  strRepText = strRepText & Sep & "<H5>Element properties (names not
selected)</H5>"
              End If

              FormElementCount = FormLevel.Elements.Length
              For IndexElements = 0 To FormLevel.Elements.Length - 1
                  If blnObjectNames Then
                    strRepText = strRepText & "<H5>Object</H5>"
                    strRepText = strRepText  & "Name = """ & _
                     FormLevel.Elements(IndexElements).Name & """"<BR>"
                    If blnElementProperties Then
                      strRepText = strRepText & _
                      GenElementPropsReport(FormLevel.Elements(IndexElements))
                    End If

                  End If
                  If blnElementProperties Then
                    If NOT blnObjectNames Then
                      strRepText = strRepText + Crlf
                    End If
                    GenElementPropsReport(FormLevel.Elements(IndexElements))
                  End If
              Next
              If FormElementCount = 0 Then
                  strRepText = strRepText & "<H5>No elements found</H5>"
              End If
            Next
        End If
    Next          '<- the end of the 'main' loop
```

Now we've reached the end of the main loop which is executed for each frame in the document being analyzed. In a complex page, with a Detailed report, this code will have run a good many times. All that remains are the formalities of tidying up the end of the report, and we can then return the string we've been building by assigning it to the function name:

```
    If blnObjectCounts Then
        strRepText = strRepText & Sep & "<H3>Summary Details</H3><UL>" _
                & "<LI>Frame count = " & (DocumentCount - 1) _
                & "<LI>Document count = " & DocumentCount _
                & "<LI>Link count = " & LinkCount _
                & "<LI>Anchor count = " & AnchorCount _
```

```
                   & "<LI>Form count = " & FormCount     _
                   & "<LI>Form Element count = " & FormElementCount & "</UL>"
        End If

        strRepText = strRepText & "<HR><CENTER><H3>End of Report" _
                 & "</H3></CENTER><HR>"
        GenerateReportBody = strRepText
    End Function
```

That about covers the generation of the report text. All the details have been stored in the
strRepText. This is returned to the **Write** method for the new document window we created in
the original Generate button click code. The only thing we haven't shown you yet, is how the
form elements are processed. The main loop calls the **GenElementPropsReport()** function once
for each HTML form element found in a document. Here's the function itself:

```
    Function GenElementPropsReport(Element)
        On Error Resume Next

        Dim TestVariant
        Dim blnChecked, blnDefaultChecked, blnEnabled
        Dim blnListCount, blnLength, blnForm
        Dim blnListIndex, blnMultiSelect, blnName, blnValue
        Dim strRepText
        Dim Crlf
        Dim Index

        Crlf = "<BR>"

        blnChecked = False : blnDefaultChecked = False
        blnEnabled = False : blnForm = False
        blnListCount = False : blnLength = False : blnListIndex = False
        blnMultiSelect = False : blnName = False : blnValue = False
```

The various Boolean variables that we are declaring here represent the typical properties that an
object *might* have. Since VBScript doesn't have a function which gives us the *type* of an object, we
just have to assume that the unknown object will have a certain set of properties, and examine
their values. Of course, an error will occur if we query a nonexistent property, so we have
protected ourselves against this by including the **On Error Resume Next** statement at the top of
this function.

Now we can check the individual properties. This section of the code determines if the assumed
property actually exists for the current object, **Element**:

```
        TestVariant = Element.Checked
        blnChecked = (Err.Number = 0) : Err.Clear

        TestVariant = Element.DefaultChecked
        blnDefaultChecked = (Err.Number = 0) : Err.Clear

        TestVariant = Element.Enabled
        blnEnabled = (Err.Number = 0) : Err.Clear

        TestVariant = Element.ListCount
        blnListCount = (Err.Number = 0) : Err.Clear

        TestVariant = Element.Length
        blnLength = (Err.Number = 0) : Err.Clear
```

```
        TestVariant = Element.ListIndex
        blnListIndex = (Err.Number = 0) : Err.Clear

        TestVariant = Element.MultiSelect
        blnMultiSelect = (Err.Number = 0) : Err.Clear

        TestVariant = Element.Value
        blnValue = (Err.Number = 0) : Err.Clear
```

Consider the case when **Element** is a text box. Attempting to assign its **Checked** property to **TestVariant** will cause an error, which, of course, is ignored because of the **On Error Resume Next** statement. At this point, we can set the relevant flag variable by assigning to it the result of a test on **Err.Number**. Because of the error, **Err.Number** will be non-zero, so the test **(Err.Number = 0)** will return **False**. Of course, if the property does exist, the test will produce **True**. Note that we also have to **Clear** the **Err** object ready for the next test.

Having tested all the properties, the remaining code just appends the results to the return string **strRepText** for each property where its flag is **True**. Notice the two small loops. Where there are groups of option buttons, or a list, we iterate through the elements so as to give as complete a report as possible:

```
    If blnValue Then strRepText = strRepText & Crlf & "Value = " & _
      IIf(IsEmpty(Element.Value), "None", """" & Element.Value & """")
    If blnChecked Then strRepText = strRepText & Crlf &"Checked = " & _
      IIf(Element.Checked, "True", "False")
    If blnDefaultChecked Then strRepText = strRepText & Crlf & _
      "Default checked = " & IIf(Element.DefaultChecked = "", "None", _
       Element.DefaultChecked)
    If blnEnabled Then strRepText = strRepText & Crlf & "Enabled = " & _
      IIf(Element.Enabled, "True", "False")
    If blnMultiSelect Then strRepText = strRepText & Crlf & _
      "Multi select = " & IIf(Element.MultiSelect, "True", "False")'
    If blnListIndex Then strRepText = strRepText & Crlf & _
      "List index = " & Element.ListIndex
    If blnLength Then
        strRepText = strRepText & Crlf & "Option Length = " & _
        Element.Length &_  Crlf & "Selected index = " & _
        Element.SelectedIndex & "<OL>"
        For Index = 0 To (Element.Length - 1)
            strRepText = strRepText & " <LI>" & Element.Options(Index).Text
        Next
        strRepText = strRepText & "</OL>"
    End If
    If blnListCount Then
        strRepText = strRepText & Crlf & "List item count = " & _
                                      Element.ListCount
        For Index = 0 To Element.ListCount - 1
           strRepText = strRepText & "List Item = """ & _
                                      Element.List(Index) & """<BR>"
        Next
    End If
    StrRepText = strRepText & "</DD></DL>" & Sep
    GenElementPropsReport = strRepText
End Function
```

While the Document Analyzer is a little limited in the reporting it does, it does cover the main features of the HTML objects you are likely to come across. However, when it comes to ActiveX controls and Java applets, the variety in object types, and the number of available properties, would make it very difficult to build a generic reporter to handle these. If you find yourself dealing with a common set of such objects, you may want to add to this function to handle those that you're most interested in.

Summary

We've used this chapter to help you think about those aspects of software development that can often take up the most time and which are, generally, the most disliked part of creating any kind of application—be it a new program or a web site. Once you introduce scripts and objects into your web pages, problem solving is more than just looking at the result in the browser and tweaking a few HTML attributes. You have to really start thinking about your pages as 'applications'.

We've looked at some of the issues that are involved in tracking down and remedying errors in your web pages. We also looked at a web page which is, itself, an application designed to help you manage your site.

In this chapter, you saw:

- How different kinds of errors can arise in your VBScript code
- Ways of tracking down bugs, and killing them for good
- How we use the **Err** object to cope with run-time code errors
- Building a debug window to make error detection easier
- A tool to analyze your Web pages and to help you manage your site

Now it's time we changed our focus to see what's involved at the server-end of the process. Before we come to look at how the server can interact with your VBScript pages, we'll consider in more depth the issues raised in the first few chapters. In particular, how do the ActiveX controls, or other objects, actually get from the server into your page and into your Windows Registry?

```
<HEAD>
    <SCRIPT LANGUAGE="VBScript">
<!--
Sub window_onLoad()
  Dim objLst
  set objLst= dimensions.
                        lstMaterials
  objLst.AddItem "Clay Bricks
                          (3x8x3.5)"
  objLst.AddItem "Stone Blocks
                          (8x8x4)"
  objLst.AddItem "Concrete Blocks
                          (8x16x
  objLst.ListIndex = 0
nd Sub
-->
    </SCRIPT>
```

Creating Your Own ActiveX Objects

The whole face of Web development has changed since Java and ActiveX hit the scene. It's no longer enough to be proficient in HTML coding techniques, and leave the other jobs to your Internet service provider or network administrator. Now, the web server and its client (the browser) have some very different tasks to perform, and you need to know a lot more about the basics of these—even if you don't intend to get closely involved in the administration side.

We're going to move on from the immediate concerns of programming in VBScript to consider how you can create and install your own objects and interface with the server. This is a huge subject area; we intend to give you an appreciation of what's involved, and some simple examples so that you are in a position to start learning more. In particular, we'll see how we can improve on the debug window we used in the previous chapter. We've produced a stand-alone object which achieves similar functionality, which you can drop straight into a page.

In this chapter, we'll be looking at the way that the browser and server need to respond so that objects, either ones you've created yourself or ones that come from other sources, are available for use in your web pages. We'll cover:

- The changing role and responsibilities of the server
- How you specify exactly which component is required in a web page
- Briefly how you can go about creating your own component objects
- The way you package, digitally sign, and install components ready for use

Even if you aren't the one who is responsible for administering your web server, you'll find some useful information in this chapter. And if you are considering an intranet for your own organization, you'll need to know a lot more about the techniques we'll be looking at here.

The Changing Role of the Web Server

The combination of the functionality of Internet Explorer, and the flexibility of VBScript, allows us to add interactivity to our web pages. In some ways, these new technologies are driving a change in Internet application development, and moving processing away from overloaded servers to desktop client machines. Consequently, the traditional role of the server is changing. It's no longer the sole processing center, and with the introduction of the **Microsoft Active Internet Platform**, it is no longer the only place for storing application code and components.

In most of our earlier examples, the server provided the HTML file which made up the page, and the other components it required—such as images and ActiveX controls. After that it had no involvement, until the browser requested another page. All the processing was done within the browser itself. In this scenario, the server is changed from being the code store *and* execution environment, to the code store only.

This requirement for the components to be made available on the client system has meant that the life cycle of Internet components has now changed dramatically. In the past, they spent their whole life on the server, being downloaded repeatedly to the client and then discarded when a new page was opened. With ActiveX controls, and other objects, they are downloaded on request, but then installed and run on the client platform directly. The next time they are required, they don't have to be downloaded from the server again. This process allows the component objects to be made available at the right time, and in the right place, so that code in your pages can operate successfully. It's generally referred to as **code download**.

What is Code Download?

In order for the script engine to utilize objects and components, they must be resident on the client machine. Internet Explorer uses a mechanism called **Internet Component Download** to control the downloading of ActiveX components and other files, from HTTP servers and local networks, to client machines. Active Internet Platform is part of the Internet Explorer installation, and it controls this process, ensuring that the components are correctly downloaded, verified for safety, and installed in the Windows Registry so as to be available in the pages.

The technology supports the download of ActiveX components (`.ocx`), executable files (`.exe`) and dynamic-link libraries (`.dll`), which are normally referred to as **portable executables**. When combined with **digital certification** and **code signing**, this process presents a robust and reliable solution to file distribution, both on locally controlled intranets and globally on the Internet. We'll be looking at these issues later in this chapter.

The Server as the Object Repository

The majority of VBScript code is developed on a client machine, so that it can be used on another client machine located elsewhere. This could be on the next desk, or in another time zone. However, we still need a universally accessible server to act as an **object repository**. No matter how hard we try, that stubborn server just won't go away! We need it to serve our HTTP requests, and store our mail and HTML pages. If our pages contain references to ActiveX objects, we need a central repository to store these objects, and the server fulfills that role. Regardless of what type of code we reference in our scripts (custom controls, executable files, or dynamic-link libraries) we need to store them in a central repository in order for them to be available, in what has now become a global environment.

The Platform-independent Server

Although, in the office environment, Microsoft Windows may seem to be the dominant operating system, this is not true of the Internet as a whole. There's also a possibility that your own server, which supports your company's intranet, is running an operating system such as VMS or UNIX. And if you are involved in design or publishing, you could well have a few Apple Macs hanging off the network as well.

Although VBScript started life in Internet Explorer, it will continue to spread through other browsers. And, of course, the millions of clients on the Internet itself are using systems based on a different architecture, as well as different browsers. While scripting languages themselves are platform-independent (providing the browser itself has an interpreter for that particular script language), the executable code of an ActiveX control is not. So we need to consider how we can provide objects which are available to all our visitors (without resorting to writing them in Java).

Getting Objects into Your Pages

In earlier chapters, we've looked at how the browser goes about finding the objects it needs when displaying a web page. In general, we've done this from a client-side point of view, but of course it's the server which has to be able to store the object and send it to the client on request. However, it's not as simple as just delivering it to the user's hard disk, like you would a zipped attachment to a mail message. It has to be properly installed on their system before it can be used in the page.

Inserting an Object into HTML Code

References to ActiveX controls are inserted into your HTML code using the **<OBJECT>** tag. The addition of the **CODEBASE** keyword to the **<OBJECT>** tag allows us to specify a source location where the component is located. If this code isn't already installed or is out of date, it can be downloaded from the server. Here's an example which inserts a pop-up menu object into the page. If the code required isn't available on the user's system, it's downloaded from **myserver.com** and installed as the page is being rendered:

```
<OBJECT
  ID="iepop1"
  CODEBASE="http://www.myserver.com/comps/iemenu.ocx#Version=9,67,5,1689"
  TYPE="application/x-oleobject"
  CLASSID="clsid:44232DD1-WW4R-21SD-FA2P-4512FFC56FT06"
  >
  <PARAM NAME="Menuitem[0]" value="Replacement Windows">
  <PARAM NAME="Menuitem[1]" value="Replacement Doors">
  <PARAM NAME="Menuitem[2]" value="Counter Tops">
  <PARAM NAME="Menuitem[3]" value="Flooring">
  <PARAM NAME="Menuitem[4]" value="Fixings">
</OBJECT>
```

However, the **CODEBASE** doesn't have to be a directory on a web server. The following tells Internet Explorer to look in the local directory **C:\Windows\System** for the file **iemenu.ocx**. The location of the **.ocx** file in this example is a local drive on the client machine:

```
CODEBASE="file://C:\Windows\System\iemenu.ocx#Version=9,67,5,1689"
TYPE="application/x-oleobject"
```

If the custom control has been developed by an Independent Software Vendor (ISV) then it will probably reside on the machine which acts as the server for the ISV's web site:

```
<! for a control located on your ISV's Web server >
<OBJECT
  ID="iepop1"
  CODEBASE="http://www.isvname.com/controls/iemenu.ocx#Version=9,67,5,189"
  . . .
</OBJECT>
```

215

You are also more likely to find the latest version here. Alternatively, if the control was developed by the IT department which builds and supports your corporate intranet, it may reside on a server somewhere within your corporate network:

```
<! for a control located in your IT department's network directory >
<OBJECT
  ID="iepop1"
  CODEBASE="file://\\yourserver\share\it\controls\iemenu.ocx"
  . . .
</OBJECT>
```

Specifying the Version of an Object

If a specific minimum version of a component is required for an application to run correctly, the **CODEBASE** directive can be expanded to include **Version** arguments. Then, if the client system doesn't contain a component which is more recent than that indicated by the **Version**, it will download the new version from the component object store, and install it.

For example, the server may have version **1,2,3,4** of a control **calc1.ocx** available, and you could specify that this is the minimum version of the control which is acceptable in your page by using:

```
"CODEBASE=http://www.myserver.com/MyFormula.ocx#Version=1,2,3,4"
```

If the browser doesn't have a copy of **MyFormula.ocx** with a version number equal to or higher than this, their browser will download and install the newer one from the server. However, if you *don't* supply a **Version** directive, the browser will only download and install that component if it doesn't already have *any* version of the component registered and installed. For example:

```
"CODEBASE=http://www.myserver.com/MyFormula.ocx"
```

will only download and install **MyFormula.ocx** if this component doesn't already exist on the client machine.

There is one other option. You can set up a selection of default directories called the **Internet search path** (these are stored in your Registry) then instruct the browser to search all of these for the *latest* version of the component. If you suspect that there are problems with a component you are using, this method means that your web page will always use the latest release of the component. The syntax is:

```
"CODEBASE=http://www.myserver.com/MyFormula.ocx#Version=-1,-1,-1,-1"
```

This option should only be used when all other options are unavailable. It can be a very time-consuming process, because it involves searching *every* server on the Internet search path for the component and comparing available version numbers. Then, lastly, the most recent of the found versions must be downloaded and installed. If many of these servers are at the other end of the Net, rather than the server in the office next door, there is an overall degradation of performance.

> *Remember that the* **CODEBASE** *attribute is only used when the browser can't find a match in the Registry for the* **CLASSID** *specified in the* **<OBJECT>** *tag (unless you've specified the* **VERSION** *as* **-1,-1,-1,-1**). *If the component already exists on the user's machine, and the* **CLASSID** *you specify matches, the browser will automatically use the local version.*

The Internet Search Path

We mentioned the set of default server directories that form the **Internet search path** in the previous section. The Windows 95 operating system allows us to specify a selection of 'default' HTTP servers or **Object Stores** which can be searched for components to download. This selection is defined in the Registry, and consists of a list of URLs which point to servers and specific server directories where components may reside.

By specifying a particular Internet search path, we can prevent the browser using the location in the `<OBJECT>` tag's **CODEBASE** parameter when **#Version=-1,-1,-1,-1**. This allows greater control of the download process, and is especially useful in intranet situations where the need for interaction with the Internet and the outside world can be totally removed.

Setting the Search Path

The Internet search path is specified in the Registry under the following key:

```
HKEY_LOCAL_MACHINE\Software\Microsoft\Windows\CurrentVersion\Internet
Settings\CodeBaseSearchPath
```

The key consists of the **CodeBaseSearchPath** keyword and a list of URLs.

```
CodeBaseSearchPath = URL1;URL2; ... URLn
```

These URLs are searched from **URL1** through **URL***n* for the most recent version of the component which is to be downloaded. They will generally point to a file which holds one or more components for downloading.

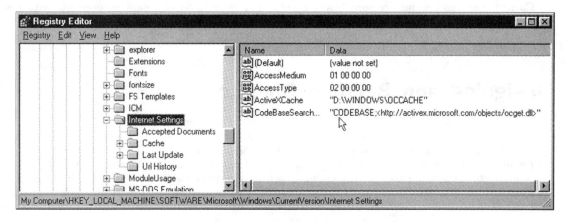

As you can see from the screenshot, the **CODEBASE** keyword can also be included in the Internet search path. This forces the download process to also look in the location specified in the **CODEBASE** parameter of the `<OBJECT>` definition in the VBScript code. The default position for **CODEBASE** is first in the path, so the object will always be loaded from the site specified in the `<OBJECT>` tag if it's available.

In the next example, however, we've moved **CODEBASE** to a different point in the path. **URL1** through to **URLn** will be searched, and only then the location specified in the **CODEBASE** parameter. The search will then continue from **URLp** through to **URLz**. It's important to remember that *all* locations will be searched until a component exceeding that specified in the **Version** parameter is found:

217

```
CodeBaseSearchPath = URL1; URL2; ... URLn; CODEBASE; URLp; ... URLz
```

Controlling Download of Objects

If you're working in a corporate intranet environment, you may want to prevent objects being downloaded into the user's system from outside the company network. By removing **CODEBASE** from the Internet search path altogether, you completely control the component download process. If **CODEBASE** is *not* contained within the path then the browser will only search the paths that are included there, irrespective of what is in the **<OBJECT>** tag of the page.

Platform Independence

In a mixed architecture environment, when using platform-dependent objects such as ActiveX controls, constructing a truly platform-independent corporate intranet becomes more complicated. It's possible for different components to be prepared for different types of client platforms, although at present only a limited number of platforms are supported.

Where there are multiple target platforms, such as the Mac and PC, careful planning can make the download process platform-independent. We'll be looking at this in detail towards the end of the chapter.

Storing and Caching Objects

At present, the download process is controlled by Internet Explorer, which has predefined directories for component storage and caching on the client machine. In the present release, components (**.ocx**) are stored by default in the **Windows\Occache** folder.

Currently, all components are stored permanently, and there is no automatic or user-driven process to delete unnecessary or unwanted components or remove references to them in the registry. No doubt this will be possible in future releases of the Internet component download software which controls the process.

Designing and Building Objects

While there are a growing number of ActiveX controls and other objects available for you to use in your pages, there will come a time when you have no option but to create your own. Perhaps the ones you can find aren't quite what you want to achieve, or are limited in the effects that they produce. It may even be that what you need is just too specialized and there are no ready-written controls out there to do the job. For example, you may have some calculation to do in a web page using one of your secret company-specific formulae. Obviously, you don't want the viewer to see how it's done...

Keeping a Secret with an ActiveX Control

You could implement a secret formula in your web page as a server-based process, by getting the viewer to supply the values needed on a normal HTML form and then submitting it to your server for processing. It would then return a new web page containing the result. However, if you want to make the page more interactive, for example, displaying the result in real time as users change the settings on a scroll bar, you need to process the information right there in the page.

If you produce an ActiveX control that can calculate the result, you can then insert it into the page and use its methods and properties in the usual way. The process is encapsulated and, unlike VBScript code, the user can't see how the calculation is done. Here's how the **<OBJECT>** tag for your new control might look:

```
<OBJECT
  ID="SecretFormula"
  CODEBASE="http://www.myserver.com/objects/MyFormula.ocx#Version=1,1,0,5"
  TYPE="application/x-oleobject"
  CLASSID="clsid:49322DD1-AF4R-28BD-FE5P-4720FCC56GD15"
  WIDTH=0 HEIGHT=0
  >
  <PARAM NAME="Temperature" VALUE="20">
  <PARAM NAME="Overload" VALUE="0.752">
  <PARAM NAME="Action" VALUE="REPORT">
  <PARAM NAME="Failure" VALUE="PANIC">
</OBJECT>
```

Then, when the user changes the scroll bar setting on the page, we can calculate the new result and display it straight away:

```
Sub hsbTemperature_Change()
   SecretFormula.Temperature = hsbTemperature.Value    'set the parameters
   SecretFormula.Overload = hsbOverload.Value
   SecretFormula.Action = txtAction.Text
   SecretFormula.Failure = txtFailure.Text
   SecretFormula.ProcessData                           'process the values
   lblResult.Caption = SecretFormula.DataResult        'display the result
End Sub
```

Developing a DebugLog Control

In Chapter 6, we used VBScript to provide a feature which is sadly missing from the current interpreter's error-handling arsenal. One of the easiest ways to find errors in any programming language is to monitor the code as it runs by dumping intermediate values and messages into a separate window, usually called a debug window.

While our VBScript example works well, it does suffer from a couple of problems. It has to redraw the whole page each time you add a line of text, because you can't append data to an existing HTML page while it's displayed. This tends to slow the process down and the redraws make the window flicker.

A better way is to implement a debug log as a separate process, which can operate invisibly. This simply means that it can update the text in the log itself, while the VBScript code in the page is running. To do this, we have to implement it as a separate component, and we've chosen to use the ActiveX control format and build it using Visual Basic 4. Although we can't create a true **.ocx** control, VB4 does allow us to build an **in-process OLE server** as a dynamic-link library (**.dll**). This is the format we'll be using for our DebugLog control. An in-process OLE server works in a similar way to an ActiveX control, but it isn't a *control* as such. It can't be manipulated using the Control Pad, like the normal ActiveX controls we've used in previous chapters can.

Using the DebugLog Control

We've supplied a sample page which uses the DebugLog control for you to try. You can use it yourself for a variety of applications, and modify it as you wish, or use it as a guide to creating your own more complicated controls. And because it's only an example, we haven't **signed** the control, so it will display a warning message each time you use it.

You can try out the DebugLog control yourself, by opening the page

`http://www.wrox.com/books/0448/code/chapter07/DebugLog.htm`

from our server. To run a Visual Basic application, your system must have certain VB run-time files installed. If you have installed VB4 itself, or any applications written with it, you will already have these files and your browser will just download our new **debuglog.dll***. If not, the run-time files will be downloaded as well. These are large files, so it can be a long process. However, it only needs to be done once.*

Loading the page will display a warning dialog, telling you that it uses an object which hasn't been certified, and then another to say there is a script in the page which will use the object. Once past these, the browser reveals a simple set of instructions, and a button. The button runs a small VBScript routine which just causes an error, then uses DebugLog to append details of the error to a text file called **wroxlog.txt**, placed in the root of your **C:** drive.

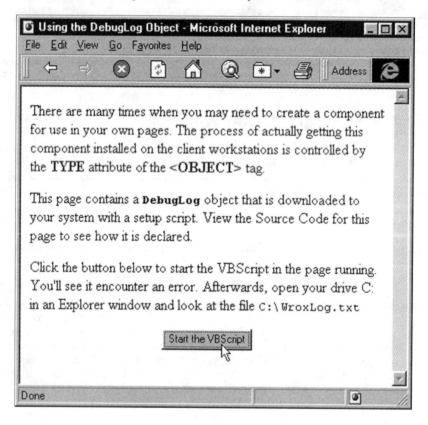

If you right-click on the page and select View Source, you can examine the HTML code that creates the page. Here's the **<OBJECT>** tag, and the code that creates the push button:

```
<OBJECT ID="dbg" WIDTH=1 HEIGHT=1
 CLASSID="CLSID:3F18BC14-2120-11D0-AB39-0020AF71E433"
 CODEBASE="http://www.wrox.com/books/0448/code/chapter07/controls/
                                                  debugLog.inf"
 TYPE="application/x-setupscript">
</OBJECT>

<CENTER>
<INPUT TYPE="Button" NAME="cmdDebugUse" VALUE=" Start the VBScript ">
</CENTER>
```

When you click the button on the page, you first see a message box telling you there's going to be an error (it's only there to show that the routine has actually run!). Then you can open the file **wroxlog.txt** and see the error text written to it.

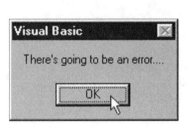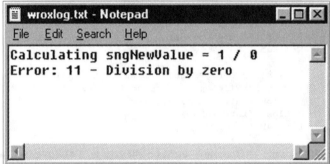

All we've done in the routine is to execute some VBScript code which causes an error. To prevent the browser showing the normal error dialog, we include the **On Error Resume Next** statement. Then we can examine the **Err** object, and print its property values (the error number and description) to the log file using the **DebugPrint** method of our new DebugLog object (which we named **dbg** in the **<OBJECT>** tag).

```
<SCRIPT LANGUAGE="VBScript">
<!-- begin to hide script contents from old browsers.
Option Explicit

Sub cmdDebugUse_onClick()
  On Error Resume Next
  MsgBox "There's going to be an error...."
  sngNewValue = 1 / 0
  If Err.Number <> 0 Then
    dbg.DebugPrint "Calculating sngNewValue = 1 / 0"
    dbg.DebugPrint "Error: " & Err.Number & " - " & Err.Description
    dbg.DebugPrint ""
  End If
End Sub
-->
</SCRIPT>
```

221

You can print other text or values to the file as well. Here, we're printing a note of what we were doing at the time the error occurred. And, of course, we could print the value of the other **Err** object properties, the value of any other object's properties, or the value of any variables we want to examine at that point, and other information such as time and date.

Designing and Building the DebugLog Control

So, having seen what the DebugLog control does, let's have a brief look at how it was created. Visual Basic 4 (except for the Standard Edition) allows you to create in-process OLE servers which, in the new terminology, are basically just ActiveX objects.

The amount of code required for such a simple object is tiny. Here's the full listing of the class file, **DebugLog.cls**, as seen in Visual Basic:

```
Option Explicit
Private strFileLog As String
Private intFileNum As Integer

Private Sub Class_Initialize()
  strFileLog = "c:\wroxlog.txt"
  intFileNum = FreeFile
End Sub

Public Sub DebugPrint(strLine As String)
  Open strFileLog For Append As intFileNum
  Print #intFileNum, strLine
  Close (intFileNum)
End Sub
```

As you can see, the only **Public** method is **DebugPrint**, and there are no **Public** properties. The **Initialize()** event, which occurs when the control is first loaded, is just used to set the file name and get a file handle. Then the **DebugPrint** method can open the file in **Append** mode, print the text which appears in its argument, and close the file again. We have given the class a name of **Log** which will form part of its programmatic ID when the object has its details placed in the Registry. All very simple stuff, especially if you're used to Visual Basic.

The only other code required is the **main()** subroutine which appears in **modMain.bas,** and because we only want to create an object from it, the **main()** routine is empty, and the application isn't run as such.

```
Sub main()
'dummy
End Sub
```

All that is left to do is set the options for the project. In Visual Basic, bring up the Options dialog and click the Project tab. You need to enter a useful project name—we've used **wxDebug**. As well as the Class name, the object will have a programmatic ID, **wxDebug.Log**, from where we can find the class ID. The project is then compiled using the Make OLE DLL File option, and the result is a **.dll** file, rather than an **.exe**. All this contains is our new **DebugLog** class, from which we can create a new object instance with an appropriate **<OBJECT>** tag in our page. Then we can use its single method **DebugPrint**.

Packaging and Signing Objects

Having produced our object, we now have to consider how we're going to get it onto the user's system. The sample DebugLog, that we built in the previous section, is itself just a single file which can simply be downloaded on demand from our own web server. However, there are several reasons why you should consider other methods of **packaging** them to get them safely to the end-user. For example, our DebugLog requires a set of Visual Basic run-time files before it will work, so we also had to provide a package containing these, so that they could be downloaded to systems where they weren't already available.

There's also the problem of security. As we saw in Chapter 3, the browser won't allow you to download and run just any object. It produces stern warning messages unless the object is **signed**, so that it is known to have come from a reputable source. By packaging the various components, we can ensure that they are all available, and that they have not been tampered with.

Obviously, when a user opens one of your pages, the various components need to be available from somewhere. If a graphic is missing, they'll see a 'hole' where it should have been. However, if an object such as an ActiveX control is missing, the page just won't work as intended. In this and earlier chapters, we've considered in depth where the objects required for a page could be stored. All we've got to do is make sure our object is actually stored there, and is in a format that the browser can understand.

Object Packaging Formats

The process of creating the files to be downloaded can range from being very simple (when only one file needs to be downloaded) to very complex (when multiple file types and versions must be copied from the server, installed in different folders, and their details added to the Registry). Each method can be fraught with pitfalls. However, careful consideration of the 'features' of each method will indicate which is preferable. There are basically three ways that you can package objects for downloading into the browser. Here, we are mainly considering ActiveX components, though Java applets can be packaged in a similar way. The object could consist of:

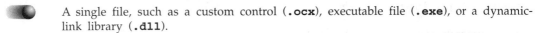 A single file, such as a custom control (**.ocx**), executable file (**.exe**), or a dynamic-link library (**.dll**).

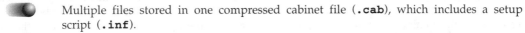 Multiple files stored in one compressed cabinet file (**.cab**), which includes a setup script (**.inf**).

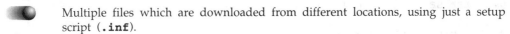 Multiple files which are downloaded from different locations, using just a setup script (**.inf**).

We'll look at each of these in turn.

> *You'll find a lot of useful information in the ActiveX SDK. You can download the complete SDK (all 13MB of it!) from:*
>
> **http://microsoft.com/intdev/sdk** or **ftp://ftp.microsoft.com/intdev/sdk**

Single Files (Portable Executables)

These are custom-developed objects (**.ocx**, **.exe**, **.dll**) which are single stand-alone files, and which don't need other files in order to execute correctly. Once they have been created, you simply place them on the server, in the appropriate directory, and then use the **CODEBASE** parameter in the **<OBJECT>** statement to point to this location. This can be local, in the case of an intranet, or an HTTP address for downloading it over the Net. Once the component has been downloaded, the browser will complete the process by automatically caching and registering the component. As we've seen earlier, the following HTML code inserts the **iemenu.ocx** pop-up menu control into a document:

```
<OBJECT
   ID="iepop1"
   CODEBASE="http://www.myserver.com/comps/iemenu.ocx"
   TYPE="application/x-oleobject"
   CLASSID="clsid:44232DD1-WW4R-21SD-FA2P-4512FFC56FT06"
   >
   . . .
</OBJECT>
```

Portable executables provide the simplest download method in terms of design and execution, but it's also the least flexible. Direct downloading of portable executables doesn't allow us to use file compression to speed up the download, or include multiple files in one download process, though it is a very easy method to set up and test.

Using the Portable Executable Download Method

All we need to do is ensure that the component is located on the server in a suitable directory which isn't password protected, and which allows public access. Then, the **CODEBASE** statement in the object declaration in our HTML page instructs the browser to retrieve the component and install and register it automatically. The **TYPE** attribute tells the browser what type of file it has downloaded and how to deal with it. Generally this has been **application/x-oleobject** for ActiveX controls, but our DebugLog sample used **application/x-setupscript**. We'll discuss this is more detail later in the chapter.

The **CODEBASE** statement should include a fully specified location which contains the component name. The location can be either a URL or a fully specified path and filename. Remember that you can specify the minimum version of the object, by adding the optional version number to the end of the **CODEBASE** as we saw earlier in this chapter.

Cabinet Files (.cab)

If you need to supply several files, or want to compress the file(s) you are using, you should consider building a cabinet file. These files can contain any number of component files (**.ocx**, **.exe**, **.dll**) and one **.inf** script file which controls the installation and registration process.

This download mechanism requires more work from the component developer than the portable executable method, but results in a more sophisticated download process. In particular, cabinet files are a popular method because they allow the use of data compression techniques to reduce the size of files to be downloaded.

Creating Cabinet Files

The **.cab** file is created using the **Diamond** tool (`diantz.exe`), which is supplied with the ActiveX SDK. The process involves three steps:

- Creating the **.ddf** file, which controls the building of the cabinet file
- Creating the **.inf** file which controls the installation at the client end
- Actually creating the **.cab** file using `diantz.exe`

Creating the .ddf File

The first step in the process is to create the **.ddf** file. This is used as the input to the Diamond tool, which ultimately creates the **.cab** file. The **.ddf** file contains the cabinet name, the names of the components to be included, and the name of the **.inf** file which will control the installation on the client:

```
.OPTION EXPLICIT
.Set CabinetNameTemplate=calc1.cab
.Set Cabinet=on
.Set Compress=on
MyFormual.ocx
MyFormula.inf
```

This example is the minimum required for a **.ddf** file. It includes the **.OPTION EXPLICIT** directive which aids in the debugging process by identifying errors in variable names. Although not mandatory, this line of code should be standard in all your files. Next, it defines the name of the cabinet file you want to create. The **.cab** extension *is* mandatory. The next directives tell Diamond that, yes please, we do want to create a cabinet file, and we would also like it to be compressed. Then, lastly, we just list the files we want to include in the cabinet file (including a path, if they're not in the same folder as Diamond.)

> The actual **.cab** file will end up in a `disk1` subfolder.

Comments can, and should, be added to **.ddf** files by using a semi colon as the first character.

```
;An example of a comment in a .DDF file
```

It's good practice to code the **.ddf** file first as it forces you to declare all components which are part of the download. The **.ddf** can then be used as a checklist when the **.inf** file is being created, to ensure all components are included.

Creating the .inf File

The **.inf** file consists of directives for the installation of the components being downloaded. It needs to be specified in the **.ddf** file, and included in the **.cab**. It's also important to remember that a **.cab** (and therefore a **.ddf** file) can only reference one **.inf** file.

The **.inf** file includes the location of the component and its **CLASSID**. Other optional parameters can include the version number, and the destination directory (i.e. the complete directory path where the component should be installed on the client machine). Here's a simple example:

225

```
[Add.Code]
MyFormula.ocx=MyFormula.ocx
MyFormula2.ocx=MyFormula2.ocx
MyFormula.dll=MyFormula.dll

[MyFormula.ocx]
file=thiscab
clsid={7823A620-9DD9-11CF-A662-00AA00C066D2}

[MyFormula2.ocx]
file=http://www.myserver.com/objects/MyFormula2.cab
clsid={132WRR13-551Q-1S44-3551-199WR6739VB1}

[MyFormula.dll]
file=http://www.myserver.com/libraries/MyFormula.dll
clsid={572QGD13-591A-1S27-8410-194TL4881N41}
```

The first section defines the components to be installed, giving a section name where more information about each one will be found. By default the file name is used for this. Within each section, you specify the location of the file to be installed, and its **CLASSID** for the Registry.

Notice how the location is specified. The component can be in the same cabinet as the **.inf** file (which will normally be the case), in a different cabinet file (which is then automatically downloaded and unpacked), or actually stored as a portable executable elsewhere, (which is then downloaded normally). If you are installing on an intranet, using a source location on the server, you can specify the normal path to the files you want to install.

Extra parameters can be added to the **.inf** file to define the file version required and the destination directory of the downloaded component. The **FileVersion** parameter allows you to specify the minimum version of the component that is required for the application to run successfully. If the client system doesn't have at least this version of the component registered and installed, the newer version will be downloaded.

```
FileVersion=4,70,0,1161
```

The default destination for downloaded components is the **Windows\Occache** directory. However, this can be overridden by using the **DestDir** parameter, which can be either **\Windows** or **\Windows\System**. To install components in the **\Windows** directory, you use a value of **10**, and to install in **\Windows\System** you use **11**.

The following example **.inf** file specifies how two particular files will be installed. The first one, **MyFormula.ocx**, will be installed into the client's **\Windows** directory from a remote web server, but only if the version already installed on the client machine is less than **4,70,0,1161**. Then it will install the file **MyFormula2.OCX** from the local server's **G:\isdept\cust\controls** directory into the **\Windows\System** directory, but only if it doesn't already exist on the client machine.

```
[Add.Code]
MyFormula.ocx=MyFormula.ocx
MyFormula2.ocx=MyFormula2.ocx

[MyFormula.ocx]
file=http://myserver.com/cabs/MyFormula.cab
clsid={7823A620-9DD9-11CF-A662-00AA00C066D2}
```

```
FileVersion=4,70,0,1161
DestDir=10

[MyFormula2.ocx]
file=file://G:\isdept\cust\controls\MyFormula2.ocx
clsid={132WRR13-551Q-1S44-3551-199WR6739VB1}
DestDir=11
```

Create the .cab File

The last task is to create the actual **.cab** file using the Diamond tool. This is found in the **/Bin** folder of your ActiveX SDK **INetSDK** folder. It's a command line argument driven program, which combines the files specified in the **.ddf** (the components to be downloaded, and the controlling **.inf** file) into a single compressed cabinet file. From the command line you type:

```
diantz.exe /f filename.ddf
```

where *filename* is the name of the **.ddf** file you created earlier. Easy!

Specifying the CODEBASE for a .cab file

Cabinet files are more complex to create and test than portable executables, however they allow you to take advantage of file compression. Careful scripting of the **.inf** file also allows some level of control over the installation process. And when you come to produce the HTML page, you just need to specify the name of the cabinet which contains your components in the **CODEBASE** attribute of the **<OBJECT>** tag:

```
CODEBASE="http://www.myserver.com/cabs/calcs.cab"
TYPE="application/x-cabinet"
```

The **TYPE** attribute is important. It informs the browser how it should use the downloaded file. In this case specifying a cabinet application ensures that the browser not only downloads the file, but also extracts its contents accordingly.

Direct Downloading with .inf Files

You've seen in the previous section how the **.inf** file in a cabinet file can be used to download components from elsewhere, as well as installing those which are included in the **.cab** file. As an extension of this method, you can actually omit the cabinet altogether and just use the **.inf** file by itself. Once this file has been downloaded to the browser, it then downloads and installs the various components separately, from one or more locations. This method also allows you to target different system architectures, as you'll see later in the chapter.

The components can be stored in other existing **.cab** files or as portable executables, and can be located almost anywhere. For example, you could specify that some of the components come from a local server on your own network, while others come from a web server on the other side of the world. All you need to do is provide the correct address in the **file=** parameter, and the unique **CLASSID**. And, like the previous example, you can use the **FileVersion** and **DestDir** parameters to control which version of a component is installed, and which folder it's installed in.

How Wrox DebugLog is Installed

In the case of our sample DebugLog control, we used this method because it requires several Visual Basic run-time files to be available on the client system. The `.inf` file on our server looks like this (note that we've omitted part of each address so that it all fits on one line here):

```
[Add.Code]
vb40032.dll=vb40032.dll
ven2232.olb=ven2232.olb
olepro32.dll=olepro32.dll
msvcrt20.dll=msvcrt20.dll
msvcrt40.dll=msvcrt40.dll
Debuglog.dll=Debuglog.dll

[vb40032.dll]
file="http://www.wrox.com/.../chapter07/controls/vbruntime.cab"
DestDir=11

[ven2232.olb]
file="http://www.wrox.com/.../chapter07/controls/vbruntime.cab"
DestDir=11

[olepro32.dll]
file="http://www.wrox.com/.../chapter07/controls/vbruntime.cab"
DestDir=11

[msvcrt20.dll]
file="http://www.wrox.com/.../chapter07/controls/vbruntime.cab"
DestDir=11

[msvcrt40.dll]
file="http://www.wrox.com/.../chapter07/controls/vbruntime.cab"
DestDir=11

[Debuglog.dll]
file="http://www.wrox.com/.../chapter07/controls/debuglog.dll"
clsid={3F18BC14-2120-11D0-AB39-0020AF71E433}
RegisterServer=yes
```

You can see that the last section of the `.inf` script specifies the single DebugLog file, `debuglog.dll`. It includes its `CLASSID`, and a `file=` line which points to its location on our server. We haven't used any version information in this case. The last line in this section, `RegisterServer=yes`, tells the browser to register the object, even though it's a `.dll` or an `.ocx`. VB automatically includes the required Registry keys and values in an OLE server when it compiles it.

Finding the CLASSID for DebugLog

However, you still need to know the `CLASSID` to put in your `.inf` file (and `<OBJECT>` tag). There are two ways you can find this out. If you are creating the component with the Enterprise Edition of Visual Basic, or most other language compilers, there is an option in the compiler dialog to produce a registry information file. Part of the file that VB produced for our DebugLog object is shown below. You can see the `CLASSID` listed in the first line, and some of the other registry entries required to make it work:

```
HKEY_CLASSES_ROOT\wxDebug.Log\CLSID =
                                {3F18BC14-2120-11D0-AB39-0020AF71E433}
HKEY_CLASSES_ROOT\CLSID\{3F18BC14-2120-11D0-AB39-0020AF71E433}\ProgID =
                                wxDebug.Log
HKEY_CLASSES_ROOT\CLSID\{3F18BC14-2120-11D0-AB39-0020AF71E433}\Typelib =
                                {3F18BC15-2120-11D0-AB39-0020AF71E433}
HKEY_CLASSES_ROOT\CLSID\{3F18BC14-2120-11D0-AB39-0020AF71E433}
                                \InprocHandler32 = OLE32.DLL
HKEY_CLASSES_ROOT\CLSID\{3F18BC14-2120-11D0-AB39-0020AF71E433}
                                \LocalServer32 = DebugLog.dll
```

Alternatively, if your compiler can't produce this information directly, you can register the file yourself and then check the **CLASSID** in the Registry afterwards. To register a component yourself, you need the program **regsvr32.exe**, which is included with Windows programming languages that have OLE or ActiveX support. Copy **regsvr32.exe** and the component you want to register into your **Windows\System** folder, then at the DOS prompt change to that folder and type:

```
regsvr32.exe debuglog.dll
```

This displays a message when registration is successful, then you can run **regedit.exe** and search in the Registry for the entry for **debuglog**, which will reveal its **CLASSID**.

Installing the VB Run-time Files

The normal set of Visual Basic run-time files are also listed in the **.inf** script, being required if not already present on the user's machine. They are only downloaded, however, if they're not already present. To make the download as quick as possible, we've compressed all these into a single **.cab** cabinet file. If the client doesn't have these files already, the whole cabinet is downloaded, expanded, and the files are installed. You might find this cabinet file useful for your own pages, if you create objects using Visual Basic 4. All you need to do is include the first five file sections from our example file in your own **.inf** file.

Lastly, here's the HTML **<OBJECT>** tag that we use to insert the control into our DebugLog example page:

```
<OBJECT ID="dbg" WIDTH=1 HEIGHT=1
  CLASSID="CLSID:3F18BC14-2120-11D0-AB39-0020AF71E433"
  CODEBASE="http://www.wrox.com/books/0448/code/chapter07/controls/
                                            debugLog.inf"
  TYPE="application/x-setupscript">
</OBJECT>
```

Notice that the **TYPE** attribute is **application/x-setupscript**, which indicates to the browser that we're using the **.inf**, or direct file, download method. You always need to let the browser know how to handle the file it downloads. In this case, it downloads the **.inf** file and uses this file to get information about the other components which are required.

Designing for Platform Independence

Unlike Java applets, which are designed to be platform-independent, ActiveX controls, and other Windows-based components, are not. The version designed for an Intel processor running Windows 95 won't be a lot of use on a Mac or one of Digital's Alpha workstations. The only way to achieve some level of platform independence is to provide several versions of the component, each compiled for that particular platform.

The key to this is the **TYPE** parameter of the **<OBJECT>** tag, which specifies the type of object required. For ActiveX controls, this is generally **application/x-oleobject**:

```
<OBJECT
  ID="iepop1"
  CODEBASE="http://www.isvname.com/controls/iemenu.ocx#Version=9,67,5,189"
  TYPE="application/x-oleobject"
  CLASSID="clsid:44232DD1-WW4R-21SD-FA2P-4512FFC56FT06"
  >
  . . .
</OBJECT>
```

However, there are a range of values which indicate exactly which platform is in use:

File Download Method	TYPE Attribute
Portable executable (**.exe, .dll, .ocx**)	**application/x-pe-**opsys-cpu
Cabinet files (**.cab**)	**application/x-cabinet-**opsys-cpu
Setup scripts (**.inf**)	**application/x-setupscript**

The **opsys** and **cpu** parts of the attribute are substituted with the operating system and the CPU of the platform that the downloaded components will be executed on.

opsys	Meaning
win32	32-bit Windows 95 or Windows NT
mac	Apple Macintosh operating system

cpu	Meaning
x86	Intel x86 family of processors
ppc	Motorola PowerPC architecture
mips	MIPS architecture processors
alpha	DEC Alpha architecture

So **application/x-cabinet-win32-x86** identifies a Windows 95/NT cabinet file designed for an Intel x86-architecture processor.

The trick is to supply different values in the **.inf** file (which could be in a cabinet or downloaded separately) for each operating system combination. In this case, the **file=** line is replaced by **file-**opsys-cpu**=**, and the values of **opsys** and **cpu** define the platform. For example:

```
[calc1.ocx]
file-win32-x86=http://www.myserver.com/cabs/intel.cab
file-win32-alpha=http://www.myserver.com/cabs/alpha.cab
file-mac-ppc=ignore
```

```
clsid={7823A620-9DD9-11CF-A662-00AA00C066D2}
FileVersion=4,70,0,1161
DestDir=10
```

Here, we've made two versions of the control available for Windows 95/NT. One is for an Intel platform, and other for Digital's Alpha systems, and we use the **ignore** keyword because we don't need to supply this file for a Mac.

When we're using the direct file download method, controlled by a separate **.inf** file, we use **application/x-setupscript** for the **TYPE** attribute. You saw this with our example DebugLog control earlier in the chapter.

Note that you can only achieve this platform independence by using the HTTP protocol to download the files, so if they are located on a local server, you'll need to use the syntax **file="file://G:\isdept\cust\controls\MyFormula.ocx"**.

Security and Code Signing

Now that we are able to download component code from any server attached to the Internet, or any local server, we have, in theory, an infinitely large and ever expanding software library. However, this isn't quite the binary heaven you might imagine, because the absolute flexibility of the download mechanism introduces security issues. In the recent past (and in Internet technology is there any other kind?), all interactive pages used some type of CGI script written in PERL, C, or other esoteric languages, running on a server.

However, the introduction of scripting languages, such as VBScript and JavaScript, have moved the execution from the server to the client machine. This means we are downloading and installing code which may well come from an unknown source. Just ask yourself this question, '*Who coded and tested the last ActiveX component your browser downloaded and executed?*'

We need to have some method by which we can identify the source of downloaded code—not just the web server itself, but the actual author or license holder. As part of this identification process it would also be beneficial if it verified that the code is legitimate, and can be traced back to the author. This makes it more likely to be 'safe', and we are less likely to end up downloading code infected with viruses, or which has the ability to destroy not only local drives, but entire networks.

Microsoft, in conjunction with VeriSign and other interested parties, have introduced an infrastructure and supporting software which will provide certification processes allowing users to download and install code with at least a certain level of confidence. The mechanism is based on two main indicators of quality, a **signing process** and **certificates of authentication**.

What is Code Signing?

Once the software is ready for distribution, it is signed and verified by the author to indicate that, as far as *they* are concerned, it is safe from potential viruses and other defects, and is of an acceptable level of quality. If the downloaded file is altered in any way during the period between signing and being downloaded to the client machine, the browser will always react by warning the user that the code has been tampered with and then allowing them to decide whether or not to install the 'unclean' code.

231

Only after this signing and certification process is the code distributed on the Net, and a certificate of authentication is attached to the component to confirm the source of the code. This process can be compared to purchasing software from a reputable distributor and then ensuring the software has a certificate of authentication from the software author. Software signing and certification will generate customer confidence in the Internet as a viable software distribution medium. Users must be confident that software obtained in this manner will not 'chew' their hard disk, or worst still compromise network stability and security.

One concern, however, is that digital code signing doesn't constitute a content **quality** assurance. In other words, it doesn't guarantee that the software will be fit for the purpose. It's simply a way of certifying that it has not been tampered with. More information on code signing and certification can be found on the Microsoft Internet site at this address:

```
http://microsoft.com/intdev/signcode/certs/
```

What Does Signed Code Look Like?

When a file which has been signed and certificated is downloaded from a server, the browser will generally display the certificate to show that this code was signed by the software's original author. The certificate gives some information about the author, and allows you to set up a default acceptance for other components at the same time.

There is a check box for the particular author, and one for the Certificate Authority (CA). You can remove the need for the certificate to be displayed in future, when downloading components digitally signed by the same author or CA, by clicking the appropriate check boxes.

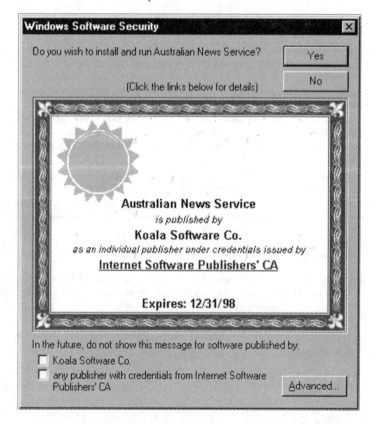

You can also control what type of warning you get by setting the options for your browser. In Internet Explorer, select View | Options, open the Security page, then click the Safety Level button. This allows you to easily set one of the three basic security states (High, Medium or None), and it controls whether to display certificates every time a component is downloaded, or only when it's source is not one specified previously, or never at all when the integrity of the component is in doubt.

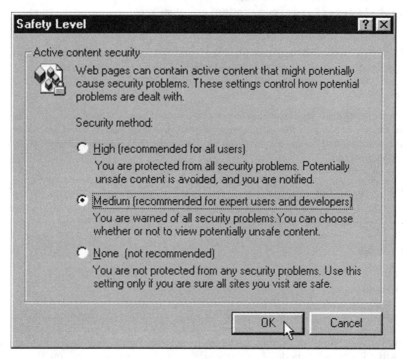

How Do I Get a Certificate?

The certification process has been set up by Microsoft and other companies, including VeriSign. They have created a **Certificate Authority** (CA) which controls the issuing of certificates and the process of digital code signing. The CA ensures that software developers are carefully vetted prior to the issuing of a digital certificate. They will also control the issuing and registration of the 'crypto-keys' used in the digital signing process, and ensure that developers are held accountable when their software causes problems on client machines.

In order to digitally sign and authenticate code, you must go through a certification process controlled by the CA. Certification has been split into two broad categories, that for large corporate software companies and a slightly less stringent process for small independent vendors. The software signing and certification process and the key signing (cryptography) technology are identical for both parties, the only major difference is in the registration process, the cost, and the level of confidence assumed by the user.

At the time of writing, certification was available in the United States and Canada only from VeriSign. VeriSign (**http://www.verisign.com**) has split software certification into Class2 and Class3 processes. Class2 is for independent vendors and requires the requester to provide a name, address, social security number, and valid credit card number; it costs $20 per annum. Class3 requires, in addition, a DUNS number. This is a corporate identification number provided by Dun and Bradstreet which ensures that the company requesting the certificate is valid. Billing information must also be provided, and the cost per annum is $400.

The Certification Process

Certification is a simple two stage process. Stage one consists of filling in an online form at **http://digitalid.verisign.com/codesign.htm**. When the form is submitted a 'key' is issued, and on acceptance a password is sent to the email address you provide.

Once you have this password you can log back into VeriSign (using it and the 'key' supplied originally), and request a set of software credentials. These credentials are your software certificates, and you now have the two components needed to digitally sign and certify your code.

> *Once you have your private key and certification credentials it is advisable to store them safely, away from your hard disk. Remember these files allow anyone who has them to digitally sign their (possibly unsafe) software with your unique key and company credentials, so ensure they are stored in a secure place and that backup copies are made.*

Having got your certification and digital key, the actual process of certifying and digitally signing your code is very simple. It uses the program **signcode.exe**, which is installed as part of the ActiveX SDK, and the process is identical for Class2 and Class3 certificate holders.

Certifying Your Files

If you are using a cabinet (**.cab**) to package your file(s), you need to add special code to the **.ddf** file to facilitate the code signing process. The line:

```
.Set ReservePerCabinetSize=6144
```

sets the minimum size for the cabinet package, to ensure digital signing components can safely be added to it after it's been created. The actual size may, however, depend on the level of certification you have and how much information needs to be contained in the cabinet. Then you can build your cabinet file as normal. Single file (portable executable) components do not, of course, require this step. In their case, the signing code is included within the original file.

Now you run the **signcode.exe** program, from your **INetSDK\Bin** folder. Although this is primarily a command line parameter driven program, if you start it by double-clicking in an Explorer window a Wizard-style application starts.

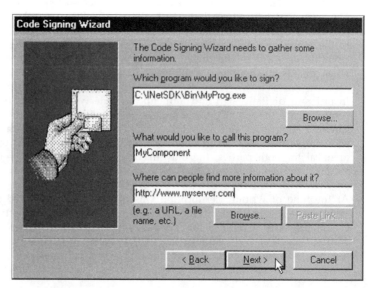

You first supply the details of your component. The field which allows you to record a URL or file name containing information is optional, however this is a useful place to put a link to a suitable web page on your server. The next page asks you to supply your code signing credentials. In our example, we've got them stored on a floppy disk which normally lives in the safe!

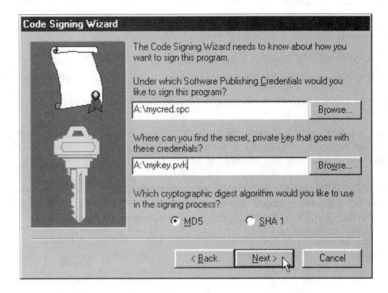

The final task is testing your newly signed file, to make sure the certification has been successful. The ActiveX SDK contains a program, **chktrust.exe**, which tests the signed file, and displays the certificate of authenticity. This is a command line parameter driven program, which requires the name of the signed file and an optional parameter which indicates which type of file this is:

```
chktrust filename.ocx           'checks a portable executable
chktrust -c cabfilename.cab     'checks a cabinet file
```

It's possible to sign the individual files within a cabinet file, instead of signing the entire cabinet in one go. Entire cabinet file signing is generally encouraged, as it speeds up the download verification process because the browser only has one certificate to examine. It also protects against tampering with the **.inf** *script files, which specify where the downloaded files are placed on the client.*

Summary

In this chapter, we've moved on from the immediate concerns of programming in VBScript to consider how you can create and install your own objects, and interface with the server. The increased complexity that ActiveX and other object technologies bring to web authoring mean there is a lot more you have to master and manage.

We've looked at the way the download process works, and how you package your controls so that they are available at the right time, and in the right place, for your web pages. We also showed you some of the background to creating your own controls, though we didn't go into a lot of details about this. Even if you don't build your own controls, there are many people who will provide them. This is likely, in fact, to be a whole new sector of the software manufacturing industry, and you'll need to know how it works to ensure you choose the correct ones, and install them the proper way.

Lastly, we looked at the ways that you can protect yourself from rogue objects. The signing and certification process is designed to ensure that only code that has been verified as being safe is downloaded to your browser.

So in the chapter, we've covered:

- The changing role and responsibilities of the server
- How you specify exactly which component is required in a web page
- Briefly how you go about creating your own component objects
- The requirements for packaging and signing objects ready for use

In the next and final chapter, we continue to look at how VBScript and the server work together. In this chapter, we've been considering a proposal that the server is now just an object repository, and that all the exciting things are happening with objects in the browser itself.

But the server still has a major role to play in today's interactive web environment. In the next chapter, you see how we have added extra functionality to the Bob's Builders Supplies application that you first met in Chapter 4. So measure up that wall you want to build, and we'll see what differences a server can make....

```
<HEAD>
    <SCRIPT LANGUAGE="VBScript">

<!--
Sub window_onLoad()
  Dim objLst
  set objLst= dimensions.
                          lstMaterials
  objLst.AddItem "Clay Bricks
                          (3x8x3.5)"
  objLst.AddItem "Stone Blocks
                          (8x8x4)"
  objLst.AddItem "Concrete Blocks
                          (8x16x
  objLst.ListIndex = 0
nd Sub
->
    </SCRIPT>
```

Bob's Building Supplies Revisited

When we left our sample Bob's Building Supplies page, in Chapter 4, it was a complete working client-side application. However, as you'll no doubt have been aware, it had some serious limitations. For example, it didn't actually collect new customers' details or recognize existing ones. Neither did it store and process the order outside the actual browser. There were also other aspects which were less than ideal in the way they were implemented. All the information on products and prices was hard-coded into the pages, being placed in the controls in the **onLoad** events of the various documents.

In the real world, the products stocked and available from a supplier change quite often, and prices change even more regularly. Keeping our web page up-to-date means continuously updating the HTML and re-coding the events in the **<SCRIPT>** sections. In fact, VBScript makes the task worse, because interactive pages are now so easy to produce that you'll probably find that you write more and more, and you'll need to keep them all up-to-date.

In this chapter, we'll be taking a broad outline view on the changing role of the server, when processing information from a web page. More importantly, we'll see how web pages are becoming more powerful through the combination of client-side processing with VBScript and the new server-side technologies, like IDC and OLEISAPI. We'll do this by adding extra functionality to the original Bob's Building Supplies application. As you design and build ever more complex VBScript pages, you'll find that you really need to understand how server interaction works, so that you can get the best out of it.

We'll be looking at:

    The changes required to our application, so that it can interact with the server

    How new technologies like IDC and OLEISAPI can help to achieve this

    An outline of the way we've added extra functionality to our sample application

First, then, we should examine what Bob's Building Supplies needs to do in the 'real world'...

Designing for Server Interaction

While this book is primarily about using VBScript in the browser, we've already started to consider some of the other aspects of using web pages with it; for example, in the previous chapter, we looked at how you can create and make available your own ActiveX controls and components. We said that the server is changing to become an **object repository**, storing the components we need to insert into our web pages. This *isn't* true, though, when your pages are designed to collect information for central processing, as in Bob's Building Supplies application where the real purpose is to collect orders.

In the Chapter 4 version of the Bob's Building Supplies application, the first thing you see on visiting the site is the main page. Here you can enter your name and address details, and build up your order using the various 'wizards' it contains. It's all very friendly and easy to use. However, working this way isn't ideal when it comes to security, or the requirements of the server. And, as we've already discussed, it can mean huge overheads in maintenance effort to keep the products and prices up-to-date.

What we want is to make sure we know who the customer is when they first enter our site, and then be able to handle and store the order they place on our server. On top of this, we would like the page itself, at least in part, to be generated dynamically. In other words, it should use a list of products and prices which are stored on our server, rather than hard-coded into the page. So it's obvious we are going to need some kind of database to accomplish all these tasks.

A New Look at the Design

It seems, then, as though there are basically three things we need to accomplish. We must:

 Get the customer's details when they first enter the site, and validate them

 Set the prices for all the products, using data stored on the server

 Store and acknowledge the orders that our customers place

If you want to try the new server-interactive version of the application, point your browser at this address:

`http://www.wrox.com/books/0448/code/chapter08/example2/logon.htm`

In our example, we aren't dynamically generating the product lists, though there is no reason why this can't be done as well. However, the principle is the same as we've used for the prices and, in fact, we use a couple of other techniques as well, which are particularly interesting.

Getting the Customer's Details

One of the main visible changes to Bob's site is the introduction of a logging-in dialog, so the main page is not now the first thing that you see. The reason why we've made this change is simple: we need to check if you already have an account with Bob (i.e. whether you have placed an order before). If you have, your billing address will be stored on our server, so we can fill in the details for you automatically. If not, the server will add your details to our database when you place an order. Now you can enter your name and account number, or just enter as a new visitor.

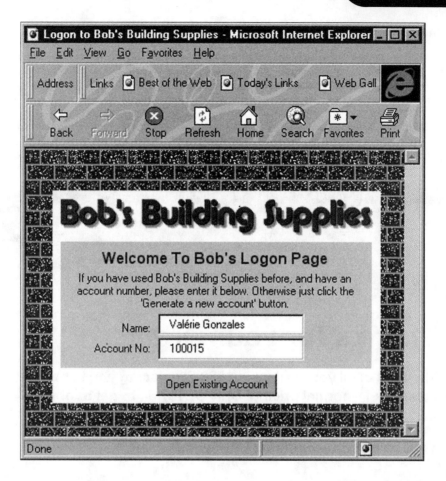

By collecting both your name and account number, we can do some basic validation, checking that they actually match an existing account on our system. In a real-life situation we would probably want to ask for a password as well, and deny access to people who didn't have the correct password, or get them to enter more information before opening an account.

Our log-in page performs several tasks when you click the button. First, it checks to see if you actually do have an account, by looking up your name and account number in our database. If you have, it automatically fills in the Account Details section of the main page.

Setting the Prices for Products

Second, the log-in page sets the prices for the products we sell. If you are a new visitor, it uses a set of default prices. However, if you already have an account, it checks to see how much you've previously spent at Bob's, then uses prices which are suitably discounted. This kind of flexibility is invaluable if you trade with a range of different people.

For example, you may want to offer different prices depending on where you've got to ship the goods to, or include local tax rates in the prices automatically. Of course, you're not limited to just setting different prices. If your page uses the server database for a list of products, you can vary the list available depending on the visitor.

Storing the Order

Lastly, we need to accept the order and store it on our database. And, of course, we need to update the total sales for your account, so that you become entitled to a discount once you've spent an appropriate amount. The order itself is assembled with VBScript in the page, and displayed in a new browser window.

When the Send this order button is clicked, the browser submits the information to our server, which then returns an order confirmation page thanking you. It also displays your account number, so that you can have all your details filled in automatically the next time you log in.

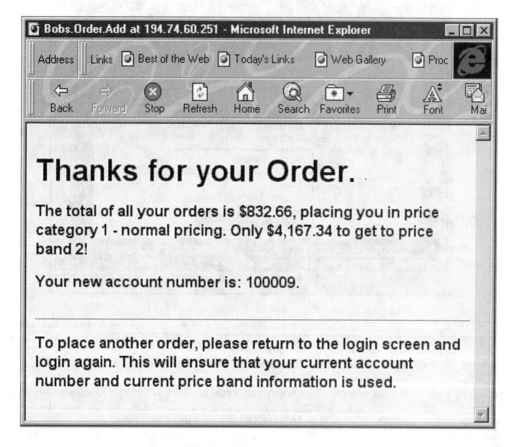

You don't need to be nervous about using this sample page. Although it stores your name and address, you won't wake up to find your driveway full of bricks and sand. We purposely haven't asked for a credit card number, or other payment details, and so you won't get a bill either. Of course, your real-life applications will need to take care of collecting payment details as well as orders!

It should now be obvious just how much this version of Bob's Building Supplies page depends on our server, both for interaction with the browser, and the database stored there. In many cases, including our application, it's the database that forms the core of the whole process. In the remainder of this chapter, we'll be looking briefly at how a web database, and other new technologies, have been used to add extra functionality to the Bob's Building Supplies application.

However, before we get too involved, we should step back and look at these new technologies in a little more detail.

Server-side Technologies

Almost without exception, web pages designed for commercial applications can benefit from interfacing with a database running on the server. It's possible for the server to create HTML documents that contain up-to-date information pulled direct from the database, and send this to the client browser. And with the appropriate interface software, the server can capture and store information received across the Web.

What is a Web Database?

Databases provide many services that are integral to the success of businesses throughout the world. Typical uses of database systems include:

- Maintaining data about customers, business strategies and policies
- Providing product specifications, ordering information, and automated technical support 24 hours a day
- Giving up-to-date statistical information, possibly collected from multiple sources
- Monitoring stock levels and instigating orders automatically
- Providing data to search engines which can quickly sort out relevant data based on an interactive query

Small databases may be installed on individual desktop computers and accessed by just one user, while larger distributed database systems can be accessed by people from different geographical locations. As the Web has grown, and more business users have become involved, much attention has been given to making this data available to the online world. On top of this, as we've seen, a database can reduce site maintenance by generating web pages dynamically, based on the data stored there.

So, a web database is essentially a normal database system, such as Access™, Oracle™, or SQL Server™, that can be accessed indirectly using current web technology as well as in the normal way over a standard in-house network. It can, of course, be run locally, rather than connected to the Web as a whole. If your company uses an intranet, it's likely you'll want to display data from the company's main database.

The Web Connection

To connect a web database to the Internet, we first have to be connected to the Internet via software running on the server, which handles requests issued by the client browsers. The server software we are using in this book is Microsoft Internet Information Server (IIS), although other servers like Website, NCSA httpd, CERN httpd are available.

On top of the server connection software, we need a software layer that issues instructions to, and retrieves data from, the database. There are various types, which differ in their level of sophistication. They include:

- Windows Common Gateway Interface (WinCGI)
- Internet Database Connector (IDC)
- Object Linking and Embedding Internet Server Application Programming Interface (OLEISAPI)

Windows Common Gateway Interface

It's long been possible to create web pages dynamically, using some kind of database or application which is running on the server. Traditionally, these use the **common gateway interface** (CGI), which is a mechanism that allows web clients to execute programs on a web server and to receive their output. Through the use of CGI programs, the server can process input from an HTML form, and can also dynamically produce HTML documents. Now, however, there are several new technologies which extend the power of the server, and make programming the interface much easier. The simplest of these is IDC.

Internet Database Connector

The **Internet Database Connector** (IDC) is a mechanism introduced with Microsoft Internet Information Server. It acts as a bridge between any ODBC data source and your client's browser. You send it several parameters, including the name of the data source, a user name and password to access it with, and an SQL query to execute against the data. IDC queries the data in the database, then inserts the results into a new, dynamically generated, web page which is sent back to the browser.

IDC is relatively straightforward, quick to set up and use, and can easily transform static web pages into dynamically generated documents. You create an Extended HTML Template (HTX) file which contains 'placeholders' for the returned data. It's this page, with the placeholders replaced by the values from one or more matching records, that's actually returned to the user as an HTML file.

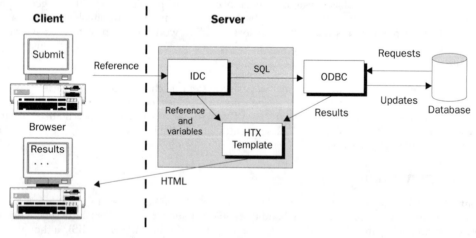

Although IDC provides easy access to any ODBC data source, the imposed execution order of HTML document, IDC script, HTX document, IDC script, etc. can be cumbersome and inadequate for larger applications.

OLEISAPI

Internet Information Server provides another method of accessing data on the server, using the **Internet Server Application Programming Interface**. In effect, you create an OLE server program, and then use its exposed methods to directly manipulate data. In fact, you can do more than just query and update a database using the API. Most modern Windows programming languages, including Visual Basic 4, let you create OLE Automation Server DLLs, and this allows you to create custom solutions based on all the functionality available in that language (apart from routines which write to the screen).

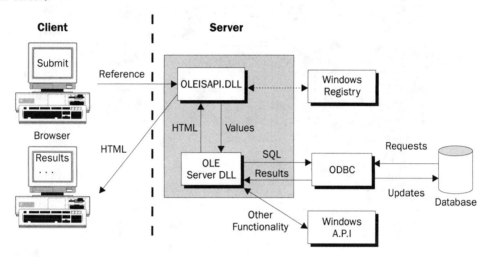

We won't be using the Common Gateway Interface in this chapter, but we can take advantage of the other two methods to add the extra functionality we want for Bob's Building Supplies application. They both come courtesy of the new Microsoft Internet Information Server (IIS), which is part of Windows NT4. The latest version can also be downloaded free from the Web at **http:/ /microsoft.com/infoserv**. Before we actually go back to our application, though, we'll take a look in more detail at how you use these two new technologies.

Introducing IDC

Internet Database Connector (IDC) is one of the easiest ways to create an interactive database-controlled web site. You can use data stored on your server to create HTML pages 'on the fly', which are always up-to-date. The obvious benefits are reduced maintenance, and increased topicality. Both are especially important on your corporate intranet, as well as your company Internet site.

IDC communicates with your database using **Open Database Connectivity** (ODBC) methods and, before you can start to use it, you must establish the correct ODBC driver software for your particular database system, and set the **System Data Source Name** (DSN). To give you some assistance with this, we've included details of setting the System DSN for a Microsoft Access database in Appendix D.

An Example of IDC at Work

To give you an idea of what IDC can do, we'll start with a simple example that you can try out. You'll find it on our web site at the following address:

http://www.wrox.com/books/0448/code/chapter08/example2/getcontacts.htm

We've placed a database containing some fictitious names and addresses on our server, which you can access using this example page. By entering all or part of a name, you get a listing of all names and addresses that match.

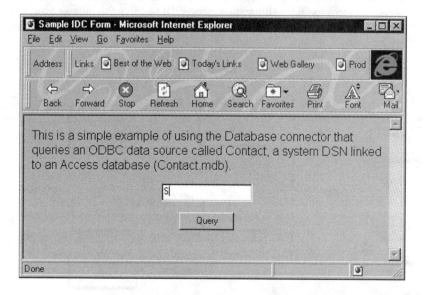

In this example, we're looking for all names which begin with '**S**'. Our database is very simple, having a single **FullName** field, so the query will match first names, rather than surnames. Here's the result of the query:

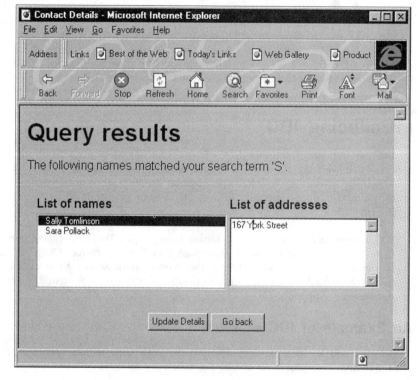

Having found a matching name and address, you can do more than this. You can select a name in the left-hand list and then change their address in the right-hand text box. Clicking the Update Details button then actually updates the value stored in the database on our server. So we have a fully interactive database query and update system available in a web page.

How the Example Page Works

The example you've just seen gives some idea of just how powerful IDC is, and how it opens up a huge window of opportunity for building web sites which can both supply and collect information. We'll work through the example, showing you each component and how they link together.

The Opening Query Page

IDC uses a **script** to specify the name of the data source and connection information, the name of a template containing the page to be returned to the client browser, and the query that is to be run against the data. This script is stored on the server, and to execute it we place its address in the **<FORM>** tag of the HTML page. The browser sends to the script the values of all the controls we've placed inside that **<FORM>** section.

In our sample page, the IDC script is called **GetContacts.idc**. Here's the HTML code that creates the page (we've abbreviated the full URL to make the code easier to read):

```
<HTML>
<HEAD>
  <TITLE>Sample IDC Form</TITLE>
</HEAD>
<BODY>
  This is a simple example of using ... etc. <P>
  <FORM NAME="Me" ACTION="http://.../code/GetContacts.idc" METHOD="POST">
    <INPUT TYPE="TEXT" NAME="NameSearch"> <P>
    <CENTER> <INPUT TYPE="SUBMIT" VALUE="Query"> </CENTER> <P>
  </FORM>
</BODY>
</HTML>
```

The Query button on the page is of type **SUBMIT**, and so clicking it fires the **ACTION** attribute in the **<FORM>** tag. The value of the text box **NameSearch** is sent to the IDC script listed there. Notice that we've decided to use the **POST** method for submitting our data. We've done this because the **GET** method has a limit of sending **1024** characters (the maximum length of the URL), which includes data submitted after the URL name. This approach also provides extra flexibility, which is even more important when using OLEISAPI rather than IDC, as you'll see later.

The IDC Script

The key component of an IDC process is the script itself. The basic form is:

```
Datasource:
Username:
Password:
Template:
SQLStatement:
+
```

The **Datasource** is the System Data Source Name (DSN) that you've specified for the ODBC database to be queried. **Username** and **Password** are used in the normal way to connect to the data source. **Template** is the name of an Extended HTML (HTX) template which is used to generate the HTML that will be sent back to the client browser. Lastly, **SQLStatement** introduces one or more SQL query statements which are to be executed to provide the results. The individual lines of the SQL statement are placed after the **SQLStatement** line, each one starting with a '**+**' symbol, and continuing on as many lines as necessary.

> *In its minimal form, the IDC script must provide at least the* **Datasource**, **Template**, *and* **SQLStatement**. *Since not all scripts are appropriate to all users, however, the execution permissions of such scripts can be set appropriately in NT Server, and controlled with the* **Username** *and* **Password** *fields in conjunction with an Access* **system.mdw** *file, or whatever security system your database implements.*

In our case, the IDC script needs to use the data source we've previously defined as **Contact**, and an SQL statement which extracts the matching customers' names and addresses. To be able to extract the correct records, we use the value sent from the **NameSearch** text box on the original page.

Referring to <FORM> Elements in an IDC Script

The values in the controls (or elements) within the **<FORM>** and **</FORM>** tags of an HTML page can be accessed in an IDC script. They become variables which you can then use in the SQL statement defined in the script. Numeric variables are accessed as *%ControlName%*, and strings are accessed as '*%ControlName%*'. In our case, we want to use the value of the **NameSearch** text box, so we refer to it as '**%NameSearch%**'.

To retrieve the matching records from the database, we need an SQL statement which selects these, and returns the contents of the **FullName** and **Address** fields. To allow us to update a record later if required, we also retrieve the value of the **ID** field, which is an **AutoNumber** type field in the database. Without going into a tutorial on SQL here, the statement we need is:

SELECT ID, FullName, Address FROM *table* **WHERE FullName Like '%NameSearch%'**
ORDER BY FullName

Since we're working with a string value, and using the **Like** operator, we must enclose the **%NameSearch%** variable in single quotes. To specify which *table* in the database we want to use, we place its name in the SQL statement. In our case, it's the table named **User**. Here's the full script:

```
Datasource:Contact
Username: sa
Template: ViewContacts.htx
SQLStatement:
+SELECT ID, FullName, Address
+FROM User
+WHERE FullName Like '%NameSearch%'
+ORDER BY FullName
```

When the script executes, the variable **%NameSearch%** is dynamically instantiated to the value of the **NameSearch** text box on the form. The SQL statement is then executed against the database, and the matching IDs, names and addresses are retrieved as a set of records.

Using Wildcards in an IDC Script

Unfortunately, the script above would only return the records which have a **FullName** field value that is identical to the text entered in the **NameSearch** text box on the form. The problem is that **wildcard pattern matching** is not specified. Normally, we would use an asterisk, appended to the text, to mean any value starting with the text we've entered. But this won't work, because the asterisk is taken to be a literal character, and is matched directly against the names.

The SQL query syntax we have to use is that of ODBC, *not* Access. In ODBC syntax, **%** is used as a wildcard character that matches zero or more characters. As such, our query now appears like this:

```
SQLStatement:
+SELECT FullName, Address
+FROM User
+WHERE FullName Like '%NameSearch%%'
+ORDER BY FullName
```

Note that if no search string is specified, for example when the user leaves the text box empty, only the wildcard character % is used in the SQL statement. This will match every record in the table.

Returning the Results to the Client

So, the script executes the SQL statement, which produces a recordset containing the ID, name, and address from all records which match the criteria in the text box on the original page. The problem now is, how do we get them back to the user on the client machine? This is where the HTX template comes in.

The **Template** section of the script contains the name of an HTX file on the server which will display the results of the query on the user's machine. It's basically just an ordinary HTML file, but there are some special properties which allow us to control exactly what is displayed, and how. In our case, the template is used to fill the controls on the page that is returned to the client. However, it is often a much simpler process than this. We'll look at the basic method first, then come back to see how it's been done in our example.

The HTX Template

For a simple example, we'll just display a formatted list of names that match in the web page we return. Each record will have an **ID**, **FullName**, and **Address** field. In the template, we use the following construct:

```
<%BeginDetail%>
  . . .
  The text to display in the returned page
  . . .
<%EndDetail%>
```

The IDC process iterates through the matching records, placing the text between the **<%BeginDetail%>** and **<%EndDetail%>** tags into the new page. If you were using Visual Basic, this could be compared to using the following code to iterate through a recordset:

```
With rsMyRecordSet
  While Not .EOF
```

249

```
            'The text to display in the returned page
        Wend
    End With
```

However, this isn't very useful, as we aren't obtaining the field values. All we're doing is printing the text once for each matching record. What we need is to insert the field values from the records into the page instead. This is done using variable placeholders in the HTX template file, which are then replaced with the actual data as the HTX is transformed into HTML and sent to the client browser.

Accessing Field Values in an HTX Template

In order to make the **<%BeginDetail%> <%EndDetail%>** construct useful, we want to access the fields of the recordset returned by the SQL statement. This is done using variable names of the form **<%*Variable*%>**, where *Variable* is the name of the field. Remember that the IDC script contained the following SQL query:

```
SQLStatement:
+SELECT ID, FullName, Address
+FROM User
+WHERE FullName Like '%NameSearch%%'
+ORDER BY FullName
```

In order to generate HTML code that would provide a list of names with addresses, the HTX file would contain the following code fragment:

```
<%BeginDetail%>
  <PRE>
    Record ID    : <%ID%>
    Contact Name : <%FullName%>
    Address      : <%Address%>
  </PRE>
<%EndDetail%>
```

The result is a formatted list of matching IDs, names, and addresses:

```
Record ID    : 10009
Contact Name : Sally Tomlinson
Address      : 167 York Street
Record ID    : 10018
Contact Name : Sara Pollack
Address      : 428 Times Square
```

Notice that we include the **<PRE>** *tags to make sure that the text is correctly formatted. Without them, the carriage returns would not be placed in the page, so all the text would appear on a single line.*

Conditional HTML Generation in an HTX Template

IDC also supports conditional HTML generation based on predicates in the HTX file template. Imagine what would happen if no records matched the search criteria specified in the text input box. It would be perfectly feasible to give an empty listing of the names and addresses, but it is much nicer to provide the user with alternative information in such a circumstance. You can accomplish this by using the **If** construct, which has this syntax:

```
<%If Condition%>
  HTML generated if condition true
[<%Else%>
  HTML generated otherwise]
<%EndIf%>
```

The square brackets represent the optional **Else** clause of the **If** statement. You can't, however, use any old expression in the **If** clause. It must be of the form:

```
<%If Value1 Operator Value2%>
```

where **Operator** can be one of the following:

EQ if **Value1** equals **Value2**

LT if **Value1** is less than **Value2**

GT if **Value1** is greater than **Value2**

CONTAINS if **Value2** is a substring of **Value1**

We want to be able to tell if there are any matching records returned by the SQL statement. To do this, we check the value of the internal variable **CurrentRecord**, which is visible to the code in the HTX file. It contains a value which is the number of records in the recordset, *after* iteration through the **<%BeginDetail%>** **<%EndDetail%>** section. If it has the value **0** at that point, we know that no names were found starting with the search string originally entered, so we can generate appropriate text for inclusion in the page:

```
<%BeginDetail%>
  <PRE>
    Record ID    : <%ID%>
    Contact Name : <%FullName%>
    Address      : <%Address%>
  </PRE>
<%EndDetail%>
<%If CurrentRecord EQ 0%>
  Sorry, no matching names were found.
<%EndIf%>
```

The HTTP Variables Available in HTX Templates

As well as the internal variables, such as **CurrentRecord**, it's possible to access the many parameters available from the IDC within the HTX template. This is done by adding **'idc.'** onto the front of the variable name. The variables in this instance are the values in the original form's control elements, when the IDC script was called. So, to access the original value in our **NameSearch** text box, we can use the syntax **<%idc.NameSearch%>** in our HTX template.

Variables are defined like this for all the elements specified between the **<FORM>** and **</FORM>** tags in the HTML document that calls the IDC script. We can use this to further enhance our HTX template, on the occasions when there are no matching names in the database:

```
<%BeginDetail%>
  <PRE>
    Record ID    : <%ID%>
```

```
      Contact Name : <%FullName%>
      Address      : <%Address%>
   </PRE>
<%EndDetail%>
<%If CurrentRecord EQ 0%>
   There are no names matching the search string <%idc.NameSearch%>
<%EndIf%>
```

Conditional Display of other Page Elements

In the second page of the example that you saw at the beginning of this section, which displays the results of the search, there are two buttons. One of these, Update Details, is inappropriate if there are no records returned from the query. So we can make the page even more user-friendly in this case by omitting that button. All we need to do is place an **If** construct in the HTX template, which contains the HTML code that creates the two buttons. It only generates the code for the Update Details button if the value of **CurrentRecord** (i.e. the number of matching records found) is greater than zero:

```
<%If CurrentRecord GT 0%>
  <INPUT TYPE="SUBMIT" NAME="cmdUpdate" VALUE="Update Details">
<%Else%>
  Sorry, there are no names matching the search string <%idc.NameSearch%>
<%EndIf%>
<INPUT TYPE="BUTTON" NAME="cmdBack" VALUE="Go back">
```

Incorporating VBScript in an HTX Template

So far in our example, we've seen how the server processes the browser's query, and how the data can be returned to the browser as normal HTML code using an HTX template. However, the example does more than this. It displays the returned information inside list controls, rather than as text on the page, and allows you to update the address for a record which has been returned.

To do this, we added extra functionality by including (yes, you've guessed) VBScript within the page that's returned to the client by the IDC process. This page is created, you'll recall, by the HTX template file. It just generates normal HTML code and sends it to the browser. So, although it's 'virtual' HTML (as we've seen with **document.write** in earlier chapters) it still appears to the browser as normal HTML code. It's coming from the server just like a normal page stored on the server's disk.

And in earlier chapters, you saw how we can include VBScript code in the 'virtual page' we produce, just by including it in the string we **write** to the document. If we include VBScript in the HTX file, the browser will parse it in the same way as a normal static page.

> Note that the VBScript *doesn't* execute on the server. It only runs after it's been loaded into the browser on the client machine.

In the case of our sample page, the HTX file contains several VBScript routines which manipulate the controls in the page it returns. As well as this, there is the code to initialize the variables, the **<OBJECT>** tags to create the list and text boxes, and other HTML code to complete the page. We don't want to show all of the IDs and addresses, so the **objLstIDs** and **objLstAddresses** list boxes have their **Visible** properties set to false in their respective **<OBJECT>** tags. All the viewer sees is a list of matching names. The two text boxes, **txtAddress** and **hidIDValue**, are used to store the currently selected address and ID value, so that we can send them back to the server when the time comes. The address text box is visible, but the ID one isn't.

Here's the part of the HTX file that creates the main **<SCRIPT>** section in the page.
ViewContacts is the name of the **<FORM>** section in the page holding the list and text boxes, so
we set up references to them to save us the effort later:

```
<SCRIPT LANGUAGE="VBScript">
  <!--  Option Explicit
  Dim objLstNames, objLstIDs, objLstAddresses, txtAddress, hidIDValue
  Set objLstNames = ViewContacts.objLstNames
  Set objLstIDs = ViewContacts.objLstIDs
  Set objLstAddresses = ViewContacts.objLstAddresses
  Set txtAddress = ViewContacts.txtAddress
  Set hidIDValue = ViewContacts.hidIDValue
```

Next, we see if there are any matching records. If there are, we insert VBScript statements which
set the first item in the list as the default, and copy the address from the hidden list box into the
visible address text box. This means that there will still be a value available if the user clicks
Update Details before actually selecting a name. Of course, this submit button isn't generated at all
if there are no records, as we saw earlier.

```
<%If CurrentRecord GT 0%>
  objLstNames.ListIndex = 0
  txtAddress.Value = objLstAddresses.List(0)
<%EndIf%>
```

What's important, though, is how a varying number of returned records is added to the list boxes
in the page.

Filling the List Boxes in the Results Page

Within a **<%BeginDetail%> <%EndDetail%>** block in the HTX template, we can insert
'placeholder' variables, which IDC replaces with actual values from the records after the SQL
statement that creates the results has been executed. In earlier examples, we simply used these
values as text for the HTML page. However, instead, we can use them to create VBScript code. In
our sample page, the HTX template contains this code:

```
<%BeginDetail%>
  <SCRIPT LANGUAGE="VBScript">
    <!--
    Option Explicit
    ViewContacts.objLstIDs.AddItem "<%ID%>"
    ViewContacts.objLstNames.Additem "<%FullName%>"
    ViewContacts.objLstAddresses.AddItem "<%Address%>"
    -->
  </SCRIPT>
<%EndDetail%>
```

Remember that anything in this section of the HTX file is repeated, once for every record which
matches the criteria in the SQL statement. The field name placeholders are replaced each time by
the values from the records, so if we've got two matches, the resulting HTML code that's sent to
the browser could look like this:

```
<SCRIPT LANGUAGE="VBScript">
  <!--
  Option Explicit
  ViewContacts.objLstIDs.AddItem "10009"
```

253

```
   ViewContacts.objLstNames.Additem "Sally Tomlinson"
   ViewContacts.objLstAddresses.AddItem "167 York Street"
   -->
</SCRIPT>
<SCRIPT LANGUAGE="VBScript">
   <!--
   Option Explicit
   ViewContacts.objLstIDs.AddItem "10018"
   ViewContacts.objLstNames.Additem "Sara Pollack"
   ViewContacts.objLstAddresses.AddItem "428 Times Square"
   -->
</SCRIPT>
```

Updating the Data Source from the Browser

Having got the complete page in front of the user, we now need to consider how we are going to manage the updating of the selected record if they click Update Details. There are two text boxes in the **<FORM>** section of the page, and all we need to do is make sure that at the appropriate time these contain the ID of the record we want to update (in the hidden one), and the new address we want to place in that record. So other VBScript routines are included in the HTX template, and hence in the page it generates. The first of these runs each time the user selects a name in the list box, and it places the value of the currently selected address into the address text box, where it can be edited:

```
   Sub objLstNames_Change
      txtAddress.Value = objLstAddresses.List(objLstNames.ListIndex)
   End Sub
```

The second routine runs when the Update Details button is clicked. This button is defined with **TYPE="SUBMIT"**, so it will send the contents of the two text boxes on the form back to the server. However, by defining a VBScript routine for it, our code will run before the actual submit action takes place. The ID of the currently selected record is copied to the hidden text box, and will be passed back to the server so that it knows which person is to have their address changed:

```
   Sub cmdUpdate_onClick()
      hidIDValue.Value = objLstIDs.List(objLstNames.ListIndex)
   End Sub
```

Lastly, because we've provided a Go Back button, we need to include the routine for this. If no matching records are returned from the server, the Update Details button is not generated. The Go Back button means that the user can easily go back to the previous Search page:

```
   Sub cmdBack_onClick()
      Window.History.Back(1)
   End Sub
```

Even though we've written code that runs when the Update Details button is clicked, the **SUBMIT** action will still take place when our code has completed. The **<FORM>** tag we've placed in the page (with the address abbreviated for clarity) is:

```
   <FORM NAME="ViewContacts" ACTION="http://../UpdateAddress.idc" method="POST">
```

So when the user clicks Update Details, another IDC script is executed, which in turn runs another SQL query against the database. However, this time it changes the address stored there, by using an **UPDATE** query rather than the **SELECT** query we saw earlier which just retrieved records.

```
Datasource:Contact
Username: sa
Template: GetContacts.htm
SQLStatement:
+UPDATE DISTINCTROW User
+SET Address = '%txtAddress%'
+WHERE ((User.ID) = Val(%hidIDValue%));
```

You can see that this SQL statement uses the values sent from the browser which represent the contents of the address text box, **'%txtAddress%'**, and the hidden ID text box, **%hidIDValue%**. And also notice that the template we've specified this time is just a normal HTML document—not a template at all. All we're doing is reloading the original page. So there can be a chain of processes which involve an HTML page calling an IDC script, which uses an HTX template to return another HTML page, which calls a different IDC script, and repeats the process.

Returning Multiple Recordsets from an IDC Script

One of the main restrictions with the IDC process is where a script contains one SQL query, but multiple **<%BeginDetail%> <%EndDetail%>** sections are required. Only the first one will actually be iterated. It may also appear that only one database process (or query) can be executed for each script. In other words, there has to be an HTML document returned after each step of a multiple-query process, which then calls the IDC script containing the next query. This is what is happening in our example, where we first retrieve the details, then use a second script to update them.

However, it's possible to include more than one SQL query in an IDC script, and match it to multiple **<%BeginDetail%> <%EndDetail%>** sections in the HTX file. Only appropriate queries, which actually return records, will match the corresponding **<%BeginDetail%> <%EndDetail%>** section. Here's a quick look at how it works. This is a section of the IDC script:

```
SQLStatement:
+INSERT INTO Staff Name, Age VALUES('%FullName%', %AgeYears%)
+SELECT Name, Age FROM Staff
+SELECT Price1, Price2 FROM Price
```

and this is part of the HTX file that generates the resulting HTML page:

```
<%BeginDetail%>
   Name:    <%Name%>
   Age:     <%Age%>
<%EndDetail%>
<%BeginDetail%>
   Price1:   <%Price1%>
   Price2:   <%Price2%>
<%EndDetail%>
```

The IDC only returns a recordset from queries that are meant to return data. In the example above, only the second and third **SELECT** queries return data, and these recordsets are matched up to the first and second occurrences of **<%BeginDetail%> <%EndDetail%>** sections in the HTX file extract shown. Notice also that the second query:

SELECT Name, Age FROM Staff

takes its input from the first query:

255

```
INSERT INTO Staff Name, Age VALUES('%FullName%', %AgeYears%)
```

which, in turn, takes its input from values returned from the `<FORM>` section of the page. So there's really no limit to the processing you can carry out if required, as long as it can take place as a series of SQL statements.

Finding Duplicated Records with an IDC Script

As an example of how you can use multiple recordsets, here's a way of finding the number of duplicated records in our database. We need a recordset composed of any duplicated names together with the number of occurrences of that name. Here's the IDC script:

```
SQLStatement:
+SELECT Name, Age FROM User
+SELECT DISTINCTROW First([Name]) AS [Name Field], Count([Name]) AS +NumberOfDups
+FROM User
+GROUP BY [Name]
+HAVING Count([Name])>1
```

The first SQL statement creates a recordset containing the **Name** and **Age** fields from all the records. In this, we'll assume we've got three records with the name John Smith. Each one holds the name and age. The second query then creates a two-field recordset which contains the name in the first field, and the number of times it appears in the **Datasource** in the second field. Because of the grouping on the **Name** field, **Count([Name])** produces a value equal to the number of records with that name.

By including the **DISTINCTROW** keyword, however, we ensure that duplicate records (with the same name and number of occurrences) will only appear once in the resulting recordset. So for John Smith, we get a single record with the value **John Smith** in the first field, and **3** in the second. The final condition in the second query then limits the records that are included to those where the number of duplicates (in the second field) is greater than **1**. Once we've got this recordset, we use the HTX template to create the appropriate HTML report:

```
<%BeginDetail%>
  <%Name%>  age: <%Age%>
<%EndDetail%>
<%BeginDetail%>
  Attention: Name <%Name%> found <%NumberOfDups%> times in the database!
<%EndDetail%>
```

The first `<%BeginDetail%>` `<%EndDetail%>` section will list all the names in the database, because the first query returns a record for each one. However, the second `<%BeginDetail%>` `<%EndDetail%>` section will only iterate through the records in the final recordset—in other words, the ones that are duplicated. When viewed in the browser, John Smith would appear as:

```
. . .
Sara Pollack  age: 29
John Smith  age: 36
John Smith  age: 24
John Smith  age: 47
Valerie Gonzales  age: 19
. . .
Attention: Name John Smith found 3 times in the database!
. . .
```

Introducing OLEISAPI

We've spent a lot of time on IDC, as it's arguably the quickest and easiest way to produce interactive, database-populated, web pages. It's also very powerful, and we've really only scratched the surface here. Thankfully, **OLEISAPI** (Object Linking and Embedding Internet Server Application Programming Interface) will take us a lot less time to introduce. However, what we can't hope to cover here is a detailed description of how it works. You'll see some implementation background later in the chapter, as we return to look at Bob's Building Supplies application.

OLEISAPI is a method of connecting applications written in normal programming languages (that can produce OLE Servers) with Internet Information Server. It uses OLE Automation to allow your own bespoke applications to manipulate the data source directly, and send information back and forth between the server and the client. It's also around five times faster than using the traditional CGI method.

In order for OLEISAPI to work correctly, you must be running Windows NT 3.51 (with service pack 4 installed), or better. Our development work is done on Windows NT4 Server. You also need a copy of the file **OLEISAPI.DLL**. The source code for this can be found on Microsoft's Developers Network (MSDN), or compiled at many web sites online. We have included a downloadable version on our site. Currently, the version from the MSDN source can only generate 4K of output, but other versions have been modified to relax this limit.

To use your custom OLE server, you place a call to it in the **ACTION** attribute of the **<FORM>** tag, so that it executes when the form is submitted. You have to specify the **class**, and the **method** in that class, that you want to execute:

```
ACTION="path to OLEISAPI.DLL/CUSTOMOLE.DLL.Class.Method"
```

We'll show you just how useful OLEISAPI is towards the end of the chapter.

Linking Bob's Page to Our Server

It's time we came back to look at how we've added the extra functionality you saw at the beginning of the chapter to Bob's Building Supplies application. We've used both IDC and OLEISAPI in the process, but for different reasons.

The new log-in page uses IDC to query the database on our server and retrieve details of the customer. This is an ideal application of IDC, though we've added quite a lot of extra functions to it by using various techniques in the IDC script's SQL statement, and in the HTX template file that creates the return page.

The return page is, in fact, the original opening page you saw when you used the application in Chapter 4. Now it's an HTX file, rather than a normal HTM file, but this makes no difference. By the time it gets to the browser, it just appears as normal HTML code.

The other change is in the way we handle an order that's placed. Because of the way the order is coded into a quite complex table, using HTML tags, it wouldn't be an easy feat to decode it using SQL statements in an IDC script. Instead, we've built a custom OLE server DLL, which accepts the complete order string, updates the database directly using the OLEISAPI interface, and then returns a 'thank you' page which it generates internally—inside the OLE server.

In this final part of the chapter, we'll outline the way in which these two new parts of the application work.

The New Log-in Page

Instead of loading the main page first, a visitor to our site now opens the log-in page instead. Here, we collect their name and account number, and use these to see if they are already in our database. The page has a **<FORM>** section, containing two hidden text controls and a **SUBMIT** button with its caption set to Generate New Account. The **ACTION** attribute of the form is an IDC script called **Logon.idc**, which is stored on our server (we've shortened the address to make it easier to read the code):

```
<FORM NAME="GetAccount" ACTION="http://.../Logon.idc" METHOD="POST">
<INPUT NAME="hidAccountNumber" TYPE="HIDDEN" VALUE="0">
<INPUT NAME="hidName" TYPE="HIDDEN">
<INPUT TYPE=SUBMIT VALUE="Generate New Account" NAME="sbtAcctNumber">
```

We could easily have used normal (visible) text controls here, but instead chose to use an ActiveX layout control with two text box controls. This means that we can use their events and properties to make the form more interactive. Here's the code in the layout control:

```
Sub txtAccountNumber_Change()
  Dim AcctNum
  AcctNum = Trim(txtAccountNumber.Text)
  If IsNumeric(AcctNum) Then        'is a number
    If Len(AcctNum) = 6 Then        'is 6 digits long
      GetAccount.sbtAcctNumber.Value = "Open Existing Account"
    Else
      GetAccount.sbtAcctNumber.Value = "Generate New Account"
    End If
    GetAccount.hidAccountNumber.Value = AcctNum
  Else
    GetAccount.sbtAcctNumber.Value = "Generate New Account"
  End If
End sub

Sub txtName_Change()
  GetAccount.hidName.Value = txtName.Text
End sub
```

All it does is copy the values of the two text boxes into the hidden controls on the form as they're changed. However, we can take advantage of the **Change** event for the **txtAccountNumber** control to change the caption on the button to a more appropriate one once they've entered enough information to log-in as a 'known' user. Because we gave the hidden account number control on the form a default value of **0** when we created it, it will always contain a numeric value.

The IDC Script for the Logon Screen

When the form is submitted, by clicking the button in the log-in page, the IDC script **Logon.idc** is executed. Here's the first part of the script:

```
Datasource: Bobs
Username: sa
Template: BobsHomePage.htx
```

The **Datasource** and **Username** parameters specify our database called **Bobs**, and give the user access to it. The **Template** parameter is the name of the HTX file which will create the returned page. Here, it's **BobsHomePage.htx** which is a modified version of the original 'main' page, **BobsHomePage.htm**, that we used in Chapter 4.

The next part of the script defines the SQL statement that queries the database and returns the values we want to use in the HTX template. We need to extract the customer's details if they already have an account, and the prices for the various products they can buy. You'll recall that we decided to offer a discount depending on their total purchases to date, and these prices are stored in the database in three different bands. So we actually have three parts to the **WHERE** condition in the statement, each using the value in the **TotalOfOrders** field in our database to decide which category the customer falls into.

We'll break the SQL statement down into parts, so that you can see how it works more easily. First, the names of the fields we want to extract the values from:

```
SQLStatement:
+SELECT DISTINCTROW AccountNo, Name, Address, Town, State, Zip, Phone, Email,
Glass, ClayBrick, StoneBlock, ConcreteBlock, ScreenBlock, DecorativeBrick, Sand,
Cement
```

Next, the names of the two tables that contain those fields:

```
+FROM Customer, Price
```

Now, the **WHERE** condition which limits the records retrieved to those which match our visitor's name and account number. The variables **%hidAccountNumber%** and **%hidName%** are taken from the values of the controls on the form that was submitted:

```
+WHERE (((Customer.AccountNo)=Val(%hidAccountNumber%)
+AND ((Customer.Name)='%hidName%'))
+AND (((Customer.TotalOfOrders)>=10000)
+AND ((Price.CatRef)=3)
```

What this is saying is: **JOIN** the selected customer record with the third record (price band 3) of the price table **IF** the customer has spent at least $10,000. Similarly, the next parts determine if the customer is in price band 2 or 3:

```
+OR (((Customer.TotalOfOrders)>=5000 AND (Customer.TotalOfOrders)<10000)
+AND ((Price.CatRef)=2))
+OR (((Customer.TotalOfOrders)>=0 And (Customer.TotalOfOrders)<5000)
+AND ((Price.CatRef)=1))))
```

The Main HTX Template File

Once we've established the customer details and the relevant prices, we can use them in the page we send back. The HTX file, **BobsHomePage.htx**, is quite complex. It not only contains all the HTML and VBScript code you saw in the original example, but it has to be able to cope with the dynamic information from our IDC script as well.

We aren't going to go into the whole process in detail, but we'll show you in outline how it works. Earlier in the chapter, we used the **<%BeginDetail%> <%EndDetail%>** section of the template, in conjunction with the **CurrentRecord** variable, to generate slightly different sections of VBScript code in the page depending on the outcome of the SQL query in the IDC script. This is the same technique that we use to create the new main page for Bob's site.

Originally, the material prices were set in the **window_onLoad** event of the main document, and the address information was always blank. In our new version, we have the values of all these (providing we found the customer in our database), and so we can set them in the page we

259

return. We do this by generating a different version of the page depending on whether we found the customer's details or not.

Detecting an Existing Customer

To decide if we found the customer, we just need to iterate through the returned records, then examine the value of the **CurrentRecord** variable in the HTX template. If there is a record, then any statements between the **<%BeginDetail%> <%EndDetail%>** sections will be executed exactly once.

If no record is returned, i.e. we have no match to the account number and name, then the **<%BeginDetail%> <%EndDetail%>** sections will just behave as if no statements exist between them. This is equivalent to **For intLoop = 1 to 0 ... Loop**, which will never execute any statements inside the loop. In effect, we're using an **If...Then** construct, like this:

If *there is a record returned* **Then**
  Input details and set appropriate flags
  Input prices
Else
  Just assign the default prices
EndIf

```
    <%BeginDetail%> <!-- If there is record then include this subroutine -->
     <SCRIPT LANGUAGE="VBScript">
     <!--
     Sub GetCustDetails()
       gstrAccountNumber = CStr(<%AccountNo%>)      'set the customer's
       gflgAccReady = gflgAccReady OR 1             'details into global
       gstrName = "<%Name%>"                        'variables, and update
       gflgAccReady = gflgAccReady OR 2             'the flag variable that
       gstrAddress = "<%Address%>"                  'shows which parts of
       gflgAccReady = gflgAccReady OR 4             'the address are
       gstrTown = "<%Town%>"                        'available.
       . . .
       'etc                                         'then fill the prices array
       . . .
       gsngPrices(0) = <%Glass%>            'glass/m2/mm thick
       gsngPrices(1) = <%ClayBrick%>        'clay bricks each
       gsngPrices(2) = <%StoneBlock%>       'stone blocks each
       gsngPrices(3) = <%ConcreteBlock%>    'concrete blocks each
       gsngPrices(4) = <%ScreenBlock%>      'screen blocks each
       gsngPrices(5) = <%DecorativeBrick%>  'decorative bricks each
       gsngPrices(6) = <%Sand%>             'sand/ton
       gsngPrices(7) = <%Cement%>           'cement/bag
     End Sub
     -->
     </SCRIPT>
    <%EndDetail%>

    <%If CurrentRecord EQ 0%> <!-- no record, so above is not included
                                  instead we include this one -->
     <SCRIPT LANGUAGE="VBScript">
     <!--
     Sub GetCustDetails()      'use default prices for a new customer
       gsngPrices(0) = 1.25    'glass/m2/mm thick
```

```
      gsngPrices(1) = 0.15   'clay bricks each
      gsngPrices(2) = 0.50   'stone blocks each
      . . .
      'etc
      . . .
      gflgAccReady = 0         'no customer name and address details set
   End Sub
   -->
   </SCRIPT>
<%EndIf%>
```

You can see that *both* subroutines are named **GetCustDetails**, but only *one* will be included in the final page. The first subroutine will be created if there is a matching customer record, and the second one if there isn't. If the first one is created and executed, it places the customer's details into global variables ready to drop into the relevant page later on, and then sets the special discounted prices for that customer. All these are variables returned by the server. If there is no matching customer record, and the second routine is created and executed, the usual default prices are used instead.

There are other, minor differences in the code that the HTX file creates, depending on whether a matching customer record was found. For example, we assume that the address supplied by a new customer is their billing address, and add that to our database when the order is placed. For an existing customer, however, we pre-populate the Account Details frame with their current billing address from our database, and assume that if they change it, the new one is the delivery address.

The Need for Absolute File References

One problem arises when you start to use IDC and HTX templates to create returned web pages dynamically. In the original version of our page, as in a normal web page, we could just put all of our source files (documents, images, etc.) into one directory. Using just the file name to reference these files automatically meant 'the current directory', i.e. the same one as the current page.

When we dynamically generate HTML from an HTX template, however, the HTML file is *virtual*. It's an amalgamation of the data returned from the database and the HTX template. In reality, it just exists as a string sent to the browser as a response, and so it doesn't have a current directory. Because of this, any references to files must include an explicit reference to the file as well as the file name. This could be **file://\\YourServer\Sharesomedir\somefile**, if they are stored locally on your intranet, or **http://www.mywebsite.com/file** to reference them over the Net itself.

We had to do this with our main **BobsHomePage.htx** file, which loads the documents into the appropriate frames in the main page:

```
</HEAD>
<FRAMESET COLS="355,*">
   <FRAMESET ROWS="50,255,*">
      <FRAME SRC="http://.../titlebar.htm" SCROLLING=NO NORESIZE>
      <FRAME SRC="http://.../wizmenu.htm" SCROLLING=NO NORESIZE>
      <FRAME SRC="http://.../intro.htm" NAME="IntroFrame" SCROLLING=NO >
   </FRAMESET>
   <FRAMESET ROWS="225,*">
      <FRAME SRC="http://.../startwiz.htm" NAME="WizardFrame">
      <FRAME SRC="http://.../customer.htm" NAME="CustDetails">
   </FRAMESET>
</FRAMESET>
</HTML>
```

261

Of course, this is only necessary in HTX template files. Other files, such as HTML documents and `.alx` layout control files, don't need to contain explicit references because they reside in, and are used directly from, a directory on the server.

Processing the Order with OLEISAPI

The other task we need to achieve is accepting, storing, and acknowledging the orders placed by our customers. Whilst we can do a lot using just VBScript and IDC, it's often necessary to have explicit control of functionality that only program code can achieve. Previously, our best option would have been to use the WinCGI, but now that OLEISAPI is available, we can achieve similar results with only a fraction of the programming effort.

We create a custom OLE server which has **methods** and **properties** to achieve the specific task we want. We call the method from the **ACTION** attribute of the **<FORM>** tag in our HTML page:

```
ACTION="http://URL/FullPathToOLEISAPI.DLL/OLEISAPI.DLL/OLEServerIdentifier
                                        .ClassName.MethodToInvoke"
```

The method itself is a **subroutine** in the class module within the OLE server, and it must accept two string parameters. We've used the **ACTION** attribute of the Order page form in our application to call the **Add** method of the **Order** class in our **Bobs** custom OLE Server:

```
ACTION="http://www.wrox.com/.../OLEISAPI.DLL/Bobs.Order.Add
```

In our custom OLE server, we've defined the **Add** method like this:

```
Public Sub Add(strRequest As String, strResponse As String)
   ...
   'code to validate the user and update the database
   'code to create the response string in strResponse
   ...
End Sub
```

Notice how the subroutine is **Public**, so that the method is visible for use outside the OLE server. The two string parameters are used to pass the values into and out of the subroutine. The first of these is a string containing all the values from the controls in the **<FORM>** section, formatted at name/value pairs:

```
Control1Name=Control1Value1&Control2Name=Control2Value...etc.
```

Inside the OLE server, the second string is set to the result we want to pass back to the browser. It's usually a string containing HTML tags which creates a confirmation and 'thank you' page in the browser. It should start with **Content-Type:text/html** to let the browser know that it's receiving an HTML document.

It's also worth remembering that the source string coming from the browser is URL encoded. This means that standard HTML tags will appear differently, and will need decoding to transform them back into HTML if required. Spaces are translated to '**+**', and special characters such as '**<**' and '**>**' and plus signs themselves are converted to '**%**' followed by their hexadecimal ASCII code. So a normal **<B>** tag would appear in the string as **%3CB%3E**.

As an example of the submitted string, we'll take a **<FORM>** containing two text boxes called **txtAccNum** and **txtCustName**. The user sets the values of these to **107562** and **Herman J.**

Goldsmith, respectively. When the form is submitted to our OLE server, the first string parameter will be:

```
txtAccNum=107562&txtCustName=Herman+J.+Goldsmith
```

Bob's OLE Automation Server

When a visitor places an order, there are a lot of specific tasks we have to accomplish to update our database. If they're a new customer, we need to generate a new customer record before an order can be placed. We also have to update the total sales figure in their customer record, and add the details of the order to the various order tables.

The problem is that what's actually coming back from the browser is one long string of HTML formatted information, basically the same as is used to generate the order page itself. This is because we created the order page using a table, and formatted the text so that it looked like a real paper-based order. All we did then was to dump the whole thing into three hidden text boxes in the **<FORM>** section of the page. When the form is submitted, the names and values from the text boxes are combined together and sent to the server as one string. And to make matters worse, it's also URL encoded. So our customer OLE server has several tasks to carry out. It must:

- Decode the incoming string, converting the **+** signs to spaces.
- Break the strings up into individual customer details and order details, stripping out the HTML tags.
- Query the database to see if it's a new customer, and if so add the address details to it.
- Add the order details to the database, then update the 'total spent to date' field.
- Create a suitable HTML coded string to create the order acknowledgment page, and send it back to the browser.

Our OLE server is created using Visual Basic 4, and the major task is to produce the various routines which carry out the operations listed here. The first two are basically string-handling jobs, a task to which VB is well suited. In the order part of the string, we use the embedded **<TR>** and **</TR>** tags to break it down into individual order lines. After that, it's relatively easy to separate out the individual field values.

Once we've got the values we need, we can update the tables in the database. Here's the routine which checks to see if the customer already exists there. It uses normal VB/VBA code to set the index for the table, then uses the **Seek** method to find a matching record. The table's **NoMatch** property returns **True** if a matching record was *not* found.

```
Function AccountExists(strAccountNumber As String) As Boolean
   Dim lngAccountNumber As Long
   tblCustomer.Index = "PrimaryKey"
   lngAccountNumber = CLng(IIf(strAccountNumber = "", 0, strAccountNumber))
   tblCustomer.Seek "=", lngAccountNumber
   AccountExists = Not tblCustomer.NoMatch
End Function
```

To add a customer to the table, we use VB/VBA methods again. Here's a sample:

263

```
WS.BeginTrans
  With tblCustomer
    .AddNew                              'add a new customer record
    !AccountNo = lngNewAccountNumber
    !Name = strName
    !Address = strAddress
    !Town = strTown
    !State = strState
    !Zip = strZip
    !Phone = strPhoneNumber
    !Email = strEmailAddress
    .Update
  End With
WS.CommitTrans
```

After this, we add the order details to the database, and update the 'total spent to date' field. The final task in our OLE server is then to create the return string, containing the HTML code for the page sent back to the browser. We need to confirm that the order has been placed, and display the (new or existing) customer account number ready for our visitor to use when they come back again. We also include a note of how they can get back to the opening page of our site.

```
Private Function CreateHTMLResponse() As String
  'Generates the HTML response that will be returned to
  'the clients browser, confirming the order.

  Dim strPriceCat As String

  If gTotalOfOrders >= 10000 Then
    strPriceCat = "3 - major price reduction."
  ElseIf gTotalOfOrders >= 5000 Then
    strPriceCat = "2 - good price reduction. Only $" _
              & Format$((10000 - gTotalOfOrders), "###,##0.00") _
              & " to get to price band 3!"
  Else
    strPriceCat = "1 - normal pricing. Only $" - _
              & Format$((5000 - gTotalOfOrders), "###,##0.00") _
              & " to get to price band 2!"
  End If

  CreateHTMLResponse = "Content-Type: text/html" & vbCrLf & vbCrLf _
              & "<BODY BGCOLOR=#FFFFC0 TOPMARGIN=30><H1>" _
              & "Thanks for your Order.</H1><P>" _
              & "<B>The total of all your orders is $" _
              & Format$(gTotalOfOrders, "###,##0.00") _
              & ", placing you in price category " & strPriceCat _
              & "<P>Your " & IIf(gflgNewAccountNumber, "new", "") _
              & " account number is: " & gAccountNumber & ".<P>" _
              & "<HR>To place another order, please return to the" _
              & "log-in screen and start again.  This will ensure" _
              & "that your current account number and current price" _
              & "band information is used.</B></BODY>"
End Function
```

All we need to do now is assign the value of this function to the second string in our original method call, so that it's sent back to the client, and we're in business.

We haven't got the space here to go into how all the code actually works. If you are using VB already, what you've seen will no doubt be familiar to you. And, if you want to learn more, look out for the Wrox Press books that cover the subject in detail— such as Beginning Access 95 VBA Programming and The Revolutionary Guide to Visual Basic 4.

Summary

In this chapter, we've seen some of the ways that the server can increase the functionality of our VBScript pages, by storing and processing information outside the actual browser. We discovered the techniques of client-side validation, which is then followed by server-side storage and processing. This tends to limit the number of connections required when you're working with complex pages, thereby improving response times and reducing Net traffic.

We looked at how the server can supply information which is dynamically generated, and always up-to-date, by taking it from a database—rather than using hard-coded information in the page itself. In situations where product availability and prices change regularly, this greatly reduces the work involved in maintaining your pages. And the techniques you've seen in this chapter, combined with those from Chapter 7, allow you to set up and manage your own intranet with the minimum of effort.

The new server-side technologies like IDC and ISAPI are making web pages even more powerful, when combined with the client-side processing available with VBScript and ActiveX components. As you design and build ever more complex VBScript pages, you'll find that you really need to understand how server interaction works, so that you can get the best out of it. To learn more, look out for the forthcoming book **Instant Web Databases with NT Server**—from Wrox Press naturally!

In this chapter, we looked at:

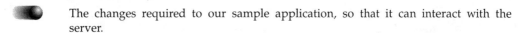

The changes required to our sample application, so that it can interact with the server.

How new technologies like IDC and OLEISAPI can help to achieve this.

An outline of the way we've added extra functionality to our sample application.

We've reached the end of the book, and you should have a solid grasp of VBScript techniques, and perhaps a better understanding of the browser itself. So fire up Control Pad now... there's a whole world out there just waiting to view your next all-singing, all- dancing, interactive web page!

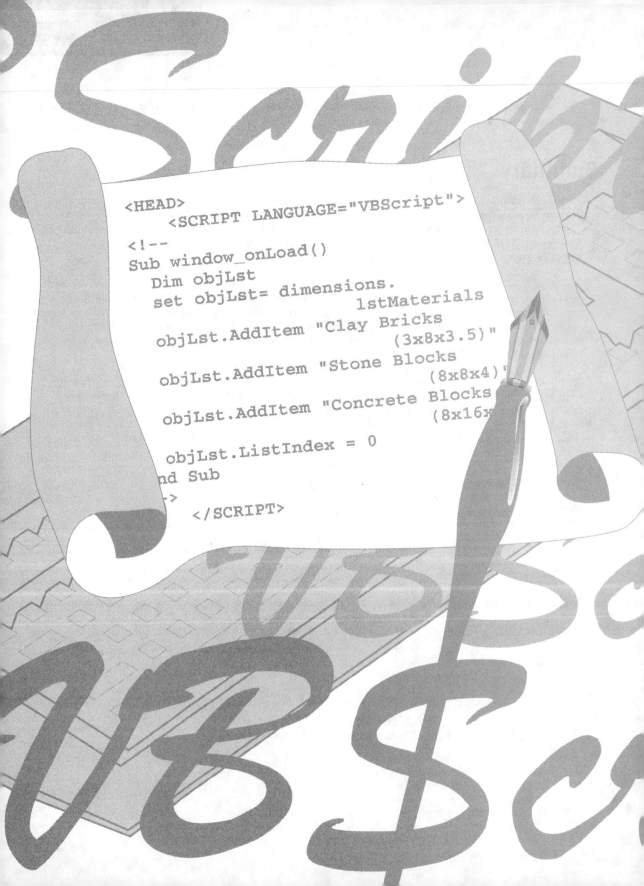

```
<HEAD>
    <SCRIPT LANGUAGE="VBScript">

<!--
Sub window_onLoad()
  Dim objLst
  set objLst= dimensions.
                        lstMaterials
  objLst.AddItem "Clay Bricks
                           (3x8x3.5)"
  objLst.AddItem "Stone Blocks
                             (8x8x4)"
  objLst.AddItem "Concrete Blocks
                            (8x16x
  objLst.ListIndex = 0
nd Sub
->
    </SCRIPT>
```

INSTANT

VBScript

Appendix A - Naming Conventions

These are the naming conventions that are applied throughout the book.

Variable Naming Conventions

Data Type	Prefix	Example	VarType()
Boolean	bln	blnAccepted	11
Byte	byt	bytPixelValue	17
Date or Time	dtm	dtmFirstTime	7
Double	dbl	dblTotalDistance	5
Error	err	errOverflow	10
Integer	int	intCount	2
Long	lng	lngFreeSpace	3
Object	obj	objListBox	9 or 13
Single	sng	sngLength	4
String	str	strAddress	8

Control Naming Conventions

Control Type	Prefix	Example
Check Box	chk	chkFullPacksOnly
Combo List Box	cbo	cboThickness
Command Button	cmd or btn	cmdCalculate
Horizontal Scroll Bar	hsb	hsbWidth
Image Control	img	imgDisplayPicture

Table continued on next page

Control Type	Prefix	Example
Label	lbl	lblDescription
List Box	lst	lstBrickTypes
Pop-up Menu	mnu	mnuSelection
Radio/Option Button	opt	optIncludeCement
Spin Button	spn	spnVolume
Tab Strip	tab	tabOptionPages
Text Box	txt	txtCustomer
Vertical Scroll Bar	vsb	vsbHeight

```
<HEAD>
    <SCRIPT LANGUAGE="VBScript">

<!--
Sub window_onLoad()
  Dim objLst
  set objLst= dimensions.
                        1stMaterials

  objLst.AddItem "Clay Bricks
                            (3x8x3.5)"

  objLst.AddItem "Stone Blocks
                            (8x8x4)"

  objLst.AddItem "Concrete Blocks
                            (8x16x

  objLst.ListIndex = 0
nd Sub
->
    </SCRIPT>
```

Appendix B - VBScript Reference

Array Handling

Dim—declares an array variable. This can be static with a defined number of elements or dynamic and can have up to 60 dimensions.

ReDim—used to change the size of an array variable which has been declared as dynamic.

Preserve—keyword used to preserve the contents of an array being resized. You can only redimension the rightmost index of a multi-dimension array.

```
Dim strEmployees ()
ReDim strEmployees (9,1)

strEmployees (9,1) = "Phil"

ReDim strEmployees (9,2)    'loses the contents of element (9,1)
strEmployees (9,2) = "Paul"

ReDim Preserve strEmployees (9,3)  'preserves the contents of (9,2)
strEmployees (9,3) = "Smith"
```

LBound—returns the smallest subscript for the dimension of an array. Note that arrays always start from the subscript zero so this function will always return the value zero.

UBound—used to determine the size of an array.

```
Dim strCustomers (10, 5)
intSizeFirst = UBound (strCustomers, 1)    'returns SizeFirst = 10
intSizeSecond = UBound (strCustomers, 2)  'returns SizeSecond = 5
```

> The actual number of elements is always one greater than the value returned by **UBound** because the array starts from zero.

Assignments

Let—used to assign values to variables (optional).
Set—used to assign an object reference to a variable.

```
Let intNumberOfDays = 365

Set txtMyTextBox = txtcontrol
txtMyTextBox.Value = "Hello World"
```

Constants

Empty—an empty variable is one that has been created but not yet assigned a value.
Nothing—used to remove an object reference.

```
Set txtMyTextBox = txtATextBox    'assigns object reference
Set txtMyTextBox = Nothing        'removes object reference
```

Null—indicates that a variable isn't valid. Note that this isn't the same as **Empty**.
True—indicates that an expression is true. Has numerical value -1.
False—indicates that an expression is false. Has numerical value 0.

Control Flow

For...Next—executes a block of code a specified number of times.

```
Dim intSalary (10)
For intCounter = 0 to 10
    intSalary (intCounter) = 20000
Next
```

Do...Loop—executes a block of code while a condition is true or until a condition becomes true.

```
Do While strDayOfWeek <> "Saturday" And strDayOfWeek <> "Sunday"
    MsgBox ("Get Up! Time for work")
    ...
Loop
```

```
Do
    MsgBox ("Get Up! Time for work")
    ...
Loop Until strDayOfWeek = "Saturday" Or strDayOfWeek = "Sunday"
```

If...Then...Else—used to run various blocks of code depending on conditions.

```
If intAge < 20 Then
    MsgBox ("You're just a slip of a thing!")
ElseIf intAge < 40 Then
    MsgBox ("You're in your prime!")
Else
    MsgBox ("You're older and wiser")
End If
```

Select Case—used to replace **If...Then...Else** statements where there are many conditions.

```
Select Case intAge
Case 21,22,23,24,25,26
   MsgBox ("You're in your prime")
Case 40
   MsgBox ("You're fulfilling your dreams")
Case 65
   MsgBox ("Time for a new challenge")
End Select
```

Note that **Select Case** can only be used with precise conditions and not with a range of conditions.

While...Wend—executes a block of code while a condition is true.

```
While strDayOfWeek <> "Saturday" AND strDayOfWeek <> "Sunday"
   MsgBox ("Get Up! Time for work")
   ...
Wend
```

Functions

Conversion Functions
Asc
AscB
AscW
Chr
ChrB
ChrW
CBool
CByte
CDate
CDbl
CInt
CLng
CSng
CStr
Hex
Oct
Fix
Int
Sgn

Date/Time Functions
Date
Time
DateSerial
DateValue
TimeSerial
TimeValue
Day
Month
Weekday
Year
Hour
Minute
Second
Now

Math Functions
Atn
Cos
Sin
Tan
Exp
Log
Sqr
Randomize
Rnd

String Functions
Instr
InStrB
Len
LenB
Lcase
Ucase
Left
LeftB
Mid
MidB
Right
RightB
Space
StrComp
String
Ltrim
Rtrim
Trim

Variable Testing Functions
IsArray
IsDate
IsEmpty
IsNull
IsNumeric
IsObject
VarType

Variable Declarations

Dim—declares a variable.

Error Handling

On Error Resume Next—indicates that if an error occurs, control should continue at the next statement.
Err—this is the error object which provides information about run-time errors.

Error handling is very limited in VB Script and the **Err** object must be tested explicitly to determine if an error has occurred.

Input/Output

This consists of the MsgBox for output and the Input box for input:

MsgBox

This displays a message and can return a value indicating which button was clicked.

```
MsgBox "Hello There",20,"Hello Message","c:\windows\MyHelp.hlp",123
```

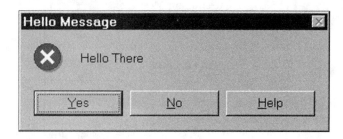

The 5 parameters are explained below:

"Hello There"—this contains the text of the message and is obligatory.
20 - this determines which icon and buttons appear on the message box.
"Hello Message"—this contains the text that will appear as the title of the message box.
"c:\windows\MyHelp.hlp"—this adds a Help button to the message box and determines the help file that is opened if the button is clicked.
123—this is a reference to the particular help topic that will be displayed if the Help button is clicked.

The value of the icon and buttons parameter is determined using the following tables:

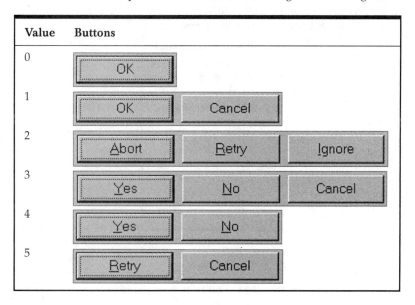

Value	Description	Icon
16	Critical Message	
32	Questioning Message	
48	Warning Message	
64	Informational Message	

To specify which buttons and icon are displayed you simply add the relevant values together. So, in our example, we add together 4 + 16 to display the Yes and No buttons with the Critical icon.

You can determine which button was clicked by the user by assigning the return code of the **MsgBox** function to a variable:

```
intButtonClicked = MsgBox ("Hello There",35,"Hello Message")
```

Notice that the **MsgBox** parameters are enclosed by brackets when used in this format. The value assigned to the variable **ButtonClicked** is determined by the following table:

Value	Button
1	OK
2	Cancel
3	Abort
4	Retry
5	Ignore
6	Yes
7	No

InputBox

This accepts text entry from the user and returns it as a string.

```
strTextEntered = InputBox ("Please enter your name","Login","John Smith",500,500)
```

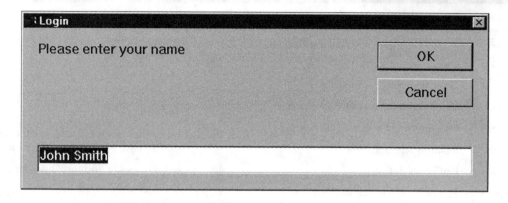

"Please enter your name"—this is the prompt displayed in the input box.
"Login"—this is the text displayed as the title of the input box.
"John Smith"—this is the default value displayed in the input box.
500—specifies the x position of the input box.
500—specifies the y position of the input box.

As with the **MsgBox** function, you can also specify a help file and topic to add a Help button to the input box.

Procedures

Call—optional method of calling a subroutine.
Function—used to declare a function.
Sub—used to declare a subroutine.

Other Keywords

Rem—old style method of adding comments to code.
Option Explicit—forces you to declare a variable before it can be used.

Visual Basic Run-time Error Codes

The following error codes also apply to VBA code and many will not be appropriate to an application built completely around VBScript. However, if you have built your own components then these error codes may well be brought up when such components are used.

Code	Description	Code	Description
3	Return without GoSub	9	Subscript out of range
5	Invalid procedure call	10	This array is fixed or temporarily locked
6	Overflow		
7	Out of memory	11	Division by zero

Table continued on next page

Code	Description	Code	Description
13	Type mismatch	424	Object required
14	Out of string space	429	OLE Automation server can't create object
16	Expression too complex	430	Class doesn't support OLE Automation
17	Can't perform requested operation		
18	User interrupt occurred	432	File name or class name not found during OLE Automation operation
20	Resume without error		
28	Out of stack space	438	Object doesn't support this property or method
35	Sub or Function not defined		
47	Too many DLL application clients	440	OLE Automation error
48	Error in loading DLL	442	Connection to type library or object library for remote process has been lost. Press OK for dialog to remove reference
49	Bad DLL calling convention		
51	Internal error		
52	Bad file name or number	443	OLE Automation object does not have a default value
53	File not found	445	Object doesn't support this action
54	Bad file mode	446	Object doesn't support named arguments
55	File already open		
57	Device I/O error	447	Object doesn't support current locale setting
58	File already exists		
59	Bad record length	448	Named argument not found
61	Disk full	449	Argument not optional
62	Input past end of file	450	Wrong number of arguments or invalid property assignment
63	Bad record number		
67	Too many files	451	Object not a collection
68	Device unavailable	452	Invalid ordinal
70	Permission denied	453	Specified DLL function not found
71	Disk not ready	454	Code resource not found
74	Can't rename with different drive	455	Code resource lock error
75	Path/File access error	457	This key is already associated with an element of this collection
76	Path not found		
322	Can't create necessary temporary file	458	Variable uses an OLE Automation type not supported in Visual Basic
325	Invalid format in resource file	481	Invalid picture
380	Invalid property value	500	Variable is undefined
423	Property or method not found	501	Cannot assign to variable
		1001	Out of memory

Table continued on next page

278

Code	Description	Code	Description
1002	Syntax error	1035	Nested comment
1003	Expected ':'	1036	'Me' cannot be used outside of a procedure
1004	Expected ';'		
1005	Expected '('	1037	Invalid use of 'Me' keyword
1006	Expected ')'	1038	'loop' without 'do'
1007	Expected ']'	1039	Invalid 'exit' statement
1008	Expected '{'	1040	Invalid 'for' loop control variable
1009	Expected '}'	1041	Variable redefinition
1010	Expected identifier	1042	Must be first statement on the line
1011	Expected '='	1043	Cannot assign to non-ByVal argument
1012	Expected 'If'		
1013	Expected 'To'		
1014	Expected 'End'		
1015	Expected 'Function'		
1016	Expected 'Sub'		
1017	Expected 'Then'		
1018	Expected 'Wend'		
1019	Expected 'Loop'		
1020	Expected 'Next'		
1021	Expected 'Case'		
1022	Expected 'Select'		
1023	Expected expression		
1024	Expected statement		
1025	Expected end of statement		
1026	Expected integer constant		
1027	Expected 'While' or 'Until'		
1028	Expected 'While', 'Until' or end of statement		
1029	Too many locals or arguments		
1030	Identifier too long		
1031	Invalid number		
1032	Invalid character		
1033	Unterminated string constant		
1034	Unterminated comment		

```vbscript
<HEAD>
    <SCRIPT LANGUAGE="VBScript">

<!--
Sub window_onLoad()
  Dim objLst
  set objLst= dimensions.
                          lstMaterials

  objLst.AddItem "Clay Bricks
                            (3x8x3.5)"

  objLst.AddItem "Stone Blocks
                            (8x8x4)"

  objLst.AddItem "Concrete Blocks
                            (8x16x

  objLst.ListIndex = 0
nd Sub
  ->
    </SCRIPT>
```

Appendix C - Properties, Methods, and Events

The History Object

Properties	Description
length	Returns the length of the history list

Methods	Description
back n	Jumps back in the history n steps, like clicking back button n times
Forward n	Jumps forward in the history n steps, like clicking forward n times
Go n	Goes to the nth item in the history list

The Navigator Object

Properties	Description
appCodeName	Returns the code name of the application
AppName	Returns the actual name of the application
AppVersion	Returns the version of the application
UserAgent	Returns the user agent of the application

The Location Object

Properties	Description
Href	Gets or sets the compete URL for the location
Protocol	Gets or sets the protocol portion of the URL
Host	Gets or sets the host and port portion of the URL
Hostname	Gets or sets just the host portion of the URL
Port	Gets or sets just the port portion of the URL
Pathname	Gets or sets the path name in the URL
Search	Gets or sets the search portion of the URL, if specified
Hash	Gets or sets the hash portion of the URL, if specified

The Window Object

Properties	Description
name	Returns the name of the current window
Parent	Returns the window object of the window's parent
Self	Returns the window object of the current window
Top	Returns the window object of the topmost window
Location	Returns the location object for the current window
DefaultStatus	Gets or sets the default text for the left portion of the status bar
Status	Gets or sets the status text in the left of the status bar
Frames	Returns the collection of frames for the current window
History	Returns the history object of the current window
Navigator	Returns the navigator object of the current window
Document	Returns the document object of the current window

Methods	Description
alert	Displays an alert message box
Confirm	Displays a message box with OK and Cancel buttons, returns **TRUE** or **FALSE**
Prompt	Prompts the user for input
Open	Creates a new window

Table continued on next page

Methods	Description
`Close`	Closes the window
`SetTimeout`	Sets a timer to call a function after a specific number of milliseconds
`ClearTimeout`	Clears the timer having a particular ID
`Navigate`	Navigates the window to a new URL

Events	Description
`onLoad`	Fired when the contents of the window are loaded
`onUnload`	Fired when the contents of the window are unloaded

The Document Object

Properties	Description
`linkColor`	Gets or sets the color of the links in a document
`ALinkColor`	Gets or sets the color of the active links in a document
`VLinkColor`	Gets or sets the color of the visited links in a document
`BgColor`	Gets or sets the background color of a document
`FgColor`	Gets or sets the foreground color
`Anchors`	Returns the collection of anchors in a document
`Links`	Returns the collection of links for the current document
`Forms`	Returns the collection of forms for the current document
`Location`	Returns a read-only representation of the location object
`lastModified`	Returns the last modified date of the current page
`Title`	Returns a read-only representation of the document's title
`Cookie`	Gets or sets the cookie for the current document
`Referrer`	Gets the URL of the referring document

Methods	Description
`write`	Places a string into the current document
`WriteLn`	Places a string plus new-line character into the current document
`Open`	Opens the document stream for output
`Close`	Updates the screen showing the text written since last open call
`Clear`	Closes the document output stream and clears the document

283

The Form Object

Properties	Description
action	Gets or sets the address for the **ACTION** of the form
Encoding	Gets or sets the encoding for the form
Method	Gets or sets the **METHOD** for how the data should be sent to the server
Target	Gets or sets the **TARGET** window name for displaying the form results
Elements	Returns the collection of elements contained in the form

Methods	Description
submit	Submits the form, just like clicking a SUBMIT button

Events	Description
onSubmit	Fired when the form is submitted

Link Object

Properties	Description
Href	Returns the compete URL for the link
Protocol	Returns the protocol portion of the URL
Host	Returns both the host and port portion of the URL (hostname:port)
Hostname	Returns just the host portion of the URL
Port	Returns just the port portion of the URL
Pathname	Returns the path name in the URL
Search	Returns the search portion of the URL, if specified
Hash	Returns the hash portion of the URL, if specified
Target	Returns the name of target window for the link, if specified

Events	Description
mouseMove	Fires an event any time the pointer moves over a link
OnMouseOver	Fires an event any time the pointer moves over a link
OnClick	Fires an event any time you click on a link

The Anchor Object

Properties	Description
`name`	Gets or sets the name of the anchor

The Element Object

The element object can be a normal HTML control, an ActiveX control, or any other control object. The properties, methods, and events supported by the browser directly, relate to the normal HTML controls:

HTML Controls

Element	Properties	Methods	Events
Button, Reset, Submit	form, name, value, enabled	click, focus	onClick, onFocus
Check box	form, name, value, checked, defaultChecked, enabled	click, focus	onClick, onFocus
Radio	form, name, value, checked, enabled	click, focus	onClick, onFocus
Combo	form, name, value, enabled, listCount, list, multiSelect, listIndex	click, focus, removeItem, addItem, clear	onClick, onFocus
Password	form, name, value, defaultValue, enabled	focus, blur, select	onFocus, onBlur
Text, Text Area	form, name, value, defaultValue, enabled	focus, blur, select	onFocus, onBlur, onChange, onSelect
Select	name, length, options, selectedIndex	focus, blur	onFocus, onBlur, onChange
Hidden	name, value	*<none>*	*<none>*

Properties	Description
form	Gets the form object containing the element
Name	Gets or sets the name of the element
Value	Gets or sets the value of the element
DefaultValue	Gets or sets the default value of the element
Checked	Gets or sets the checked state of the check box or the radio button
DefaultChecked	Gets or sets the default checked property of the check box
Enabled	Gets or sets whether the control is enabled
ListCount	Gets the count of elements in the list
MultiSelect	Gets or sets whether the combo is multiselect or not
ListIndex	Gets or sets the list index
Length	Gets the number of options in a select element
SelectedIndex	Gets the index of the selected option, or the first one selected when there is more than one object selected
Options	Gets the `<options>` tags for a select element, with these properties: defaultSelected — The currently selected attribute index — The index of an option length — The number of options in the selected object name — The name attribute of the selected object selected — Used to programmatically select an option selectedIndex — The index of the selected option text — The text to be displayed value — The value attribute

Methods	Description
click	Clicks the element
Focus	Sets the focus to the element
Blur	Clears the focus from the element
Select	Selects the contents of the element
RemoveItem	Removes the item at index from the element
AddItem	Adds the item to the element before the item at index
Clear	Clears the contents of the element

Events	Description
onClick	Fired when the element is clicked
OnFocus	Fired when the element gets the focus

Table continued on next page

Events	Description
OnBlur	Fired when the element loses the focus
OnChange	Fired when the element has changed
OnSelect	Fired when the contents of the element are selected

InternetExplorer Object

Here's a few of the common properties and methods of the **InternetExplorer** object:

Properties	Description
LocationName	Returns the short name of the current document
LocationURL	Returns the URL of the current document
MenuBar	Sets or returns the display state of the menu bar
StatusBar	Sets or returns the display state of the window's status bar
StatusText	Sets or returns the text content of the window's status bar
ToolBar	Sets or returns the display state of the tool bar
Visible	Displays or hides the application
Left	Sets or returns the left position of the application window
Top	Sets or returns the top position of the application window
Width	Sets or returns the width of the application window
Height	Sets or returns the height position of the application window
FullScreen	Displays the application using the whole screen

Methods	Description
GoBack	Equivalent to clicking the Back button
GoForward	Equivalent to clicking the Forward button
GoHome	Equivalent to clicking the Home button
GoSearch	Equivalent to clicking the Search button
Navigate	Sets the URL of the file to display
Quit	Quits the application
Refresh	Equivalent to clicking the Refresh button
Stop	Equivalent to clicking the Stop button

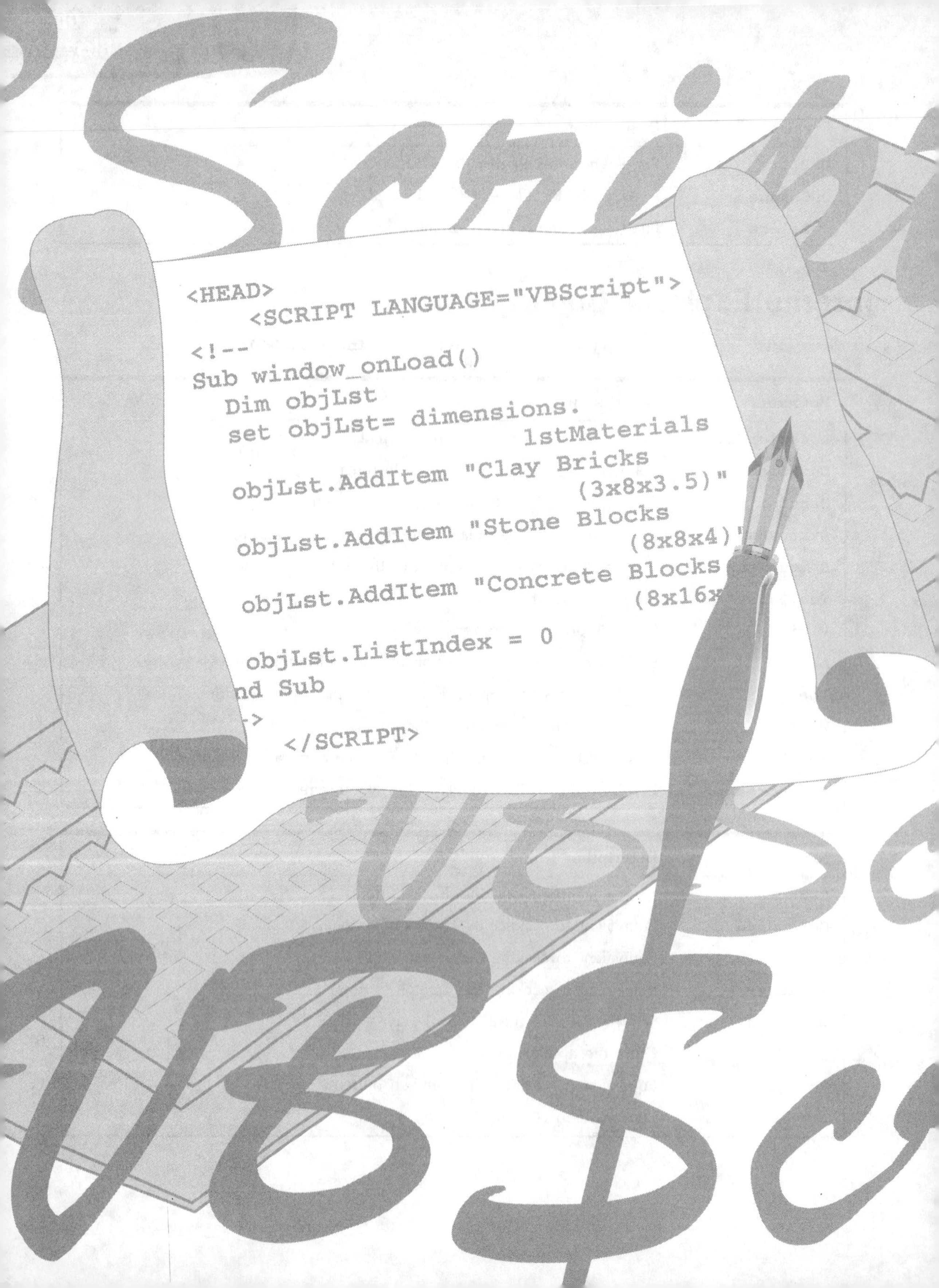

```vbscript
<HEAD>
    <SCRIPT LANGUAGE="VBScript">

<!--
Sub window_onLoad()
  Dim objLst
  set objLst= dimensions.
                           lstMaterials

  objLst.AddItem "Clay Bricks
                           (3x8x3.5)"

   objLst.AddItem "Stone Blocks
                           (8x8x4)"

    objLst.AddItem "Concrete Blocks
                           (8x16x

   objLst.ListIndex = 0
nd Sub
-->

    </SCRIPT>
```

Appendix D - Preparing the Server

Setting Up a System Data Source Name

To use **Internet Database Connector** (IDC) on Internet Information Server (IIS) you need to set up access to the data source by providing the correct system **Data Source Name** (DSN).

 Launch the ODBC Administrator program by double-clicking on its icon in Windows' Control Panel. The Data Sources dialog shows a list of the currently installed ODBC drivers. Here, we're using an Access database, so we select the Microsoft Access Driver (***.mdb**) entry from the list. If you are using a different database system, you'll need to select the appropriate ODBC driver. If an entry for it is not present, you will need to install the driver from your original setup disk, or a disk provided by the database vendor.

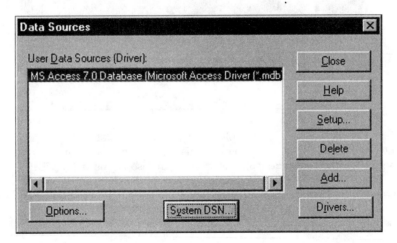

We are going to set up a system Data Source Name which will allow our database to be accessed by (potentially) all users on the network. Clicking on the System DSN button displays the System Data Sources window which lists all of the system DSNs currently installed.

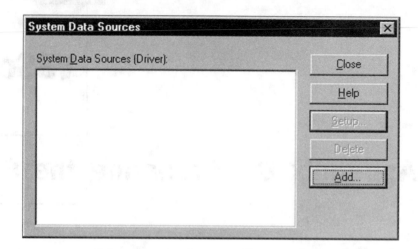

To set up a new system DSN, click on the Add button to show the Add Data Source window. We want to create an Access system DSN, so we've selected the Microsoft Access driver from the list.

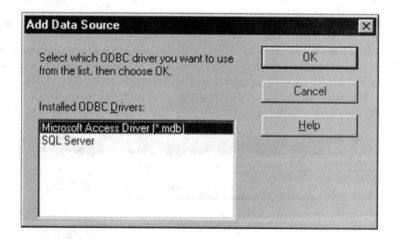

Click OK to open the ODBC Microsoft Access 7.0 Setup dialog. We now have to enter the name of the data source. This will be the name that our IDC scripts will use as the **Datasource** parameter, and can also be used for ODBC connections in OLE automation servers. We also select the path where our database resides either by typing it in directly, or clicking the Browse button. Because we are using an Access database, we have the opportunity to repair and compact the database. We can also use a **System.mdw** database to restrict user access, if required.

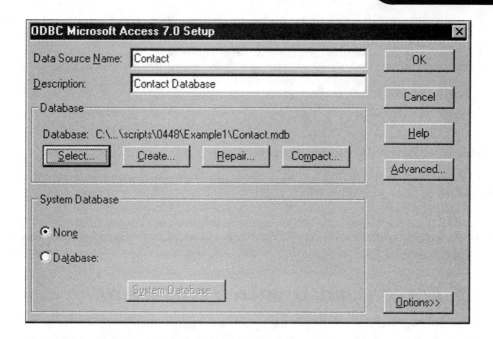

When you've entered all the details, click on OK to return to the System Data Sources screen again. Now our new System DSN is shown.

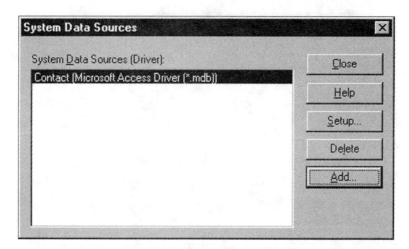

Registering the Server on NT

Before we can use an OLE server across the network or the Internet, we must first register it so that it is known to the system it will be running on. We need to have a copy of all the necessary VB4 support files (such as **VB40032.DLL** and **MFC4.DLL**, etc.) for our OLE automation server to work properly. The easiest way to do this is to use the application setup wizard that comes with VB4. Installing our automation server using the setup files created by the wizard will ensure that the appropriate components are correctly installed and registered.

If you update the OLE server component on a regular basis, it is desirable to disable IIS caching. By default, IIS performs caching to ensure that our OLE server is kept in memory as soon as it's been loaded in once. To disable caching, set the value of the key `HKEY_LOCAL_MACHINE\SYSTEM\CurrentControlSet\Services\W3SVC\Parameters\CacheExtensions` to **0** (Extension Caching disabled) with `regedt32.exe`. This prevents Access Denied messages when attempting to overwrite the OLE server.

To update the OLE server, stop the WWW service under IIS. Then deregister the original OLE server so that the system no longer knows about it. This is done using `regsvr32 /u` *DLLpath&name* from the DOS prompt (`regsvr32.exe` comes with Visual Basic 4 and other tools). Your new server can be created and used to replace the previous version. Now register your new OLE server using `regsvr32 DLLpath&name` at a DOS prompt. Finally, restart the WWW service.

Once your OLE automation server is fit for industrial use, set the value of the key `HKEY_LOCAL_MACHINE\SYSTEM\CurrentControlSet\Services\W3SVC\Parameters\CacheExtensions` **to 1 again** (Extension Caching enabled) in order to improve WWW service performance.

Setting Access and Launch Permissions

Once we've installed and registered our OLE server, we must make sure that NT will allow it to be accessed and launched when it is called. We use `dcomcnfg.exe` from the `WINNT\System32` folder to alter the permissions. After running it, select the Default Security tab from the Distributed COM Configuration Properties window.

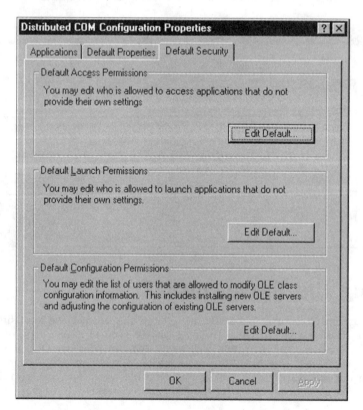

The items of interest here are the Default Access Permissions and Launch Permissions. We must use each one to add registry values that will allow us to run our OLE server uninhibited. The process is similar for each, so we'll just show you the process for access permissions. Select the Default Access Permissions button, and the Registry Value Permissions window opens.

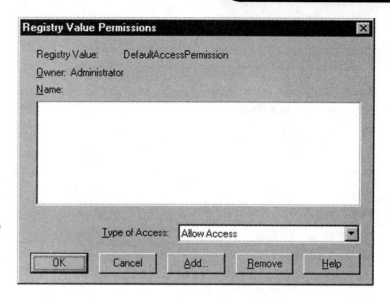

We want to allow the system to launch our OLE automation server. From the Registry Value Permissions window, select the Add button. The Add Users and Groups dialog then provides a list of groups.

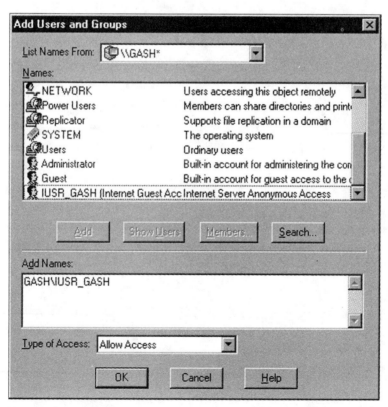

The server itself is treated as a user as far as access and launch permissions are concerned. To make this special user available, select Show Users and an entry IUSR_*MachineName* appears in the list. Select this item and change the access type to Allow Access. This will allow internet guests access to the OLE server (so it can be used by IIS).

In a similar manner, the launch permissions have to be set so that the methods in the OLE server can be run when invoked.

```
<HEAD>
    <SCRIPT LANGUAGE="VBScript">
<!--
Sub window_onLoad()
  Dim objLst
  set objLst= dimensions.
                        lstMaterials
  objLst.AddItem "Clay Bricks
                        (3x8x3.5)"
  objLst.AddItem "Stone Blocks
                        (8x8x4)"
  objLst.AddItem "Concrete Blocks
                        (8x16x
  objLst.ListIndex = 0
nd Sub
->
    </SCRIPT>
```

INSTANT

VBScript

Index

C

309

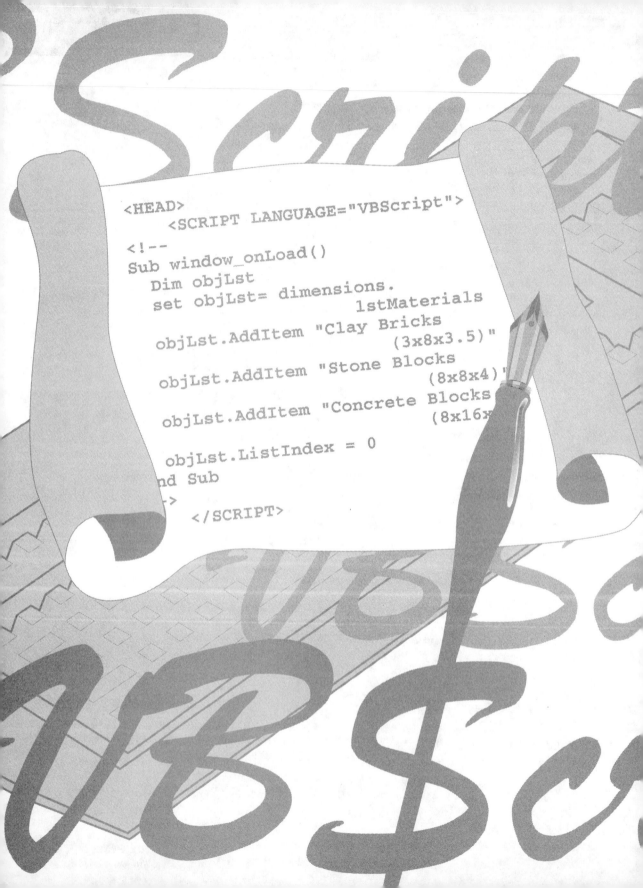

```vbscript
<HEAD>
    <SCRIPT LANGUAGE="VBScript">
<!--
Sub window_onLoad()
  Dim objLst
  set objLst= dimensions.
                        lstMaterials

  objLst.AddItem "Clay Bricks
                        (3x8x3.5)"

  objLst.AddItem "Stone Blocks
                        (8x8x4)"

  objLst.AddItem "Concrete Blocks
                        (8x16x

  objLst.ListIndex = 0
nd Sub
  ->
    </SCRIPT>
```

Beginning Linux Programming

Authors: Neil Matthew, Richard Stones
ISBN: 187441680
Price: $36.95 C$51.95 £33.99

The book is unique in that it teaches UNIX programming in a simple and structured way, using Linux and its associated and freely available development tools as the main platform. Assuming familiarity with the UNIX environment and a basic knowledge of C, the book teaches you how to put together UNIX applications that make the most of your time, your OS and your machine's capabilities.

Having introduced the programming environment and basic tools, the authors turn their attention initially on shell programming. The chapters then concentrate on programming UNIX with C, showing you how to work with files, access the UNIX environment, input and output data using terminals and curses, and manage data. After another round with development and debugging tools, the book discusses processes and signals, pipes and other IPC mechanisms, culminating with a chapter on sockets. Programming the X-Window system is introduced with Tcl/Tk and Java. Finally, the book covers programming for the Internet using HTML and CGI.

The book aims to discuss UNIX programming as described in the relevant POSIX and X/Open specifications, so the code is tested with that in mind. All the source code from the book is available under the terms of the Gnu Public License from the Wrox web site.

Professional SQL Server 6.5 Admin

Authors: Various   ISBN: 1874416494
Price: $44.95 C$62.95 £41.49

This book is not a tutorial in the complete product, but is for those who need to become either professionally competent in preparation for Microsoft exams or those DBAs needing real-world advice to do their job better. It assumes knowledge of databases and wastes no time on getting novices up to speed on the basics of data structure and using a database server in a Client-Server arena.

The book covers everything from installation and configuration right through to the actual managing of the server. There are whole chapters devoted to essential administrative issues such as transaction management and locking, replication, security, monitoring of the system and database backup and recovery. We've used proven techniques to bring robust code and script that will increase your ability to troubleshoot your database structure and improve its performance. Finally, we have looked very carefully at the new features in 6.5, such as the Web Assistant and Distributed Transaction Controller (DTC) and provided you with key practical examples. Where possible, throughout the book we have described a DBA solution in Transact SQL, Visual Basic and the Enterprise Manager.

Wrox Press
http://www.wrox.com/

Instant SQL Programming

Author:Joe Celko   ISBN: 1874416508

Price: $29.95 C$41.95 £27.99

This is the fastest guide for developers to the most common database management language. If you want to get the most out of your database design, you will need to master Structured Query Language. SQL is the standard database language supported by almost every database management system on the market. This book takes you into the concepts and implementation of this key language quickly and painlessly, covering the complete ANSI standard SQL '92 from basic database design through to some of the more complex topics such as NULLS and 3-valued logic. We take you through the theory step-by-step, as you put into practice what you learn at each stage, gradually building up an example database while mastering essential techniques.

Revolutionary Guide to Visual Basic 4 Professional

Author: Larry Roof   ISBN: 1874416370

Price: $44.95 C$62.95 £49.99

This book focuses on the four key areas for developers using VB4: the Win32 API, Objects and OLE, Databases and the VB development cycle. Each of the areas receives in-depth coverage, and techniques are illustrated using rich and complex example projects that bring out the real issues involved in commercial VB development. It examines the Win32 API from a VB perspective and gives a complete run-down of developing multimedia apps. The OLE section includes a help file creator that uses the Word OLE object, and we OLE automate Netscape Navigator 2. The database section offers complete coverage of DAO, SQL and ODBC, finishing with a detailed analysis of client/server database systems. The final section shows how to design, code, optimize and distribute a complete application. The book has a CD including all source code and a hypertext version of the book.

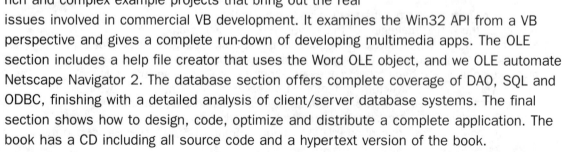

Instant HTML

Author: Steve Wright   ISBN: 1861000766   Price: $15.00 C$21.00 £13.99

This book is a fast paced guide to the latest version of the HTML language, including the extensions to the standards added by Netscape and Microsoft. Aimed at programmers, it assumes a basic knowledge of the Internet. It starts by looking at the basics of HTML including document structure, formatting tags, inserting hyperlinks and images and image mapping, and then moves on to cover more advanced issues such as tables, frames, creating forms to interact with users, animation, incorporating scripts (such as JavaScript) into HTML documents, and style sheets.

The book includes a full list of all the HTML tags, organised by category for easy reference.

Professional ISAPI Programming in C++

Author: Michael Tracy   ISBN: 1861000664   Price: $40.00 C$56.00 £36.99

This is a working developer's guide to customizing Microsoft's Internet Information Server, which is now an integrated and free addition to the NT4.0 platform. This is essential reading for real-world web site development and expects readers to already be competent C++ and C programmers. Although all techniques in the book are workable under various C++ compilers, users of Visual C++ 4.1 will benefit from the ISAPI extensions supplied in its AppWizard.

This book covers extension and filter programming in depth. There is a walk through the API structure but not a reference to endless calls. Instead, we illustrate the key specifications with example programs.

HTTP and HTML instructions are issued as an appendix. We introduce extensions by mimicking popular CGI scripts and there's a specific chapter on controlling cookies. With filters we are not just re-running generic web code - these are leading-edge filter methods specifically designed for the IIS API.